D1507489

THE COURAGE TO BE PROTESTANT

The Courage to Be Protestant

Truth-lovers, Marketers, and Emergents
in the Postmodern World

—Ⓜ—

DAVID WELLS

WILLIAM B. EERDMANS PUBLISHING COMPANY
GRAND RAPIDS, MICHIGAN / CAMBRIDGE, U.K.

© 2008 David Wells
All rights reserved

Published 2008 by
Wm. B. Eerdmans Publishing Co.
2140 Oak Industrial Drive N.E., Grand Rapids, Michigan 49505 /
P.O. Box 163, Cambridge CB3 9PU U.K.
www.eerdmans.com

Printed in the United States of America

12 11 10 09 08   7 6 5 4 3 2

Library of Congress Cataloging-in-Publication Data

Wells, David.
The courage to be Protestant: truth-lovers, marketers, and emergents
in the postmodern world / David Wells.
p.   cm.
Includes bibliographical references.
ISBN 978-0-8028-4007-3 (pbk.: alk. paper)
1. Evangelicalism.   2. Protestant churches — Doctrines.
3. Postmodernism— Religious aspects — Christianity.   I. Title.

BR1640.W43   2008
230'.4 — dc22

2007043599

Scripture quotations are from The Holy Bible, English Standard Version, copyright ©
2001 by Crossway Bibles, a division of Good News Publishers.

To

The staff of Rafiki

*who care for orphans in Africa with
such skill, compassion, and Christian dedication*

Contents

—m—

Preface   xiii

I. The Lay of the Evangelical Land   1

The Map   2

   Doctrine   2

   Culture   3

Classical Evangelicals   4

   The Beginnings   4

   Two Weaknesses   7

     DOCTRINE SHRINKS   7

     THE CHURCH VANISHES   10

Marketers   13

Emergents   15

   Conversing Together   15

   Being Open   17

The Fall of the Empire   18

   Are You an Evangelical?   18

   If Not Evangelical, What?   19

CONTENTS

II. Christianity for Sale   **23**

Thank You, Corporate America!   25

     Getting Up to Business Speed   25

     Marketing Megachurches   27

Sale: Prices Slashed!   28

     Catering to the Customer   28

     A Moment's Reflection   31

     Wal-Mart Churches   36

     Down with the Traditional Church!   39

A Word of Praise   41

     Evangelical Stagnation   42

     Engaging Culture   44

Excuse Me!   44

     Wrong Result   44

     Wrong Calculation   48

     Wrong Analogy   50

     Wrong Customer   54

The Bottom Line   57

III. Truth   **59**

The Self Is Disconnected   60

Our Modernized World   63

     Craft   63

     Community   64

     Family   65

The Changing World Inside   67

     We Live Alone   67

     Postmodern Selves   69

     Power   71

What Is Truth?   72

Contents

Christian Truth   75

    Biblical Baseline   75

    Muddled Emergents   77

    Biblical Heartbeat   80

    Evangelical Adventures   85

Truth Engagement   89

A Better Way Forward   92

    One Truth   93

    Integrity   95

IV. God   **97**

The Lost Center   99

    Thinking Biblically   99

    Evil   100

    Sin   102

The Culture's Answer   104

    Emptiness   105

    The Gathering Storm   105

    Postmoderns Emerge   107

    Nothing Makes Sense   109

    God Dies, We Die   111

    Reinvented Selves   112

God and Modernity   116

    Being Recentered   116

    Being Private   118

The Inside God   120

    What Does Nearness Mean?   121

    Misunderstanding God's Nearness   123

The Outside God   124

    God Above   124

CONTENTS

God as Holy	125
And So . . . ?	126
There Is a Law	127
There Is Sin	128
There Is a Cross	129
There Is Conquest	130
There Is Obligation	130
V. Self	**135**
In Pursuit of the Self	136
The Nation Signs On	138
Virtues to Values	143
Virtues	143
Values	146
Character to Personality	147
Personality Emerges	147
Self-Marketing	148
The Commerce of Images	150
The Fallout	151
Nature to Self	153
Nature	153
Nature Dies	154
Self Emerges	155
Rights	156
Loss	160
Guilt to Shame	162
Shame	162
Guilt	162
Healing Ourselves	163
A Different Universe	165

Contents

Rupture — 166

Reconciliation — 168

It's Not Just about Me — 169

About the Salt — 170

Where We Stand — 172

VI. Christ — **175**

Christian and Pagan Paths — 176

From Below — 179

The Facts — 179

The Church's Failure — 180

The New Journey — 182

Secular but Spiritual — 186

How Spiritualities Work — 187

NATURE — 188

SIN — 191

SPEAKING — 191

From Above — 192

Above but Incarnate — 193

CHRIST'S DESCENT — 193

AN AGE DAWNS — 194

Above and Reigning — 197

IN CHRIST ALONE — 198

DOES THIS PREACH? — 202

CHRIST'S RULE NOW — 204

VII. Church — **209**

Trouble in the House — 210

Middling Standards — 210

Be Appealing! — 213

Losing the Church — 214

CONTENTS

My Critics   217

The Church's Two Sides   218

  Visible and Invisible   218

  What Is Hidden   220

  Forget Rethinking the Church   222

  Distance and Impact   223

Marks of Authenticity   226

  Word of God   226

   SUFFICIENT   226

   DOCTRINE   228

   PREACHING   229

  Sacraments   233

  Discipline   237

Into the Depths   242

  Who Builds the Church?   242

   GOD IS SOVEREIGN   244

   WE ARE CAPTIVE   245

   MEANS OF GROWTH   245

  Let God Be God over the Church   246

Index   249

Preface

—∿∿—

T his book started out as a simple summary of the four volumes
that had preceded it. All books, however, develop a life of their
own, and this has been no exception.

I needed to update what had been said in the previous volumes
because some of it had been begun more than a decade ago. In addition
to this, I had to compress these volumes into a single account. How
does one reduce 1,100 pages to 250?

Once this work got under way I found myself not so much com-
pressing as recasting all that I had done and then updating it. The result is that this book is less a summary and more an attempt at getting
at the essence of the project that has engaged me over the last fifteen
years. And, hopefully, it will be more accessible than the previous
books, not to mention less taxing on readers!

The project began with *No Place for Truth; or, Whatever Happened
to Evangelical Theology?* (1993). That book was followed by *God in the
Wasteland: The Reality of Truth in a World of Fading Dreams* (1994),
Losing Our Virtue: Why the Church Must Recover Its Moral Vision (1998),
and *Above All Earthly Pow'rs: Christ in a Postmodern World* (2005). Run-
ning through these four books have been five main doctrinal themes:
truth, God, self, Christ, and the church. It is these five themes that I am
taking up here. Since this is so, I am not, for the most part, document-
ing the literature and research upon which this book rests since that
has already been done. It therefore has no footnotes.

I spent the spring of 2007, while on sabbatical, in Westminster College, Cambridge. I am most appreciative of the kind and generous hospitality that was extended to me during this time. It was there, in their magnificent library, with its extraordinary collection, that I spent many happy hours working on this manuscript. During my time in Cambridge I also worked at Tyndale House. I am grateful for this opportunity.

Books begin, Winston Churchill said, as an adventure, turn into a toy, then an amusement, then a mistress, then a master, then a tyrant, and just before you are about to capitulate finally, you decide instead to declare your independence by killing the monster. It gets sent off to the publisher! So it was here.

Eerdmans has been the publisher of each of these five volumes. Eerdmans has been a most helpful, proficient, and competent publisher. I wish to express my sincere gratitude to them.

CHAPTER I

The Lay of the Evangelical Land

Humpty Dumpty sat on a wall.
Humpty Dumpty had a great fall.
All the king's horses and all the king's men
Couldn't put Humpty together again.

It takes no courage to sign up as a Protestant. After all, millions have done so throughout the West. They are not in any peril. To live by the truths of historic Protestantism, however, is an entirely different matter. That takes courage in today's context.

That is the argument I will make in this book. But it needs to be made not only with postmodern culture in mind but also with contemporary evangelicalism in mind. The truths of historic Protestantism are sometimes no more welcome in evangelicalism than they are in the outside culture.

This is quite a remarkable thing. After all, the emergence of the evangelical movement following World War II has been a success story. So what has happened?

Evangelicals started out at the beginning of this period, let us remember, with nothing. They were few in number, not welcome in the academy, were ridiculed wherever Enlightenment attitudes were ensconced in the culture, and were on the outside of all the power centers in American society. In a very few years, though, this all began to change. Their churches grew and multiplied; they built institutions, started organizations, entered the academy, became a political constituency to be reckoned with; and they have reached out to those in need in a multitude of impressive ways. Indeed, so successful have they become that they have been granted a kind of grudging, cultural acceptance in America, though this is not of course the case in Europe. Never has the evangelical gospel been more widely heard than it is today, and never has the reach of evangelicals been so great.

And yet, at the very moment when the evangelical movement seemed to have arrived at this pinnacle, it started to fall apart. It is now separating into three quite distinct constituencies. Because this story explains where the front lines are, I will briefly describe these three constituencies before I get into the substance of this book. In the chapters that follow I will return to these issues a number of times.

The Map

Let me now start drawing my map of what is happening.

The evangelical world is now dividing into three rather distinct constituencies. Actually, it is dividing into many, many subconstituencies as well because this rather amazing empire of belief is fragmenting across the board. So my map with only three major constituencies portrays the land as it looks from afar, not up close. The important point here, though, is that two of these constituencies are new, and, like large icebergs, they are separating from the others. They are, as I see it, transitional movements. They are the stepping-stones away from the classical orthodoxy of the earlier evangelicals and, however unwittingly, toward a more liberalized Christianity. In due course the children of these evangelicals will become full-blown liberals, I suspect, just like those against whom the evangelical grandparents originally protested.

Doctrine

What is now dividing the evangelical world is not what used to divide it. The older distinctions were doctrinal. Doctrinal differences were what pitted Baptists against pedobaptists, premils against amils, Congregationalists against Presbyterians, Arminians against Calvinists, ordainers of women against nonordainers, and tongues speakers against cessationists. These issues are still alive and they still stir passions. I have a position on each one, and I think they are important inasmuch as each is an attempt at finding the teaching of the Word of God.

What is different is that these are not the differences that seem to matter today. The older map was drawn by differences of *doctrine.* When all is said and done today, many evangelicals are indifferent to doctrine — certainly they are when they "do church." Privately, no doubt, there are doctrines that are believed. But in church . . . well, that is different because, many think, doctrine is an impediment as we reach out to new generations. These older debates, therefore, give us no access to what shapes many evangelical churches today. The map needs to be redrawn. What is rearranging the evangelical territory now?

Culture

In the last two or three decades evangelicals have discovered culture. That actually sounds more flattering than I intend. I would welcome a serious discussion about culture. We should be exploring what it is and how it works, rather than just looking at polls to see what is hot. A serious engagement with culture, though, is not what most evangelicals are about.

What they want to know about culture is simple and easy to unearth. They want to know what the trends and fashions are that are ruffling the surface of contemporary life. They have no interest at all in what lies beneath the trends, none on how our modernized culture in the West shapes personal horizons, produces appetites, and provides us ways of processing the meaning of life. All of that seems like pretty complex and useless stuff. Pragmatists to the last drop of blood, these evangelicals are now in the cultural waters, not to understand what is there, but to get some movement. They are there with their surfboards trying to get a little forward motion as each tiny ripple makes its way toward the shore. This quest for success, which passes under the lan-

3

guage of "relevance," is what is partitioning the evangelical world into its three segments.

Again and again the issue that has emerged, as a result, is whether evangelicals will build their churches *sola Scriptura* or *sola cultura*, to use the formulation Os Guinness proffered in *Prophetic Untimeliness*. Actually, to be quite honest, the question is raised by only a few on the sidelines, and in many evangelical churches the question barely even makes sense. It sounds a bit like someone wondering about Manny Ramirez's swing after he has just hit multiple home runs in the same game.

Nevertheless, it is the question that *should* be raised again and again, no matter how little sense it makes. What is the binding authority on the church? What determines how it thinks, what it wants, and how it is going to go about its business? Will it be Scripture alone, Scripture understood as God's binding address, or will it be culture? Will it be what is current, edgy, and with-it? Or will it be God's Word, which is always contemporary because its truth endures for all eternity?

Of course, I know that the issue does not present itself in this way. Evangelicals who live *sola cultura* all claim to be living *sola Scriptura*. So it is very important for us to be able to untangle these questions and see them for what they are. I will try to do so as the book progresses.

Now, though, I need to be more specific about my three constituencies. We need to see how the older, classical evangelicalism first mutated into a segment of marketers and then mutated again into a segment of emergents. The marketers make up my second major evangelical constituency, and the emergents my third.

Classical Evangelicals

The Beginnings

The first constituency, though, is classical evangelicalism. This is what took shape and form immediately following the Second World War, both in Europe and in the United States. What stood out about it, and what still does, is its doctrinal seriousness. Indeed, its churches reflected this, rather than trying to hide it, as the marketers do today, and this kind of seriousness could be heard, Sunday by Sunday, in the sermons that were preached.

In the United States this preoccupation with doctrine was one of the consequences of the bitter disputes with liberalism at the beginning of the twentieth century. Liberals said Christianity was about deeds, not creeds. They said it was about life, not doctrine. Their conservative opponents, the fundamentalists, insisted that Christianity was about creeds as well as deeds. It was about doctrine as well as life. They came to define their distinction from liberalism, as they should have, in terms of their creeds and doctrines.

It is true, of course, that these fundamentalists also came to think as many other cognitive minorities have. They felt endangered and they protected themselves, oftentimes, by walling themselves off from everyone else. It was not a good defensive measure.

Eventually, however, fundamentalism, with its oppositional attitudes, the schisms it sowed, and the intellectual isolation it made for itself, began to die down. Its replacement in the 1950s and 1960s was neoevangelicalism led by Harold Ockenga, Carl Henry, and Billy Graham in the United States and by John Stott, J. I. Packer, Martyn Lloyd-Jones, and Francis Schaeffer in Europe. They, and many like them, set about building a movement with institutions, publications, and ministries, the whole of it intent on reengaging modern life and, for those with a will to do so, reentering the older denominations to reclaim them. This coalition was built around two core theological beliefs: the full authority of the inspired Scripture and the necessity and centrality of Christ's penal substitution.

What this meant for them was that faith that was biblical would, of necessity, be doctrinal in its form. This, in fact, was so much more than simply asserting the inspiration of Scripture and its inerrancy. In the early days of the movement, a whole way of thinking grew out of this primary commitment. It meant that being biblical in tone and content was central. From this grew churches that valued biblical truth and Christian life that sought its nourishment in the Word of God. The publications from these early days, the books that were published, and the sermons that were preached all bear this out.

Like all such movements, this one also had its symbols. Most prominent were the National Association of Evangelicals (NAE), founded in 1942, and *Christianity Today,* started in 1956. Their purposes, respectively, were to give organization and then voice to this new evangelical life. The former was an alternative organization to the liberal National Council of Churches (NCC). The latter was an alternative voice to the liberal journal *Christian Century.*

It is ironic to see the paths these two magazines have taken. *Christian Century* has, since then, retained its intellectual integrity, despite the sagging fortunes of its liberal constituency. It has been bloodied over the last couple of decades, but it remains unbowed in its liberal persuasion. *Christianity Today,* by contrast, and despite the swelling ranks of evangelicals it serves, has been far less steadfast. Its role, in one sense, has never been easier. But it has found its direction in recent years, not by theological conviction, but by testing which winds are prevailing.

As for the NAE, it is now a shadow of its former self. Actually, even a truly viable organization, which the NAE is not, would have difficulty representing the sprawling evangelical empire today.

Like many things Christian, after a while the vision of the original evangelical leaders faded. The strength, discipline, and direction they had given to the movement was lost in the next generation or two. Evangelicalism continued to sustain many who simply lived off the capital others had generated. The presses continued to roll, the Christian colleges continued to graduate students, *Christianity Today* continued to report, but the capital was not being sufficiently renewed. Slowly but inexorably this great movement has begun dissipating.

And yet, much is still strong, noble, self-sacrificial, and commendable in this world. Its most visible symbols, no longer representing the best in evangelical life, and no longer speaking for them, may actually raise more questions than are justified. The fact is, there are still many who think evangelicals should be doctrinally shaped, who love the Word of God, who value biblical preaching, who want to be God-centered in their thought and life, who do live upright lives, and who are not ashamed of their roots in the Reformation. They are the ones who are sustaining the missionary enterprise today and the ones in whom one finds an older, and quite admirable, piety that still lives on.

It would be quite unrealistic to think that evangelicalism today could look exactly as it did fifty years ago, or a hundred, or five hundred. At the same time, the truth by which it is constituted never changes because God, whose truth it is, never changes. There should therefore be threads of continuity that bind real Christian believing in all ages. It is some of those threads, I believe, that are now being lost.

My view on this, I should say at the outset, is a minority position. The changes I am about to describe have the potential, I believe, for undoing the movement and many of its great gains. Others take a different view. They say we are seeing evangelicalism coming to terms, as it should, with its culture, shedding what has become obsolete and beginning to take its own world more seriously. It is now growing up.

Before elaborating on these different perceptions, which I will in the chapters that follow, I want to explain what I think has happened. This will make sense, I hope, of the whole book.

Two Weaknesses

Although a multitude of voices, competing views, different agendas, different theological perceptions, different programs, and different ways of "doing" church now fills the evangelical world, all of it, I think, can be traced back to two inherent weaknesses in the classical evangelicalism that emerged after the war. These weaknesses constitute the soil in which first the marketers and now the emergents are taking root.

DOCTRINE SHRINKS

What is the first of these weaknesses? To become a cohesive movement, evangelicalism had to agree on essentials and agree to allow differences on nonessentials, doctrinally speaking. That is what happened. The essentials were the authority of inspired Scripture and the centrality and necessity of Christ's substitutionary work on the cross.

Through the 1950s, 1960s, and even 1970s, much else besides the two core principles was part and parcel of evangelical belief and practice. There was, however, a tacit agreement that liberty would be al-

7

lowed in all these other matters provided that the core principles were honored. As long as the center held, as long as the grounds of unity were strong, the diversity of beliefs in church government, glossolalia, baptism, and the millennium could be sustained. At the time, this seemed quite safe because the core at the center was strong and because evangelicals took seriously all the surrounding beliefs, too.

What happened, though, was that this doctrinal vision began to contract. The goal that diversity in secondary matters would be welcomed quite soon passed over into an attitude that evangelicalism could in fact be reduced simply to its core principles of Scripture and Christ. In hindsight, it is now rather clear that the toleration of diversity slowly became an indifference toward much of the fabric of belief that makes up Christian faith.

In the 1970s and 1980s, on every side and in almost every way, it was becoming clear that ways of doctrinal thinking were wearing very thin. The capacity to think doctrinally was being lost as new leaders emerged, as the leadership of the evangelical world shifted from the older pastor-theologians to the newer entrepreneurial organization builders, and as churches began to reflect this change in their attitudes and worship. And, of course, it was a shift mirrored in *Christianity Today.*

The erosion in biblical ways of thinking at first passed almost unnoticed. Nevertheless, after a while it was hard to miss the fact that this was happening. No doubt there were many specific causes. Campus organizations were undoubtedly reducing Christian faith to its most minimal form. And as serious biblical preaching in the churches diminished, ignorance of biblical truth became commonplace. But the largest factor in this internal change, I think, was that evangelicalism began to be infested by the culture in which it was living. And then Christianity became increasingly reduced simply to private, internal, therapeutic experience. Its doctrinal form atrophied and then crumbled. This was the situation I sought to address in my book *No Place for Truth; or, Whatever Happened to Evangelical Theology?* which came out in 1993.

The slide that occasioned that book, however, has continued. Indeed, it has gathered speed and momentum. Here, though, we need explore the inevitable result in only one area. What had started out as a strategy for building the evangelical movement in fact ended up weakening the whole surrounding fabric of belief. And it is now worse than that. This weakening process did not stop at the periphery. It has entered the central core.

The unraveling of evangelical truth was signaled initially in an odd series of definitional tags that became evident in the 1980s and 1990s. That was when a whole series of hybrids emerged: feminist evangelicals, ecumenical evangelicals, liberal evangelicals, liberals who were evangelical, charismatic evangelicals, Catholic evangelicals, evangelicals who were Catholic, and so it went. The additional tag — be it feminist, Catholic, or charismatic — signaled that the additional interest was at least as important as the core principles of what defined who an evangelical was. Indeed, the additional interest usually said far more about the person's interests than anything else. The core principles, in fact, were losing their power to shape people, define the movement, prescribe who was and who was not an evangelical.

This weakness has now grown and become more aggravated. It is clear for all to see in the way the marketers do their business. It is being documented by George Barna in poll after poll. I will take this up in the following chapter.

The last time I walked over the bridge that links Zambia and Zimbabwe, just below the Victoria Falls, I watched a bungee jumper launch himself into space from the center of the bridge. The waters beneath are some four hundred feet down, full of froth and crocodiles. This is Africa. Equipment of the kind he was using may not be tested regularly and replaced on schedule. In fact, what I saw were cords that appeared already to have been overused. They were very frayed, and I wondered how long it would be before an intrepid bungee jumper did not make the return journey to the bridge's edge and simply continued into the churning waters in the gorge far, far below.

Something like this has happened in the evangelical world. The cords plaited together out of the formal and material principles became frayed and then, for an increasing number, snapped. They are no longer able to return the jumpers to the fellowship.

THE CHURCH VANISHES

The second major weakness followed from the first. It had been a matter of choice for evangelicals whether or not their two core principles from the Reformation would be seen within a particular confessional tradition and lived out primarily in an ecclesiastical context. For some they were, but increasingly and for many more, they were not.

This became especially clear in the 1980s, by which time business-minded entrepreneurs were the leaders in evangelicalism. By then the overwhelming majority of religious organizations in America were evangelical, and of these, the overwhelming number had been created after the war.

Parachurch organizations have, during these years, served the evangelical cause in amazing and beneficial ways. Indeed, when the church has stumbled, it has often been a parachurch organization that has emerged to pick up what the church was failing to do. In the early postwar years these organizations stood outside the churches organizationally but lived within the church functionally. They lived to strengthen the life of the churches. They were part and parcel of this great, evangelical coalition. And certainly it was not as common earlier as it became later for these parachurch organizations to become private empires such as we have seen, for example, in many of the television ministries.

In the 1980s, though, evangelicals began to think of the whole of evangelical faith in *para* terms. That was the striking departure that happened at this time. It was, in a way, simply the outworking of the first weakness. As doctrine shrank, eventually this shrinkage came to include the church, and it then passed over into this second weakness.

The churches themselves were not attacked — at least not initially. But evangelicalism began to think of itself apart from the church. This was not simply a matter of organization but of attitude.

And this sentiment has only accelerated as the marketers began to play the market. Past traditions of believing, distinctive church architecture, doctrinal language, and the formalities of traditional church life all seemed like baggage that needed to be shed as rapidly as possible. Suddenly it was becoming an embarrassment.

But along with these changes came something else. Whereas previously the churches had been a focal point for Christian believers, now they lost that place. As unlikely as it seems, many churches in a sense disappeared. They became entirely parachurch in nature!

The leaders of this marketing enterprise understood that they were in a market, and religious customers had choices. The choices that began to be offered by way of competition, however, were all along the lines of not being churchy. This new direction was mightily re-inforced by the emergence of the television ministries, especially in the 1980s, not to mention the pervasive availability of religious videos. Church life subsided in importance for many people, if only because on Sunday morning they could, and often did, "go to church" in their living rooms in front of their television sets. One whole segment of the evan-gelical world decided to practice Christian faith as if the whole notion of the church needed to disappear. Evangelicalism was becoming *para* in mentality, and the local church was about to become its chief casu-alty.

This disappearing trick would never have been possible if evan-gelicals were still thinking in doctrinal terms. But they were not.

The truth is that without a biblical understanding of why God in-stituted it, the church easily becomes a liability in a market where it competes only with the greatest of difficulty against religious fare available in the convenience of one's living room and in a culture bent on distraction and entertainment. Few demands are made by televi-sion preachers, or on borrowed DVDs, and every pitch for a financial contribution is subject to death by the mute button. That cannot be said of the preacher in a church! This conquest by the market, accom-plished silently and without any fanfare, has not only greatly dimin-ished the church but, one has to say, has also greatly diminished what it means to be a Christian believer.

The constant cultural bombardment of individualism, in the ab-sence of a robust theology, meant that faith that had rightly been un-derstood as personal now easily became faith that was individualistic, self-focused, and consumer oriented. That was the change to which the church marketers attuned themselves. Instead of seeing this as a weakness to be resisted, they used it as an opportunity to be exploited. Increasingly, evangelical faith was released from any connections with the past, from every consideration except the self, and was imbued with no other objective than entrepreneurial success. As the evangelical experience was thus cut loose, it became increasingly cultural, increasingly empty, and increasingly superficial.

This development has continued to evolve. One of its more interesting facets has been the growth of house churches both in the United States and in Britain. These are, of course, reproducing the very first forms of Christian life that the book of Acts records (e.g., Acts 2:46-47), though the early Christians also met outside homes (3:1; 5:12). No doubt today there are good house churches as well as those that are not so good. These "independent home fellowships," as George Barna calls them, had an average size of twenty in 2007, in the United States.

Whether they were called fellowship groups, or care groups, or simply Bible studies, these "home fellowships" used to *complement* the local church's other activities. Now, what supplemented the local church has itself become the church. In fact, the church itself has gone. And with what consequences?

It is difficult to generalize since these "home fellowships" do vary. They seem to do well at encouraging friendships and mutual support. They may not do so well, though, in transmitting the full body of biblical teaching, especially those parts that are difficult or uncongenial because the small size of these fellowships and the bonding between people actually make this more difficult. And what of the sacraments? Biblical discipline? Reaching out to outsiders who are not a part of the group?

At this point, though, it is sufficient to see, at least from my point of view, that the mutations within evangelicalism in recent decades have occurred because of its weaknesses. From the earlier classical evangelicals have come the marketers and then the emergents. In the marketers, doctrine vanished and then the church. Among the emergents, doctrine also vanished but then, by way of reaction, there has been an attempt to recover a new sense of church. But without a clear sense of biblical truth, what is being drawn up in the net of recovery is often a strange mixture of ideas, traditions, and practices. It is these developments I need to explore a bit further before we look at the major themes in this book.

Marketers

The older, classical evangelicals created a movement with institutions, ministries, and publications. The marketers rode on the back of this. They capitalized on all the achievements of the classical evangelicals, but they did so for their own purposes and success. They are my second major evangelical constituency.

The church marketers are those who have followed the innovations in "doing" church pioneered by Bill Hybels at Willow Creek Community Church in 1975. They have been egged on by Barna and his never ending flow of polling numbers. What was begun then has since been copied all over America. It has morphed into new forms and been exported to other parts of the world. Of course! This is America!

This approach, it is said, is seeking to preserve the old evangelical message while delivering it in new ways. Its strategies have been borrowed from the corporate world. The key idea is that there is a market for the Christian message. They utilize marketing techniques and proven entertainment formats to penetrate that market.

This innovation seemed to be the train that was leaving town three decades ago, and pastors by the thousands scrambled to get aboard. Here was the magic formula for success. Though a genuine passion for evangelism no doubt lay somewhere in the experiment, it was also wrapped in the most stunning cultural naïveté. It was entirely predictable that this experiment would, in due course, crest and then lose its attraction, though there are always stragglers who keep chasing trends long after they have ceased to be fashionable. That is what is still happening.

What was so awe-inspiring about this to evangelicals went largely unnoticed outside their fellowship. In early 2007, Barna found that the icons in this movement, Bill Hybels and Rick Warren, were almost entirely unknown to the broader public. Hybels was unknown to 96 percent of people and Warren to 83 percent. Inside the evangelical world, though, these are giants, goliaths, bestriding all things churchly.

This was, you see, the very latest thing. Here was a newly invented and freshly minted church world. It was a church world completely reconfigured around the sales pitch. Here was the gospel product as sleekly fashioned and as artfully sold as anything in the mall or on television. Here also were churches smelling of coffee and reverberating with edgy music. There were bright and exciting videos. And the professional singers rivaled any one might hear in Vegas. It was all put together in a package to please, entice, entertain, relax, grab, and enfold potential customers, and worm its way into their hearts. There was, however, a generational focus. The generational target for the marketers has been the boomers. The music is contemporary. Usually, though, "contemporary" is no later, musically speaking, than the 1970s or early 1980s, because that is where boomers find their comfort zone. Rap or heavy metal would not be cool.

What results, all too often, beneath all the smiling crowds, the packed auditoria, is a faith so cramped, limited, and minuscule as to be entirely unable to command our life, our energies, or, as a matter of fact, even much of our attention. One church advertises itself as a place where you will find "loud music" and "short services." It has a "casual atmosphere" but, it wants us to know, it also offers "serious faith."

This is always the rub in this experiment: the form greatly modifies the content. The loud music and short services are part of the form, but the form, put together to be pleasing, actually undercuts the seriousness of the faith. The form is in fact the product, and in this market the sale has to be done quickly and as painlessly as possible because the customers all have itchy feet. That greatly militates against the seriousness any church wants to have. And that is why a deep chasm has opened between the church marketers and historic Protestant orthodoxy. It is less that the truths of this orthodoxy are assailed than that they are seen to be irrelevant to the building of the church. They are, it is believed, an impediment to its success.

Not only are the bare bones of this approach now showing, but it has to reckon with the fact that people have also become bored with it. They want something new. It has been mainstreamed. The marketing approach has become conventional in the American evangelical world, so now, people are thinking, it is time to move on. Frankly, there is no judgment more to be feared than this: you are now passé. That weighs more heavily even than words coming from the great white throne at the end of time. Imagine that! Passé.

What has happened is not unlike the way fashion migrates socially and then loses its attraction. Devotees of hip-hop culture, for example, are set apart by their getups, their tattoos, their piercings, jewelry, hoodies, off-kilter baseball caps, and pants that look like they were made by a drunken tailor. But what happens when the middle class — or worse yet, the middle-aged — also begin to sport tattoos on their sagging skin, let their pants sag halfway down their thighs, and sport hoodies as well? The answer, of course, is that youth culture has a legitimate complaint. They have been robbed! Their distinctiveness has been lost! Their cachet on the street has been diminished! It is time for them to move on, fashion-wise. So it is here.

When the evangelical world became Willow Creek–ized, the sun began to set on Willow Creek. Its cachet went down the tubes. If Willow Creek could not move on fashion-wise, others not quite so wed to its particular mode of doing things could. And so it has happened. I will return to this theme in the next chapter because the word has not reached as many ears as it needs to that the sun has set on this experiment.

Emergents

The third constituency in the evangelical kingdom would be straining the definition of "evangelical" to the breaking point if its leaders were not themselves distancing their world from evangelicalism. This constituency is made up of a loose coalition of churches that came together during the 1990s and now constitute the so-called emerging church. Here, far more than was the case among traditional evangelicals, there is a continuum in the core beliefs that is so wide that it might be wise to distinguish between the emergent church, on the one end, and those who are simply emerging on the other.

Conversing Together

They are, however, all linked together in a "conversation," live on the Web. Anyone who lived through the earlier era when Protestant liberals were so dominant in the churches recognizes all too clearly what this conversation is about. It is one we have heard before.

Emergents, as I shall call them, are about deconstruction. This is an important point. They have not sought to be movement builders because that, in a way, would defy their essential posture of pulling away from everything else. They are skeptical of power and its structures. They are not pulling in toward each other either. They are simply talking, and a few are writing books.

What they are against is often clearer than what they are for. However, they are united in thinking that classical evangelicalism, especially in its Reformed configuration, is part and parcel of modernity. By this they mean that it is rationalistic. And by that they mean it imagines that people can actually know truth with some certainty. That, they believe, is pretentious, fraudulent, and arrogant.

What emergents are against in the Willow Creeky, marketing movement is its emptiness, loss of personal connections in its monster-sized churches, and capitulation to consumerist modernity. This produces a reduced, skinny Christianity with no depth and no mystery. Emergents are *postmodern* in these ways, they say, not modern, and their style is often attuned more to Gen X and the millennials than to the boomers. They think of themselves, too, as being postconservative rather than simply evangelical.

The emergents' deconstruction of traditional evangelical belief and this reincarnation of the Willow Creek mind-set is in fact at the confluence of several other developments. The shorthand for this is to say that emergents are postconservative and postfoundational. The most obvious consequence of this is that a different understanding of the authority and function of Scripture has . . . well, emerged. It is much looser and less definitive than what has prevailed in most of the church's life.

Emergents — at least those who read theology — seem to have stumbled on the postliberals, and this is what is now driving this new understanding of the function of Scripture. They have taken up this fad as if it were the most current, cutting-edge expression in contemporary thought, though in the academic world it has already disappeared.

Being Open

The name most associated with the postliberals is George Lindbeck. He proposed a way of viewing Scripture that did not require belief in the actual truthfulness of its language. Rather, Scripture functions more like a traffic cop whose business it is to ensure that everyone moves around in a reasonable way. Not only so, but Lindbeck also wrested the interpretation of Scripture from the individual and placed it in the hands of the community. It is not hard to see why emergents have taken a shine to this.

Growing out of this is a far more "open" attitude to other faith traditions such as Eastern Orthodoxy and Catholicism. Emergents are doctrinal minimalists. They are ecclesiastical free spirits who flit around a much smaller doctrinal center and are often obliging of cultural and generational habits. By their very posture they are resistant to doctrinal structure that would contain and restrict them.

Emergents also think more about networking with each other than about working together under the same truth as evangelicals once did, more about salvation experienced in community than in individualistic ways, more about the suffering on earth now than the suffering in eternity later. They are not eager to engage (post)modernity critically. Indeed, they are as much submerged beneath it as they are emerging from it. Rather than distancing themselves from their own cultural world because they have been impelled to do so by Christian truth, they are more intent on simply huddling with fellow human sufferers. They may be willing to critique society for its social ills, but they are reserved about making judgments on private behavior such as homosexuality. What is emerging is clearly a rather different attitude about evangelical faith and practice than was seen before. We did, however, see these same attitudes in the older Protestant liberalism.

All of this, it seems to me, is a version of "offsetting." Offsetting is what the environmentally conscious do. They worry about their carbon footprint. How, then, are they going to take a vacation that requires flying since that would also involve a significant use of jet fuel with all the carbon left behind after the burn. Easy! In Britain, for example, there are businesses that cater to those of sensitive consciences. Buy your ticket from them and they will plant a tree for you. That is offsetting.

Here, among the emergents, am I mistaken in thinking that a different kind of offsetting is happening? The loss of truth is being offset by increasingly adventurous experiments in worship and by various attempts at recovering a lost sense of mystery. My view is that this kind of offsetting is an illusion. There is no offset for the loss of truth. There can be only a cover-up of what has taken place. When our knowledge of God's truth is diminished, our understanding of God is diminished, and no amount of contrived mystery through ancient liturgies or gathering in the presence of dim, flickering candlelight can compensate for this loss.

Emergents, too, are standing outside the house that Ockenga, Henry, Graham, Packer, Stott, Lloyd-Jones, and Schaeffer built in that earlier generation. The difference is that they know they are standing outside the house, whereas the seeker-sensitives, the marketers, still imagine they are living inside it.

The Fall of the Empire

Are You an Evangelical?

These, then, are my three major evangelical constituencies: classical evangelicals, the marketers, and the emergents.

Can the evangelical Humpty Dumpty ever be put together again? I think not. What was started in the 1940s, both in America and in Europe, has had a wonderful run, has created a multitude of churches and parachurch organizations, an immense and impressive array of scholarship, seminaries, colleges, social relief, missionary work, and a massive enterprise in believing. However, today it is sagging and disintegrating.

In Britain, in 2006, a survey revealed that only 59 percent of evangelicals wished to be known as such. In the United States, too, the evangelical label has become problematic. *Christianity Today*'s take on this situation is quite revealing. The problem, it believes, is that the evangelicals are lumped together by the media; all are seen as holding the beliefs of the religious right, all still confused with fundamentalism; and all are being tarred and feathered by a hostile, secular press. What is needed, this once-admired journal argued, is a counteroffensive. A charm offensive to combat the negative images.

My view is just the opposite of *Christianity Today*'s. I do not blame the secular press for what has happened to the public image of evangelicals. Nor do I think it is helpful to say that this is just a war of images.

The truth is that evangelicals have brought this bad press upon themselves. There have been just too many instances of obnoxious empire-building going on, too much in evangelicalism that is partisan and small, too much pandering to seekers, and too much adaptation of the Christian message until little remains. Too many of its leaders have been disgraced. There have been too many venal television preachers. There are too many of the born-again who show no signs of regenerate life. For many people, the word "evangelical" has become a synonym for what is trite, superficial, and moneygrubbing, a byword for what has gone wrong with Protestantism.

Those who still think of themselves as being in the tradition of historic Christian faith, as I do, may therefore want to consider whether the term "evangelical" has not outlived its usefulness. Despite its honorable pedigree, despite its many outstanding leaders both past and some in the present, and despite the many genuine and upright believers who still think of themselves as evangelical, it may now have to be abandoned.

If Not Evangelical, What?

If the word "evangelical" has outlived its usefulness, what is the alternative? Here, I am flummoxed. My own labels are too ponderous to be used widely. I am reaching out for help. I am advertising for a new label!

Let me tell you how I, at least, have thought. And there are many who are like me. Whatever label emerges will have to cover a number of the aspects that are important to us.

I am, of course, a biblical Christian first and foremost. But that does not make a sufficient distinction because all Christians, across the spectrum, from conservative Catholics to liberal Protestants, think of themselves as in some sense biblical. Can I be more specific?

How about a historic Christian? That used to have some punch. In an earlier generation liberal Protestants, otherwise known as modernists, argued that Christianity had to be adjusted to the modern world. They said it was no longer possible to believe the Bible as it stands because it came out of the ancient world that we no longer inhabit. Biblical teaching all had to be updated. A synthesis had to be produced between the best thought in the Bible and the best thought of the modern world.

To say, then, that one was a *historic* Christian was to call into question the entire argument of liberal Protestantism. It was to say that one was a Christian in the same way that Paul had been. It was to align oneself with those who had sought to follow biblical truth as Augustine, Calvin, Luther, and Edwards did. And being historical in this way was both impossible for liberals to claim and, in fact, undesirable for them to be.

As a matter of fact, this kind of argument about historic Christianity has much the same punch today as it always had, but few know it. In the emergents we are more and more hearing the old modernists' argument. The point of pressure then was the intellectual world that had enshrined Enlightenment ideals. The point of pressure now is the popular culture of the postmodern world. Modernists adapted Christianity to high culture. Emergents are adapting it to popular culture. Emergents, however, have never heard about the modernists, so the point of being a *historic* Christian is entirely lost on them.

Worse than that, one suspects, is the fact that emergents really have no historical categories. History for them, one suspects, goes no further back than the rock music of the Beatles. This is the music from the "olden days." The point I am making is therefore quite incomprehensible.

What about a historic Christian of a Reformational kind? Now, unfortunately, we have two meaningless descriptors, not just one: "historic" and "Reformational." Singly or in combination, as they say in the PR world, they do not sell.

In this book I am nevertheless going to think of myself as a biblical Christian first and foremost, as in continuity with Christians across the ages who have believed the same truth and followed the same Lord. The period in which these truths were brought into the most invigorating, health-giving focus was the Reformation. I therefore think of myself as Reformational in the sense that I affirm its *solas*: in Scripture alone is God's authoritative truth found, in Christ alone is salvation found, it is by grace alone that we are saved, and this salvation is received through faith alone. Only after each of these affirmations is made can we say that salvation from start to finish is to the glory of God alone. These affirmations do not stand simply as solitary, disconnected sentinels, but they are the key points in an integrated, whole understanding of biblical truth. This is what gives us a place to stand in the world from which to understand who we are, what the purposes of God are, and what future lies before us. These are the things that historic Protestants believe, and that is what I am.

This is what I think offers the only real hope for our postmodern world. Not only so, but it carries in it the best help for the evangelical world in its wounded and declining state today. I do not know what the evangelical future will be, but I am certain evangelicalism has no good future unless it finds this kind of direction again.

This will take some courage. The key to the future is not the capitulation that we see in both the marketers and the emergents. It is courage. The courage to be faithful to what Christianity in its biblical forms has always stood for across the ages. So, let's begin exploring what this might mean for us today.

CHAPTER II

Christianity for Sale

Church Marketing: The process of communicating the features and benefits of the Church's product (relationships) in a compelling manner that helps people take their next step in pursuing the Church's product (relationships).

CHURCH MARKETING SOLUTIONS

Therefore, we are ambassadors for Christ, God making his appeal through us. We implore you on behalf of Christ, be reconciled to God.

2 CORINTHIANS 5:20

It is Easter morning 2006. And there, lurking in the shadows, is a figure rarely seen in church. It's Superman. Yes, Superman! He who leaps tall buildings in a single bound as he pursues evildoers.

No, wait a minute. It's not him. Actually, it's only the senior pastor. The senior pastor all decked out as Superman, ready to communicate the gospel to a new generation.

Superman, you see, is a "Christ figure" who is peculiarly adapted to conveying the Christian message to generations raised on *Sesame*

Street, cartoons, and superhero action figures. So, on this day the pastor was poised to begin his instruction in a new series on how to "leap" over discouragement, "overcome" doubts, "defeat" odds, and "rise" from the ashes as Superman had on many occasions.

Spiritual feats of this magnitude seem much more likely, wouldn't you agree, when prompted by the sight of a resplendent Superman in his tights and regalia? This is a video-crazed, image-driven, picture-conscious culture, not a literate one. Our minds are entirely inert, lifeless, and useless until prodded into action by the sight of something eye-popping. Images are the fuel that, when injected into the motor, kick it all into life. Without them our minds are as limp as deflated balloons. Well, that at least is the theory invoked by those who want to do stunts like this.

Is this an anecdote plucked from an obscure part of the evangelical vineyard in America? Did it really happen? Is it so bizarre as to be unrepresentative? This incident actually happened in a church that received a Rick Warren award for church of the year. Besides, this co-opting of showbiz, this transformation of Christianity into entertainment, is rapidly becoming the norm today, not the exception. Pastors are straining to outdo each other in becoming as chic and slick as any show in Las Vegas.

I pity satirists who might be tempted to try to tweak these segments of the evangelical world. Theirs is a mission impossible. It can no longer be done. No matter how indelicately they might exaggerate, no matter how much they might embellish to make a point, no matter how many descriptions they might offer of the tasteless things that are happening, it will most likely be met with only a yawn and a bored question: "So . . . ?" Nothing seems improbable. None of it, in fact, ever seems exaggerated and none of it seems improper. It has now become impossible to insult some evangelicals. How the *Wittenburg Door* stays in business, I do not know.

Thank You, Corporate America!

Getting Up to Business Speed

This stunt was just one instance of what has become a kind of mass experiment in how to "do" church differently. It is being pushed along by the sense that things are stagnating in the evangelical world and the ways of "doing" church in the past won't work with the newer generations. That being so, churches must change their way of doing business or face extinction.

This thought of a market is of course at the heart of the new approach. It is borrowed from the business world.

Over the last three decades a consensus has emerged among the market-defined, market-driven, and seeker-sensitive that the "traditional" church is like a product now rendered obsolete by the passage of time and the onrush of innovation. Traditional churches are thinking in terms of few choices and few products — and the products are those they have always offered. Indeed, those in liturgical traditions have their most public products and choices prescribed for them.

The circumstance of the market is that no one stays in business without taking account of their customers. Traditional churches, whether liturgical or not, are disregarding their consumers if they stay their course. That is now a common assumption. Customers, after all, are sovereign. They will take their business elsewhere if businesses do not adjust to their interests and desires. This is as true in the church as it is in the mall. The church, then, plainly must rethink itself. Indeed, it needs to reinvent itself.

What happens in the corporate world has not been lost on many of our church leaders today, especially those who are American. Increasingly, they are thinking like corporate CEOs who pursue market share, and market domination, with a kind of cold, calculating, ruthless, and steely zeal.

Pastors, as a consequence, are now receiving invitation upon invitation from experts offering them help in getting up to business speed. In 2000, for example, pastors were invited to "an innovative, one-of-a-kind" conference experience. The fact that it had been held the previous year does take the bloom off the "one of a kind" bit, but never mind.

Here, pastors would be motivated by "Disney-proven approaches." More than that, they would learn "strategies and tactics" used at Disney World to ensure "customer loyalty."

A typical conference along these lines was carried out in association with the NAE in 2001. It was advertised as "Marketing 101." It was offering help for the befuddled among the church's leaders, those who had the uneasy sense that the world was passing them by. It tapped into their apprehension that their own church just might be dying on the vine. Now, however, they could find the new ideas they needed.

At this conference they would receive marketing hints from the "corporate giants." They would be armed with "image strategies from corporate ad. agencies." They would return home with the know-how to take their "church to the next level." And the really, really good thing about all of this was the assurance that God is "the best marketer of all time." So, with God's extensive and successful know-how in the business world available to them, what could they possibly lose by going? Actually, the question should be stated more firmly: If God is the marketer par excellence, how can we afford not to be in the business game ourselves?

And it is not only the evangelicals who see in this new strategy the pot of gold at the end of the rainbow. Here is the very lifeline that the liberals need to bring back their desultory churches! In Scottsdale, Arizona, an "open and affirming," but also liberal and sagging, church has found here its methodology of salvation, metaphorically speaking. This church, too, has given up on the traditional church. Actually this happened a long time ago, so this is not a new move. But this church, too, is looking for spiritual experiences, "not prepackaged dogma." Of course not! Who would want dogma prepackaged like hot dogs? This church is out there seeking seekers who "like jazz and rock, not hymns and Bach." Heavens, no! Please, no hymns. This is the very place for those who find "sermons boring" and who want worship that is "uplifting, not preachy and condemning." Right. Who wants to be condemned, anyway?

Here is a methodology for success that has deliberately cut itself loose from questions of truth. Anyone, therefore, can get on this bandwagon.

Marketing Megachurches

The internal architecture of the evangelical church began to change when pastors flocked to join the Hybels business experiment. In our shorthand, we speak of this innovation simply as what the "mega-churches are doing." That, of course, is quite inaccurate because it blurs two things that are not necessarily related. It lumps together size and the method of growth. The method is one learned from the corporate world, and, however inadvertently, it is hostile to theology. However, not all megachurches are business enterprises and not all are hostile to theology. Indeed, some are very traditional. It is important for us to understand some of these distinctions.

In the United States megachurches are defined as congregations that top 2,000 in membership; in Korea they have to be much larger to qualify for the "mega-" title. Churches of 2,000 and larger are not new. What is new is the number of them relative to the rest of the church world. In 2005 in the United States, 1,210 Protestant churches were at least this big, with some of the larger churches having weekly attendances of 20,000 to 30,000. In 1960 there were only 16 megachurches. Five decades ago megachurches were not in the national spotlight; now they are. What has changed, then, is the proportion of the church world that is now "mega-," the press attention it is receiving, and the overtly, unashamedly pragmatic modus operandi.

One recognizes this new direction in church life, or, more specifically, in how Christianity is being practiced on the marketing end of things, as soon as one sees it. These marketing megachurches boast vast auditoria, stripped of all religious symbols such as the cross, fitted out with comfortable chairs, and focused on a giant, technologically snazzy screen up front. This serves as a song sheet, as the Bible if that is needed, and sometimes as a backdrop while the speaker speaks, showing pictures of mountains, bubbling brooks, and tranquil lakes. It also serves as the speaker's connection to the . . . well, audience. Actually, this screen may also serve *as* the preacher. In 2005 over 1,000 churches in the United States were using DVDs each week, flashing up a message originally delivered somewhere else, at another time, and before a different audience. This, remember, is the video generation that moves seamlessly between a movie theater, a BlackBerry, a sitcom, and what happens in church. Perhaps technology will soon make most pastors redundant.

These marketing megachurches are sports arenas, country clubs, and corporate headquarters all rolled into one. Within they are, simultaneously, sold-out rock concerts and TV one-on-ones. However, these visual changes are the mere tip of the iceberg. Changes that are far more profound lie beneath the surface, in fact within the church's soul. Here, the very meaning of Christian faith is being reconfigured for a new generation. And the means of doing it is marketing. Proponents of this approach constantly reassure themselves that what is being changed is only the form of Christian faith, not the content. Biblical faith is not being modified but only its manner of delivery. The gospel is undisturbed but the church is simply finding new ways to speak about it to new, sometimes jaded, sometimes disaffected, generations. The church is just showing its willingness to become "all things to all people."

That is the apologetic, but it is not quite as simple as that. However innocent are the intentions, the form is actually affecting the content in this experiment. The methodology is transforming the faith that is being sold. That is what we need to see. But we first need to get inside this approach and think about how it is all put together.

Sale: Prices Slashed!

Catering to the Customer

If we are going to market the church and its gospel, where are we going to start? We start, of course, with our customer. What does the customer want?

The conventional wisdom is that seriousness is the death knell of successful churches. In an age of entertainment, such as our age is in the West, we have to be funny, engaging, likable, and light to succeed. So, seriousness must be banished. Preserve the taste but cut the calories.

That is the recipe seeker-sensitive strategists and pastors are following. It is their response to their perception of this changing public, and it matches the change Miller Brewing Company made from regular beer to Miller Lite when Americans became more weight conscious. If Miller can follow the changing habits of American consumers, so can our leading evangelical pastors!

Regular Christianity, many now think, does not go down easy and smooth; Christianity Lite does. A church that is serious, that is still regular . . . well, what can one say? It will stand out like an organ stop, if that still makes sense now that organs are becoming as rare as dodo birds. And how better to signal the change than by replacing the old-fashioned sermon with a personal chat from a barstool, or by replacing the serious discourse from the pastor with a drama whose very format carries with it a sense of entertainment?

There really is no end to the innovations that are possible as churches think of different ways to attract and accommodate consumers. Some churches, for example, allow those who attend to express themselves on walls devoted to sacred graffiti. Those who come can draw, paint, and sloganize their feelings into life. And how about a table laden with Play-Doh from which to build shapes that express how they are feeling that day? These are the tricks of marketing du jour. This is probably not what Jesus had in mind when he said his Father had hidden truth from the "wise" and revealed it to "little children" (Matt. 11:25)!

One of the ways of making the experience of going to church more pleasant is to offer choice. Consumers want to be able to choose the style of music they hear, the kind of worship they participate in, and to have a say in what they hear from the barstool up front. (The barstool, by the way, is what replaced the Plexiglas stand in many avant-garde churches, which, in turn, had replaced the pulpit.) Having a wide array of choices, after all, is the way the world is going.

It once was that a person who wanted to listen to music went to a public performance and there listened to the whole selection played by the orchestra or band. Then came records, which made it possible, though not convenient, to select one of the songs and not listen to the others. However, it required some effort and dexterity. Then came CDs, in which the selection of the song was so much easier. Finally, in came iPods, where the unwanted songs do not even appear and do not have to be selected "out." Why can't we have something like this in the church? That is what I, the consumer, really want. I want to be able to select what I hear and choose what I do in church. Why should worship not be customized, consumers and pastors alike are asking?

This, in fact, is exactly what a number of churches are now facilitating. They are aiming to please. Instead of offering the set two-, three-, four-, or five-course meal for everyone, they are letting people choose which aspects of worship they want. Customers can choose between different themes in worship, or different activities, or different styles in different parts of the building. It is much more like a buffet than a set meal. That way people can choose which aspect of worship suits them best on that particular day. If all they want to do is pray, then let them pray in a room in the building. If they want to watch a video, let them watch a video.

This, however, does give a slightly different meaning to the thought about the (single) people of God, meeting to express their *common* worship of the *same* God all at the *same* time, does it not?

Our customers, we also need to understand, are ill at ease in religious buildings. They do not want to be preached at and find hearing of their sin quite dismal; they do not want to sing boring music and don't understand the old hymns anyway. They come to be inspired and uplifted and are fish out of water unless they can mingle freely, coffee in hand; they feel most natural in an environment that bears more than a passing resemblance to the late-night comedy shows. If they are out of the old church groove — or were never in it — they are now into the relational groove. They want to connect.

And the amenities? What began as a simple recognition by church marketers that parking should be convenient, signs evident, and bathrooms clean has somehow begun a migration. In many churches this meant that what was once merely acceptable had to become first-rate instead, like stepping into a five-star hotel. Four Seasons Community Church. So it has happened all over the American church world at the cost of millions and millions of dollars.

It is simply impossible to describe the sense of bafflement that non-Westerners feel about all of this, especially when so many of them scramble to find an evening meal and have no sanitation, and their churches have no amenities at all. Should Christian churches really be *so* different in different places in the world? One wonders.

A Moment's Reflection

The yearning for relationships, into which these churches are trying to tap, is undoubtedly real. We do not have to understand it to recognize it. As a matter of fact, very few marketers show any interest in understanding it, and even if they understood it they wouldn't know how to analyze it. They simply recognize that it is there. But it is worth pondering further even if the marketers are interested only in using it.

This sense of disconnectedness is of course an irony. Never before have the lines of communication between people been more numerous, more efficient, or more used; e-mail, text-messaging, and cell phones are ubiquitous in our culture. We are the Wired Generation living in a mostly electronically mediated world. However, have you noticed that while everyone is speaking, no one is really listening? We are swamped by voices. So many want our time and attention that for our own protection we shut out most of them. And while we are surfing the Internet, e-mailing, watching television, or playing video games, we are doing it all alone. We are wired, but we are also more lonely and have fewer confidants than ever before. The Putnam thesis of the 1960s is correct: we are in touch with everyone potentially, but we know and are known by almost no one in particular.

This need has even led to the development of what is called "affective computing" in which a virtual person is created by a computer. This "person" responds to the real person using the computer with expressions of understanding and sympathy, thus giving the illusion of human companionship. That, apparently, is about as close as many people are getting to the real thing. We are increasingly very alone. So, what is happening?

No doubt the children of divorced parents, or children whose parents never married and then split or, perhaps, never identified themselves, understand why they have a sense of hollowness, of not being rooted anywhere, of not belonging, of being free-floating. However, this yearning for connection, for community, is an experience that almost everyone has in Western, modernized societies, not only those whose family bonds have been disrupted or broken. What has happened is that modernization — the rearrangement of our societies around cities for the purposes of production, consumption as a defining factor in life, the omnipresence of technology, and our enlarged means of communications — has cut most of us loose from the communities that used to define our world and in which we were anchored psychologically. Being part of a community, such as a small town, once gave us our way of seeing life. That has all changed. Today 93 percent of Americans live in cities of 50,000 or more, and in 1999, for the very first time, the world became urbanized, meaning that more people lived in cities than in rural areas. Not only that, but we are also living in an increasingly globalized context economically, informationally, and psychologically.

This has produced innumerable consequences. At the most obvious level, our clothes are, more often than not, made in Asia, or at least outside America. Our cars are assembled from parts made around the world, and there is a flourishing trade in body parts that are removed from some and sold to others around the world. And not only are body parts shipped around, but so, too, are drugs and illegals, fruit pickers, nannies, and young women for sexual use. The world is ever more tightly wrapped, national boundaries are less and less relevant, and information has become instantaneous and global. In this sense we have become citizens of the world, every day, and all the time, whether we like it or not.

For example, cartoons published in Europe in 2005, which some viewed as disrespectful to Muhammad, sparked riots in a number of Muslim countries in Asia, Africa, and the Middle East. Much the same thing happened the next year, 2006, when Pope Benedict XVI gave a lecture in a German university. Much of it was a critique of the Enlightenment rationalism that has captured the West. But it did include a brief, verbatim quotation from a fourteenth-century dialogue in which a Byzantine emperor contended that Islam had not made a positive contribution and was by nature violent, and rejected what the emperor presumed to be Islam's idea that conversions should be brought about by the sword. The Islamic world erupted. Turkey objected, ambassadors to the Vatican were recalled, a radical sheik in Somalia led a chorus of the outraged who said that the pope should be assassinated, a thousand Pakistani scholars demanded that he be ousted, Palestinians in Gaza and the West Bank firebombed several churches, mobs raged in Indonesia, and clerics in Iran demanded that the pope apologize.

What is of interest here is not so much that Muslims themselves seemed, to some, to encourage the idea of Islam as intrinsically violent, but that the incident demonstrated yet again how tightly laced together the world is by information. As globalization takes hold, as information flies, and as products cross national boundaries as if they were not there, it is the psychological consequences that probably impact the church more deeply than any others.

Today we inhabit the *world,* not just our community, our small town, or our corner of the countryside. We are knowledgeable of all the great shaping and shaking events of life almost as they happen, in Indonesia, Brazil, Australia, France, China, or Botswana. And this sense of being a citizen of the world is greatly exacerbated by the many forces in life that militate against our belonging to any one place. We are those, for example, who are carried by the economic tides from job to job, from place to place. We are those whose families have been dispersed like confetti in the wind, part blown in this direction, part in that. What is the bottom-line effect of it all? What is the psychological impact? It is loneliness. Loneliness is the modern plague. This is the plague of being disconnected, of not being rooted, of not belonging anywhere in particular but to everything in general. It is the affliction of being alone, of being unnoticed, of being carried along by an indifferent universe. Commitment — actual commitment, real bonds, a real sense of belonging, not just the *idea* of commitment — has become a precious stone, rare, much sought after and, when found, treasured.

That we experience so little sense of belonging, and have no natural communities of which we are a part, is probably what explains the fact that 40 percent of Americans regularly attend a small group. These run the gamut from small support groups for the divorced or addicted to discussion groups, reading groups, Bible study and prayer groups. These groups serve extremely important functions, whether they are religious in character or not. Among those who attend, for example, 82 percent said they felt they were not alone because they were part of the group, regardless of its character; 72 percent found encouragement in the midst of life's conflicts; 51 percent were happy to have others around them with whom they could share happy events in their lives; and 38 percent found others who could help them make difficult decisions. The functions of local communities, in which most people once

33

lived, have now been taken over by these small ad hoc groups. Undoubtedly they are meeting profound psychological needs, the needs everyone has, since we are all created as social beings, made to connect. These needs are almost as important as, and may be more important than, the reason the group exists, which is to study the Bible or to discuss investments, and so forth. But because these groups are strictly voluntary, they are inherently fragile. They can evaporate in the twinkling of an eye. They can evaporate overnight since every meeting is a matter of *choice* for those who come.

Marketers have rightly sensed this loneliness, this yearning to be connected. It is part of the fabric of modernized life. But so, too, is the sharp-edged competition that our capitalism demands. This, too, spills over into the church.

Consumers today, given the abundance of information at their fingertips, are in the driver's seat. It is their right to take their business anywhere they want. This is what fuels the competition between the retailers. The retailers and manufacturers have to ride the waves of change that course through the capitalistic world with astonishing frequency. It is consumers who demand this kind of constant change, and it is the capitalistic enterprise, always in search of an edge, that sustains it. The result is that change is faster, deeper, and more pervasive today than ever before, so much of it driven by technology, particularly the computer and now the Internet. The corporate world has had to learn how to ride this storm.

Marketers have sensed this, too. I have seen very little serious analysis of it from within their world, but they have sniffed an opportunity and are out to exploit it.

The Industrial Revolution, beginning in the eighteenth century, mechanized production. This had two effects. In Britain, for example, in the first half of that century, prices on cotton goods dropped by 90 percent while production rose more than 150-fold. It is this remaking of life, not simply in cotton goods but across our lives, that has been accelerated in recent decades by the computer. Initially, this tool simply did what people had always done, except more accurately and quickly. It was initially used mainly for tasks like keeping government records, keeping track of appointments, or booking airline tickets. However, just as the railroads connected factories and commercial centers in the

Industrial Revolution, so now, Peter Drucker has argued, are the computer and the Internet repeating this feat in an entirely different and more far-reaching way. They are creating virtual commerce. If the railroads shrank distance, the Internet eliminated it, making businesses compete nationally and even globally.

Everything is changed when those in the market for a house, for example, can inform themselves of every house in a neighborhood, city, or suburb and can "visit" any they wish to see virtually. When area auto dealers must compete for business beyond their region because their competitors are making offers directly to consumers in their backyard via personal computers, this changes the old regional dominance and loyalties. It is competition that drives change, which dramatically shortens the shelf life of all products, which makes obsolescence a circumstance more dreaded in the business world than the judgment of God, and which also creates enormous instability in the workplace. It has made mincemeat of many a career. Competition threatens laggards and the incompetent. Competition rewards the nimble, the cutthroats, and the entrepreneurial.

One of the unintended consequences of all of this is the advent of online shopping. As people have gained confidence in doing this, and as time becomes more and more scarce, the malls seem more and more uninviting. The point and click of the computer mouse seems preferable to the time and effort needed to make the purchase the old-fashioned way. In America, between 2001 and 2006, the number of online shoppers increased threefold with estimated sales online in 2006 of $200 billion. Who foresaw the effect this e-commerce would have on our social world and even on our own psychology?

Competition also explains the fact that, in a dog-eat-dog world, businesses acquire each other. Size is a means to market dominance. Not only is there an internal economy of scale that happens as enterprises swallow up one another, and not only does the holy grail of greater efficiency seem more attainable, but also competitors are put out of business. The larger the business, it is hoped, the more efficient the production or service, the greater the market penetration, the greater the dominance, the more healthy the bottom line, and the happier the investors. Big businesses can do things that small businesses cannot. Wal-Mart can offer a greater variety of goods, at a lower price, than can the mom-and-pop shops that once lined Main Street. Wal-Mart's very distinct edge is its variety and its lower prices.

These, the inhabitants of a modernized world, are the church's customers, at least in the West. So why not pitch to them? Why not compete for them? Why not bring into the church the proven techniques of market penetration? Why not speak the language of the marketplace, which is the language of the capitalistic West, and sell, sell, sell?

Why not pitch the church to these consumers as a product, as an experience that will meet the needs they are experiencing in this kind of world? Why not try to "reach" these generations of the disconnected and disaffected? Why not adapt what the church is, and what it has to offer, to these inhabitants of a postmodern world with all their loss of connections, their inward aches and pains, their loss of meaning, their loss of absolutes, and their heightened anxiety amidst all of life's changes and tensions? Why not give them as much choice as possible?

The business world has had to find ways of coming to terms with the new consumer. Can the church fail to do so and survive? One of the chief lessons the corporate world has learned is that the customer must be treated delicately. That, the church is now learning.

Wal-Mart Churches

The evangelical church, or at least a good slice of it, is nervous, twitchy, and touchy about consumer desire, ready to change in a nanosecond at the slightest hint that tastes and interests have changed. Why? Because consumer appetite reigns. And consumer appetite and consumer rights go hand in hand. These rights and appetites are very much alive in what used to be called the pew. Those who attend churches are now like any other customers you might meet in the mall. Displease them in any way and they will take their business elsewhere. That is the fear that lurks in many a church leader's soul because they know that is how the marketplace works.

Like customers everywhere, those who show up in these churches are sovereign. Let us make no mistake about that. They rule. Accepting this fact has become the key to becoming cutting-edge in cultural terms. A mailer from a church in Mesa, Arizona, in 2006, for example, read: "Is your life everything you want it to be? You hear all kinds of offers of ways to improve your life, but do they work? God is offering you a way to make your life everything you truly want it to be." So, there it is! The difference between this offer and the others is that this one works. Here the customer can match self-perceived need with a product. And bingo! Success!

With this kind of thinking in the air, we in the church today are leery of speaking of a Christian faith that is too demanding because of the prospect of offending our market(s). We take care not to cross these lines when speaking from our barstools, or from behind our Plexiglas stands if they have not yet been replaced.

This is a curious thing, is it not? It brings to mind the haplessness of parents in a home where the children have, amidst sullen moods and a creeping sense of the cruel injustice that has been inflicted on them, decided they will take it no longer. It begins with thoughts, the rebellious mists that shroud the mind and hold off the sun's light and warmth. But soon the thoughts become seeds, and the seeds, finding fertile soil in the internal wounds suffered during the journey to adulthood, begin to germinate. The parents, sensing something is amiss, scour their minds to think of what they have done wrong and, understanding little of the labyrinthine coils of the adolescent psyche, decide to back off and take the path that inflicts the least pain. Poor things. They are only trying to do the best they can, but unfortunately they do not quite understand that they are staring down the gun barrel of a stickup artist. They are about to be robbed. Out of their good intentions, space is enlarged around the child, latitude is allowed, rules are rescinded, rebukes are stifled except in rare cases, and expectations are lifted. However, parents being parents, they are never entirely out of the woods with these children because, try as they might, they are never fully successful in setting their children free.

What is interesting about this painful tango of parent and child is that the more the demands and expectations of the parents are moderated, the *more* onerous and intolerable do the children find those that remain! In fact, the few that remain become more objectionable than the many, taken together, that once were there. Parental moderation only excites fresh cries of outrage and pain. Even more disaffection follows. Murderous glances, defiant behavior, black moods follow each other like clouds shifting across a stormy front. The parents, baffled at this unreasonable behavior, retreat even more. But the further they retreat, the more intense becomes the resentment! Nothing less than their total, abject surrender is acceptable. And when they do yield and hold aloft their white flag of surrender, they are despised even more deeply!

Am I being unreasonable in thinking that there are some parallels to the contemporary church here? Not, of course, that the pastors are the parents and the congregations are the children. That is a Catholic idea. The parallel, though, does seem to hold at the point of who has the psychological edge.

It would be quite wrong to suggest that pastors and other leaders in a local church have an authority that operates with near certain infallibility, or that what they think should be beyond question, or that their teaching, if they still offer such in church, cannot be questioned. All should be held to account before the same standard that is the Word of God.

By the same token, no congregation can take to itself this authority, and that is what is happening implicitly as consumer impulses take root in the evangelical psyche. All consumers, we need to remember, are *sovereign,* and the consuming impulse, once it enters a church, makes individual preferences the deciding factor, the driving factor in what that church becomes. These preferences become the standard by which the church is measured.

The moment disaffection with the church's music, message, style, ethos, amenities, programs, or parking lot(s) begins to take root in a congregation, these new market-savvy pastors fear, they can anticipate dark glances directed toward the front of the church signaling consumer dissatisfaction. The glances will then mature into displeasure, the displeasure will become a seed, the seed will germinate in the internal soil that is ready to receive it, and the decision to walk away will be made. That is the (post)modern version of damnation, at least from a pastor's point of view!

Market-savvy pastors, sensing this, back off. They lift demands and expectations, making Christianity light and easy. They hire new staff who specialize in knowing how to make worship fun, not to mention funny. Polls and soundings are taken each week, just as they are by the major retailers, to see if things are "on target." Poor things. If only they knew that their congregations, too, have become stickup artists! Or, to change the picture, what is happening here is that the individual has invested his or her desires with a kind of sovereign authority that runs roughshod over everything else, including the Word of God.

Never mind. Is it not better to have these people in the church on their own terms than not at all? Is it not possible that they will hear something there that might "click" with them? Why offend them, then, and guarantee that their weekends will be spent away from church? So, make it all as simple as an advertisement, as pleasing as an ice cream in the heat of summer. Make it as easy on the mind as a relaxing show on television. Only give something that works. Do not talk doctrine. Do not hold forth about anything that takes serious effort to follow. Do not sound churchy.

Down with the Traditional Church!

This new direction is, needless to say, carried on side by side with an attack on the traditional church. This attack has become incessant from the church marketers, as indeed it has also from emergents, and it is, on its face, quite curious.

It is true that some traditional churches are desultory, dispirited, boring, dull, lifeless, inept, small, disheartened, or otherwise dying. One does wonder, though, why such a dead dog keeps getting kicked, sometimes quite viciously, by the church marketers. "If you have found church to be as painful as a trip to the dentist and twice as boring . . ." begins a typical attack that is also a solicitation of interest in this new breed of church-doing. Another advertisement for a megachurch, with the traditional church in mind, says church "is about avoiding hell . . . not sitting through it every week."

But if the traditional church is so inept, so out-of-it, so not-with-it, so passé, so completely washed up, so painful, and so boring, why not let it die peacefully? Why keep on kicking it?

Because the real target is not the traditional church but the traditional theology it lives by. This belief system is at the heart of the tradi-

39

tional church's life that seeker-sensitives are after. It is not that they want to deny it or reject it, but it is something of an embarrassment to them. At least in their own churches, they want to *conceal* it. They want it hidden, kept in the background, made to disappear from what they are doing. It is rather like a family secret. Family secrets are true, but they should be kept private. They should not be divulged.

This is a delicate dance. For seeker-sensitives, by their own reckoning, traditional evangelical belief is their dance partner but, in building their churches, they cannot be seen dancing with their partner. They must dance alone, theologically speaking. Actually, in place of the old partner is the new one. The new partner is the customer. It is the customer who is their theology!

These churches cannot live without traditional evangelical belief, if they still want to think of themselves as evangelical, but they also want the freedom to be independent of evangelical beliefs in constructing their churches. They do not deny the doctrines, for the most part, but these are not owned publicly because that would exclude their churches from the market dynamics.

Across much of evangelicalism, but especially in the market-driven churches, one therefore sees a new kind of leadership among pastors now. Gone is the older model of the scholar-saint, one who was as comfortable with books and learning as with the aches of the soul. This was the shepherd who knew the flock, knew how to tend it, and Sunday by Sunday took that flock into the treasures of God's Word. This has changed. In its place is the new "celebrity" style. What we typically see now, Nancy Pearcey suggests, is the leader who works by manipulating the feelings of the audience, enhancing his own image with personal anecdotes, modeling himself after the CEO, and adopting a domineering management style. He (usually) is completely results-oriented, pragmatic, happy to employ any technique from the secular world that will produce the desired results. And this leader has to be magnetic, entertaining, and light on the screen up front.

However, this is turning out to be not as easy as it once seemed. Pastors who run out of funny, inspiring, clever, and entertaining material increasingly are turning to the Internet to buy it all prepackaged. Would one not think that this material would lose its genuineness in transition? And its freshness? Never mind. If it works, if the audience is pleased, the goal has been reached. After all, don't all entertainers have ghostwriters working behind the scenes to produce their jokes? Why shouldn't pastors?

It is worth noting that this is where the seeker-sensitives and the emergents have diverged. The former have looked to corporate America and its proven strategies for market penetration in doing their church business. The cost, though, is that the large, booming success that results is often quite depersonalized and invariably emptied of serious thought.

It is true that many in today's world are comfortable with impersonal structures. They do not mind being anonymous, an unknown in a large crowd. And they take in stride the slogans and little inspirational thoughts that fill the air all the time. After all, that is life in our big, modernized cities. However, these large structures only deepen the sense of not belonging we carry with us much of the time. Why, then, would we want to experience this in church, too? And why would we content ourselves with having yet one more product plugged to us in church when we are bombarded by products and telemarketers all week? This is a point of acute vulnerability for the marketing churches.

That is what the emergents have sensed. Rather than large, empty church structures filled with the rhythms of the marketing world, emergents have gone to small, connected groups, to networking, to being deinstitutionalized if that is what it takes, to relationships. This, as I have suggested, resonates with a loss that is very deep and painful in the (post)modern psyche. People want to connect and to be connected.

However, while the emergents are intent on making connections, they do not want to make those connections across generations. They are niche-driven. The niche is Gen X. Emergent churches are typically made up from the same social slice. They are as look-alike as the marketing churches are for those of another generation.

A Word of Praise

Like so many matters in life, however, there are two sides to this story. The other side is that many who have taken up the tools of marketing have done so out of desires that could be laudable. The first of these is a desire to see Christian faith, which is apparently flagging, begin to grow again. The second is to engage postmodern culture.

Evangelical Stagnation

On the first point, it is probably impossible to know exactly what the spiritual realities are in America today. This, I know, sounds quite non-sensical. Do we not have polls? Has not George Barna delivered the goods for us? Barna indeed has been busy. However, polls are at best only approximations of very complex internal realities.

There are several complicating factors here. Answers to questions sometimes change depending on how the questions are phrased, and in any case, polls can read only the self-understanding that people have. The reading they give may or may not be accurate. Furthermore, many of the questions are not framed in biblical ways. The results may in fact tell us quite accurately how people are reading themselves but may also be quite inaccurate in telling us about the actual situation from a biblical perspective. In that sense polls can be misleading.

The only numbers we have to go on, though, all indicate that evangelical Christianity has stagnated. In 1976 Gallup startled America with his discovery that 32 percent claimed to be born again. In subsequent polls over the next three to four decades, this statistic has remained the same with minor variations, though Barna's numbers recently have shown a change.

However, both Gallup and Barna now think of the born-again in two categories, the committed and the not-so-serious. Indeed, Barna sees "evangelicals," who are more serious, as a subset of the "born again," who are less so. Evangelicals are those who not only claim to be born again but also evidence a high(er) degree of commitment and hold to a core of basic biblical beliefs such as the reliability and author-ity of the Bible, the fact that salvation is by grace, not by works, and that it is found uniquely in Christ. In 2007 he reported that while 38 percent considered themselves born again, only 8 percent actually met his doctrinal criteria for an evangelical. In 2005 it was 7 percent, in the next year 9 percent.

In 2006, 45 percent claimed to be born again, even though 21 percent of those were "unchurched." And evangelicals, by his definition, made up about only one-fifth of the total of those claiming spiritual rebirth. What is of particular interest in Barna's polling are some of the demographics.

Those who met his stricter, doctrinal criteria in 2007 were more likely than those in the looser category of the merely born again to be college graduates, white, with a higher income, and sixty years old or older. This more well-to-do and educated sector, Barna's evangelicals, is clearly fading off the scene. My conclusion from these numbers is that the postwar reconstruction of evangelical faith is now receding because its capital has not been renewed in the generations that have followed. No wonder church marketers have sniffed the wind and decided they won't have much success pitching a more doctrinally shaped faith in the marketplace today!

The 45 percent of Americans claiming to be born again is the highest number yet reported. This would suggest that born-again believing is growing. This is contrary to what the church marketers have been saying. However, much "born again" religion is simply cultural spirituality that has no doctrinal moorings, inspires little or no Christian commitment, and often opposes itself to the institutional church and to Christian truth. As a slice of American religion, it is interesting. As a barometer of Christian believing, it should be taken with a grain of salt.

The more significant number here is the 9 percent (or maybe 7 percent) of Americans whom Barna sees as evangelical. What is striking about this number is how minuscule it is. This is hardly an army about to capture the nation's soul, seize positions of power, and dominate all the cultural institutions! How groundless are the fears that are constantly making the rounds of the secular media! If they knew how small the giant actually was, and how toothless, their panic would subside like a spent summer storm.

I therefore applaud the marketers for their concern. As far as we can tell from these numbers, evangelical faith is stagnating. They have seen that.

43

Engaging Culture

I also applaud the marketers' desire for cultural engagement. That is to put as positive a construction as I possibly can on what they are doing. Yet it is also clear that their desire to engage culture is really a desire to exploit it, to use it for their own advantage. And yet, their desire is not altogether amiss.

No one should take issue with a church being sensitive to outsiders. On the contrary, this is simply about being considerate. Every church should put itself in the shoes of an outsider who visits for the first time, who knows nothing about Christian faith, and who is introduced to it at this first visit. With what impressions will that person leave? Those in this situation do notice whether it is easy to find their way into the sanctuary, whether they feel confident in leaving their children in the nursery, and whether they are met by friendliness. The effort to meet people on their own turf in this way is entirely laudable.

However, despite these two main virtues, so much of this rethinking of the church, this effort at finding new ways to "do" church, has rested on naïveté so enormous, so breathtakingly unrealistic and untrue, that it puts the rest of the church, who may have noticed what the marketers are up to, in quite an awkward position. What do you say to a friend doing embarrassing things in a public place? Do you keep silent and simply hope, for his or her sake, that others will not notice? Or do you risk embarrassing that person by telling him or her that what he or she is doing is not acceptable?

I have chosen to tell.

Excuse Me!

Wrong Result

The first mistake the church marketers made was refusing to see that what they had been doing had miscarried.

In 1991, 88 percent of evangelical pastors said they were favorably disposed to this new approach on the grounds that it worked. And subsequently, the overwhelming majority, in small or large ways, became seeker-sensitive. The problem, however, is that the approach that seemed so promising at the beginning has not worked. And the truth is that it *cannot* work because it is so internally flawed.

We were alerted to the issues we are going to find here. In America 45 percent say they are born again but only 9 percent, and maybe only 7 percent, give any evidence of Christian seriousness by way of minimal biblical knowledge for making life's decisions. The marketing megachurches are not entirely responsible for this situation, but they have done nothing but accelerate it. Everywhere in the marketing approach theology and Bible knowledge are downplayed, and then we are dumbfounded when commitment evaporates and ignorance reigns! The gelding is castrated, as C. S. Lewis observed in another context, and yet we expect it to be fruitful.

We need look no further than the way those involved in this experiment speak of the unconverted. In virtually all church-marketing literature, non-Christians are no longer unconverted, or unsaved, or those not-yet-reconciled-to-the-Father, or those who have not come to faith, or those who are outside of Christ. No, they are simply the unchurched. Those who were once the unconverted have become the unchurched. This spares us the embarrassment of uttering theological truth. And that is the tip-off that something is amiss here. What is amiss is that the Christianity being peddled is not about theological truth.

Christianity is not just an experience, we need to remember, but it is about truth. The experience of being reconciled to the Father, through the Son, by the work of the Holy Spirit all happens within a worldview. This worldview is the way God has taught us in his Word to view the world. That is why the Bible begins with Genesis 1:1 and not with John 3:16. It begins by setting out the distinction, as against paganism, between Creator and creation. It then lays out an understanding of God in his nature and redemptive works as well as an understanding of who humans are in their nature and in their fallenness. All of this sets the stage for the coming of Christ, for his incarnation, life, death, and resurrection. It is on this basis that God's wrath is assuaged, our sin is judged, our alienation is overcome, and we who are by nature unrighteous are made righteous in Christ. This happens only because of his grace and only through the empty hand of faith by which all of this is received. A Christian worldview, then, is one that rests upon a biblical understanding of the world, God, ourselves, and the redemptive work of Christ.

In our churches, however, only 9 percent of born-againers in 2005 had this worldview in even a modest sense. As for the others, they used what they had to make life's decisions. It was a confusing hodgepodge of ideas, many hostile to biblical faith, and this was rarely ever contradicted or corrected by anything they heard in their churches, Barna observed. Evangelicals, the more doctrinally shaped end of the born-again world, were more knowledgeable, but even here, only 51 percent in 2006 said their beliefs trumped all other considerations when making decisions in life. That means that, at best, their worldview played only a part in how they understood life. I would guess that when their beliefs collided with the needs of the workplace, or competing religious viewpoints, they acted on those beliefs only half the time. Of these same evangelicals, Barna also discovered that while 70 percent believed that moral truth is absolute, only 60 percent relied on Scripture when making their decisions.

Evangelicals are the more biblically serious of Barna's subjects. What of those who are simply born again? Are we surprised to learn that the differences in moral behavior between them and those who are entirely secular have almost disappeared? In 2007 the chief difference is that born-againers are not as involved in musical piracy, 2 percent as opposed to 7 percent. Maybe this is not even a reflection of their ethical sense. Maybe they just don't like the music.

It is not always a simple matter to explain complex decision-making. Yet one has to say that the decline in Bible knowledge in the churches has to be a large factor in the disintegrating moral culture of Christian life today. Bible knowledge has declined drastically in the churches as Sunday school programs are eliminated, expository preaching becomes unfashionable, and the practices of daily prayer and Bible reading vanish with a prior generation.

It seems rather clear, then, that the market defining most churches today is the one in which people are seeking some spiritual connection but, at the same time, are opposed to things religious. By that, they have in mind doctrines to be believed that they have not defined for themselves, moral norms to be followed that they have not set up for themselves, and corporate practice that is expected. Skip the religion; give us the meat and potatoes of what is spiritual, they are saying. That is what these marketing churches are attempting to do. So, it is no great revelation that those who are fed this trashy diet are frequently those with no worldview and in whose life biblical doctrine has little place.

Perhaps the crowning disappointment in this whole undertaking is the dismal failure of the worship services that were considered the marketers' pièce de résistance. In fact, eight of ten believers do not experience the presence of God in their worship at all. Is this really such a stunning outcome to services in which the centrality of truth has disappeared, biblical categories have been lost, and the entertainment ethos dominates everything?

George Barna was one of the primary architects of this new approach to "doing" church. He was in on the ground floor three decades ago. As the church's most assiduous poller, he undoubtedly expected by this time to be the bearer of good news once his marketing strategies were widely adopted, as they have been. It has not turned out that way. It has fallen to him to be the most important chronicler of his own failure.

Leaving behind this long trail of failure as if it had never happened, Barna has nevertheless struck out in a new direction with the same old panache, bravado, and undented self-assurance. The evangelical world has neither gasped nor blinked. In 2005 he published his book *Revolution,* which predicted that the church in the coming decade would lose much of its "market share," but never mind, because now it could climb aboard a different cultural trend and succeed even more spectacularly. Now, serious spiritual revolutionaries can simply cut themselves loose from every local church. Just walk away! Permanently. And find biblical Christianity elsewhere.

What is resulting from Barna's approach is barely recognizable as Christian today. And that is what makes the desire of some of the leading American marketing pastors to export their experiment to the rest of the world almost incomprehensible. It certainly is an expression of unbounded chutzpah.

The truth is that no matter how proficiently we learn to "do" church for the Western, affluent, highly individualistic market, we are doomed to failure. Indeed, the more proficient we become, if that proficiency requires that we denude ourselves of theology, the more certainly we doom ourselves to failure. The method is inherently flawed. If it succeeds in replicating itself at all, it will only be replicating its own failure. That is what the marketers have failed to see.

Wrong Calculation

While I applaud the concern that leaders in this movement have expressed over the stagnation of evangelical faith, I am also certain that fear is driving it. Fear of the (post)modern world. This is the second mistake the church marketers have made. They are building on a miscalculation.

Church marketers are on the run before postmoderns, fearing that unless they make "adjustments" in how Christian faith sounds, and what it looks like, and what it asks for, certain extinction awaits it. Actually, this fear is not entirely misguided.

The truth is that Christianity is leaving the West. Here, in the West, Christianity is stagnant, but in Africa, Latin America, and parts of Asia it is burgeoning, at least statistically. The statistical center of gravity of the Christian church worldwide has moved out of Europe and is now found in northern Africa. The face of Christianity is changing as a result. It is no longer predominantly northern, European, and Anglo-Saxon. Its face is that of the underdeveloped world. It is predominantly from the Southern Hemisphere, young, quite uneducated, poor, and very traditional. The question Westerners need to ponder is why, despite our best efforts at cultural accommodation in America, God seems to be taking his work elsewhere. Is there a lesson lurking somewhere in this story?

Evangelical pastors in America are now scared. That, I know, is not the appearance. *Au contraire!* These market-driven churches give every appearance of being on top of the world, of being cocksure.

But let us deal with reality here. Evangelicals today are fearful, but they are fearful of all the wrong things. They are deeply apprehensive about becoming obsolete, of being left behind, so to speak, of being passed by, and of not being relevant. Never mind that they should first and foremost be relevant to God and his truth. That seems like a small consideration as long as they are relevant to the latest ways of being and behaving in this (post)modern culture.

This, of course, was the fear that haunted the older generation of Protestant liberals, so many of whom began their lives in evangelical homes. They were overwhelmed by the need to be relevant to the culture. The culture they had in mind was what we think of as "high" culture. Their conversation partner was the Enlightenment. It was the purveyors of Enlightenment thought in the universities, in literature, in the arts, and of course in the sciences with whom they sought an intellectual truce, a working compromise. From this capitulation — for that is what it was — was born many a synthesis in which elements from Christian faith and elements from the humanistic world were drawn together into a single package that was Christian in name and humanistic in much of its substance. The downfall and wreckage of the mainline denominations in North America in the second half of the twentieth century, as well as their counterparts in Europe, bear eloquent testimony to the impossibility of accommodating Christ to culture in this way.

This lesson, however, is entirely lost on most evangelicals today. The reason is partly that they are treading a different path and so they do not see the parallels. Theirs is not the accommodation to high culture, as was the liberals'. That culture was suffused with intellectual pride and humanism, with rationalism and hostility to Christian faith. It is now dying. The Enlightenment, from which much of it arose, has all but collapsed, as has the Christianity that had made itself into an ally.

The parallels between these older liberals and today's evangelicals are not in the culture to which they are accommodating but in the *process* of accommodation. Behind each is the same mind-set. The difference is only in *what* is being accommodated. And the dangers are all concealed beneath the apparent innocence of the experiment. The fact is, however, that evangelical Christianity today is as endangered by its postmodern dance partner as the earlier liberals were by their Enlightenment partner.

The miscalculation here is enormous. The born-again, marketing church has calculated that unless it makes deep, serious cultural adap-

tations, it will go out of business, especially with the younger generations. What it has not considered carefully enough is that it may well be
putting itself out of business with God. And the further irony is that the
younger generations who are less impressed by whiz-bang technology,
who often see through what is slick and glitzy, and who have been on
the receiving end of enough marketing to nauseate them, are as likely
to walk away from these oh-so-relevant churches as to walk into them.

This is the second major mistake our church marketers have
made. They have miscalculated.

Wrong Analogy

The third mistake market-driven pastors and strategists have made is
to use the wrong analogy. The analogy du jour is between the way proficient marketers like Pepsi do their business and how the church should
do its business.

There are, in fact, two main parallels that some in the church
have seen. First, Christ was incarnate. He was not a celestial rabbi, giving his teaching from afar. He took on our flesh and bones, entered human life, lived under its limitations, and learned the language and habits of his own culture. He gave his teaching in its terms, in ways that
listeners could readily understand. His teaching was contextualized.
Our church life, our message, should be, too.

Our context today, at least in the West, is principally one of commerce and consumption. To speak in the language of consumption, to
use its speech and ways, is to speak contextually. It is to speak the language everyone understands. It is to enter the culture and mind-set of
twenty-first-century Westerners. It is to meet them on their own terms,
incarnationally, just as Jesus met the people of his own day. That is the
logic.

The second parallel is between marketing and evangelism. In
marketing, much time, effort, and expense are spent investigating in
exactly which social pockets, which generational habitats, the product
will find its most likely consumers. Marketing is built on serious research. Once the target audience has been identified, then the product
advertisements are honed to connect with the most likely buyers.

What is being sold is a combination of information about the product and promises about its benefits. These promises about the product are trying to connect with the consumers' deep yearnings, yearnings to be seen as successful, or important, to be cutting edge, or enviable. This is a time when we prefer to be envied for what we have rather than admired for who we are. So the sale is clinched. What is bought may be a product, but along with the product is bought a sense about life, a new look, an upgrade, having the latest and best, the appearance of having arrived, success, or being someone.

The parallels with evangelism are not of course exact, but a great many evangelical churches have signed off on this analogy. And their church staffs are now geared up for this new challenge. Now, churches are likely to be led by former CEOs, advertising executives, corporate managers, few of whom have, or want, a theological education. The skills that made them successful in the business world make them successful in the church world. That, at least, is what is assumed.

The gospel is a product, evangelism is about selling it, and church (pastoral) staffs are there to make it all happen. In the market-driven churches, this is preceded by market research that identifies the most likely customers. It turns out that these are not typically in the cities but in the suburbs, not the older suburbs but the newer ones, not among the poor but among the well-to-do middle class. Surprise!

In both forms of marketing — in the world and in the church — the result is an exchange of goods. In the one, a new sound system, a new BMW, or the latest and most alluring perfume. In the other, eternal life.

So, what is wrong with this? What is wrong if it clearly works? After all, some churches that have marketed themselves and their product, the gospel, have grown rather astoundingly, though those that have failed rarely get noticed. Can we argue with success?

I believe that we can. More than that, I believe, in this case, that we should. What we have here are churches reconfigured around evangelism that abandon much of the fabric of biblical faith to succeed. They have taken a part of that faith, modified it in deference to consumer impulse, and then made of that part all that there is to Christian faith. Here is a methodology for success that can succeed with very little truth; indeed, its success seems to depend on not showing much truth. After all, evangelical churches aren't the only ones walking this road — some liberal mainline churches are trying to do so, too, taking a page out of this playbook. So are some Catholic churches. And in Los Angeles there is the nine-thousand-member Agape International Spiritual Center, which makes no pretense to being Christian but has enjoyed great success by emulating the Willow Creek model. It boasts a million friends worldwide and casts itself in the New Thought–Ancient Wisdom tradition of spirituality, happily melding in its worship the "ohm-m-m's" of Eastern religion and the praise choruses of Christian churches. Now, that's what you call blended worship!

Success can be had along marketing lines, but truth is not an intrinsic part of that success. There is the formula. Does that not raise a red flag? Is the gospel not about truth? The Christian message is not about anything else than the "truth of the gospel" (Gal. 2:5), the "truth [as it] is in Jesus" (Eph. 4:21). Gospel truth, biblically speaking, is not a formula, not simply a relationship, not just about spirituality. It is about the triune God acting in this world redemptively, in the course of time, in the fabric of history, and bringing all of this to its climax in Christ. The message of the cross is the message that corresponds to what God actually did in space and time. And this is all a part of a whole. The whole is all that God has unveiled of himself and of how he views the world.

That is where this gospel really parts company from the way in which products and services are marketed in our modernized world. These products and services are nothing more than products and services. They are simply there for our use. The gospel is not. The gospel calls us not to use it but to submit to the God of the universe through his Son. A methodology for success that circumvents issues of truth is one that will rapidly emancipate itself from biblical Christianity or, to put it differently, will rapidly eviscerate biblical faith.

That, indeed, is what is happening because the marketing model, if followed, empties the truth out of the gospel. First, the needs consumers have are needs *they* identify for themselves. The needs sinners have are needs *God* identifies for us, and the way we see our needs is rather different from the way he sees them. We suppress the truth about God, holding it down in "unrighteousness" (Rom. 1:18). We are not subject to his moral law and in our fallenness are incapable of being obedient to it (Rom. 8:7), so how likely is it, outside of the intervention of God through the Holy Spirit, that we will identify our needs as those arising from our rebellion against God? No, the product we will seek naturally will not be the gospel. It will be a therapy of some kind, a technique for life, perhaps a way of connecting more deeply with our own spiritual selves on our own terms, terms that require no repentance and no redemption. It will not be the gospel. The gospel cannot be a product that the church sells because there are no consumers for it. When we find consumers, we will find that what they are interested in buying, on their own terms, is not the gospel.

Furthermore, when we buy a product, we buy it for our use. When we accept Christ, he is not there for our use but we are there for his service. We commit ourselves to him in a way that we do not commit ourselves to any product. There is a world of difference between the Lord of Glory, the incarnate second person of the Godhead, and a Lexus, a vacation home, or a trip to the Bahamas. The marketing analogy blurs all of this, reducing Christ simply to a product we buy to satisfy our needs. What is destroyed along the way are the biblical doctrines of sin, of the incarnation, and of redemption. The marketing analogy is the wrong analogy. It is deeply harmful to Christian faith. This harm is immediately apparent when we see that it has produced a kind of spirituality that is indistinguishable from the spirituality in the culture. That spirituality is predominantly non-Christian.

This cultural spirituality, to which I will return in a later chapter, is hostile to Christian faith. Christian faith is about revealed truth, doctrine that is to be believed, moral norms that should be followed, and church life in which participation is expected. Our cultural spirituality wants none of this.

But that has not stopped many of the megachurches from trolling in these waters because of the marketing model. The success they achieve is had by being "religious" as little as possible. Religious words have, as a result, more or less disappeared in these churches, words like "justification," "atonement," "judgment," "holiness," "incarnation," "sanctification," and "glorification." If the words have gone, so too have the doctrines of which the words were a part and by which the doctrines were taught. It is the *benefits* of believing that can be marketed, not the *truth* from which the benefits derive. So, market the one and forget the other! Here is the pragmatism that has been a hallmark of American evangelicalism. Here is an antidoctrinal mood that cannot be squared with a biblical mind-set.

What pastors and strategists have seen here, though, is something that is going to work. They thought they could sell spirituality. They apparently also thought that what makes this spirituality distinctively *Christian* is initially unimportant. It can be picked up later by osmosis once a person is in the church. This seems to be the best explanation of the fact that in these churches are many who say they are born again but who have no biblical worldview, whose views are a motley selection of what they have picked up along life's way, some biblical but many not.

The fact that this situation is getting worse rather than better delivers a strong message. It is that the analogy at work here is mistaken. It is damaging Christian faith.

Wrong Customer

There is a fourth mistake that the market-driven, seeker-sensitive churches have made. They have in their crosshairs the wrong customer.

In his book *Surprising Insights from the Unchurched and Proven Ways to Read Them,* Thom Rainer has raised an intriguing question about this customer. He noted that all the research of the 1990s had focused on the unchurched, those who had not been to church except on special occasions such as funerals and Christmas services. Was it possible, then, that the market-driven churches were reconfiguring themselves around a customer who in fact would *never* come in their doors? Was it possible that they were adapting themselves to a market to which they would mostly never have any access? Would it not be far more pertinent to look at the *formerly* unchurched, those who had not been coming to church and then started to come? What drew them? What were they looking for? This line of thought yielded a picture quite different from the prevailing wisdom found through much of the church-marketing literature.

What were these people looking for in a church? If we believe all the church-marketing hype, we would have to conclude that potential

54

customers wanted, above all else, not to hear issues of truth and belief. These should be avoided like the plague. These are matters, the prevailing wisdom says, that should be hidden from seekers because they are so dreadfully off-putting.

Not so! In fact, 90 percent of those in Rainer's studies said the preaching was important to them, and not just any preaching. Almost the same percentage, 88 percent, said that what they came to hear was *doctrine*. The beliefs of the church were important to 91 percent. They wanted to know what the church believed. They wanted to have this laid out for them — with *conviction*. This was their preeminent concern. The next issue of importance, the friendliness of people, was far down the list — only 49 percent cited it. Is this such a revolutionary discovery? Should we really be so amazed that people would like to know what Christians think and whether, in this age of jaded, faded, transient beliefs, there actually is something that can be believed for all time?

Furthermore, what is to be gained if we are so intent in reaching out to the unchurched that we then unchurch the reached? Certainly, what is happening today is that the reached of an earlier generation are being unchurched. So, not only is this approach generationally destructive but it is also trafficking in something of a fraud. The price of marketing is that the church hide its nature and biblical Christianity hide its face. So, what is there to learn in these churches? Why would anyone want to stay?

Rainer's findings confirm what others have argued. Rodney Stark and Roger Finke asked a similar question in *The Churching of America, 1776-1990*. How can we explain the fact that at the time of the Revolution only 17 percent belonged to a church, by the time of the Civil War it was 37 percent, and by 1980 it was 62 percent? What explains this steady conquest of the American soul? And what explains why some churches succeed and others do not, some gain ground and others lose it?

Their answer was that in a free society there is a market for religion. It works like the market for goods and services, which is what the seeker-sensitives also think. But what Stark and Finke said was that the content of the faith, its *doctrine*, had in the past been vital to the success of Christian churches and not, as the seeker-sensitive imagine, an impediment to success. Specifically, they argued that churches that flourish exhibit a high degree of distinction from the culture, of cognitive dissonance. Failure often has followed the disappearance of this distinction and distance. The reason is that people in the past have been looking for something different, something that cannot be had under a secular guise. Churches that have offered this have flourished. Churches that lose their distinction from the surrounding culture have failed and disappeared.

Seeker-sensitive churches are assuming the reverse. They are assuming that doctrine is really peripheral and that the level of tension felt over and against the culture should be minimized if they are to succeed. This is what is being visually represented in those churches that are trying to look just like the buildings people enter during the workweek. This is also why seeker services have greatly de-emphasized the religious dimension, removing pulpits, abandoning traditional sermons, hymns, offerings, or anything else that seems too religious. The great mistake of these marketers has been to read the needs of the consumer as being "spiritual" (in the contemporary sense) but not theological, as being psychological but wanting little to do with truth. In fact, these seekers are not just interested in techniques of survival in life. They want to understand if there is meaning in life that transcends the mere business of surviving.

Marketers also have tried to capitalize on the trendy generational studies of the last two decades. Have we not all heard generalizations about boomers and Gen Xers? Can we not all conjugate these differences? Boomers are this . . . Xers are that. These studies heighten generational differences, often fuel generational antagonisms, and overlook what people as people have in common. What we all have in common is that we all are made in the image of the same God. Those who are redeemed — if I may use biblical language — are redeemed by the same Christ, are regenerated by the same Spirit, and have the same truth and goals. Generational distinctions change none of this. When what was generationally distinctive became the total focus, red flags should have gone up instantly. Instead, churches could only drool over the sudden prospects of the extraordinary success that seemed just around the corner.

So it was that churches shaped themselves first to the boomers, who were perceived to have the money, and then to the Xers when the market became too crowded in boomerland. And no one stopped to ask what would happen to the churches that were successful. Does this strategy not undermine the very nature of the gospel message? If it is successful, it will make churches that are uni-generational, in all likelihood of the same social stripe and color, all alike, white consuming boomers intent on their own satisfactions. Is this really what Christianity is about? Does not the gospel call into fellowship those whom a society divides? There, side by side, should we not see the rich and the poor, men and women, powerful and marginalized, boomer and nonboomer all united in the same Christ by whom they have all been bought?

The Bottom Line

A disconnect is now evident between the biblical orthodoxy that is professed and the assumptions off which seeker churches are building themselves. The reasons for this are now obvious.

First is a marketing strategy that assumes that the *benefits* of believing are what people are after, not the belief itself — as if one could have the one without the other! But never mind, this is what makes the sale.

Second, to pursue this strategy these churches have had to make another assumption. This one is related to human nature. Their way of doing church assumes the (Pelagian) view that human beings are not inherently sinful. A majority of 52 percent of born-againers in fact reject the idea of original sin outright. In their disposition to God and his Word, it is assumed, (post)moderns are neutral. That being so, they can be seduced into making the purchase of faith as though it were any other kind of purchase. That all of this is deliberately undoctrinal is seen as the key ingredient to success. Is this not how America has always succeeded, by being pragmatic?

There is a yearning in the evangelical world today. We encounter it everywhere. It is a yearning for what is real. Sales pitches, marketed faith, the gospel as commodity, people as customers, God as just a prop to my inner life, the glitz and sizzle, Disneyland on the loose in our churches — all of it is skin deep and often downright wrong. It is not making serious disciples. It cannot make serious disciples. It brims with success, but it is empty, shallow, and indeed unpardonable.

It is time to reach back into the Word of God, as we have not done in a generation, and find again a serious faith for our undoubtedly serious times. It is now time to close the door on this disastrous experiment in retailing faith, to do so politely but nevertheless firmly. It is time to move on. It is time to become Protestant once again.

CHAPTER III

Truth

—ᘔ—

All that is solid melts into the air, all that is holy is profaned.

KARL MARX

Sanctify them in the truth; your word is truth.

JOHN 17:17

T ruth is hot today. Hotly disputed, that is. And this is . . . well, true, right across a wide front. Doubts about truth are aired in rarefied intellectual circles and heard in movies. It is a question in law journals as in the wider popular culture. And even in the church. Everywhere we are hearing the same uncertainties about the very possibility of truth.

In the church it is tempting to exploit these uncertainties, and many are falling prey to this temptation. The temptation is that sounding diffident about truth, about whether we can know the truth, does have its attractions today. It establishes an immediate bond with those in our postmodern culture. Postmoderns have become very leery about truth and about those who think they know it.

This apparent gain by way of a connection, however, is more than matched by a loss. What makes for a bond with culture makes for a rupture, I will argue, with the ways of God. This chapter is going to explore this uncomfortable juxtaposition of relevance and irrelevance.

I will be exploring several themes. What in the culture has led us to such a jaundiced view of truth? Why do so many Americans believe neither in truth nor in morality that is absolute? In the light of these answers, we then need to ask ourselves how we should think about truth. What is the biblical teaching on truth? That teaching will then raise for us a perplexing question. In the light of the Bible's teaching on truth, why is the church that professes this truth so untouched by it?

The Self Is Disconnected

We begin with the basic facts. A great American majority, at least two-thirds in some readings and much higher in the younger age segments, does not believe in any kind of absolute truth. It is no surprise to learn, then, that almost half of America thinks that the Bible, the Koran, and the Book of Mormon all have the same spiritual truths.

These figures are echoed in the church, too, so it comes as no surprise to learn that American Christians rate themselves high on relationships and low on Bible knowledge. The Bible, after all, is the source of the truth God has given us. Of the seven characteristics Barna selected for measuring spirituality in 2005, Bible knowledge came out the lowest.

This is part of our picture today. We are spiritual. We want relationships, but we do not want to be religious. Bible knowledge is increasingly considered part of religion in this growing and damaging separation of spirituality from religion. This explains why so many of our churches, especially the most prominent marketing megachurches, give the impression that Christianity is about many things, but truth is not one of them.

If we can accept this baseline of understanding, both about our wider society and the American church, then the question that most naturally arises is why this is so. How have we arrived at this position in our culture, and why is the church also walking down this road?

There are, no doubt, many aspects to any satisfying answer. But if

I may paint with a broad stroke, I would say that the answer to the cultural question lies in a combination of two things: the way we are experiencing the modernized world and the way we are thinking about life. In fact, these have come to coincide so that what we think is reinforced by how we are experiencing our world. Our social context, to put it more formally, powerfully shapes our internal consciousness.

My conclusion is that absolute truth and morality are fast receding in society because their grounding in God as objective, as outside of our self, as our transcendent point of reference, is disappearing. There is nothing outside the individual that stands over against the individual, that remains as the measure for the individual's actions, the standard for what is right and wrong, or as the test of what is true and what is not.

In the pages ahead I will return to this theme again and again from different angles. I am talking about what is called the "autonomous self." It does have a connection with the earlier individualism that was so much a part of the American story. However, it is not simply individualism. It is what has happened to individualism in our highly modernized world. It is how individualism now looks in its postmodern dress.

These are, I know, fighting words. Postmoderns are allergic to individualism. They pillory it as part of the rotten fruit of modernity. They think of themselves as not being modern in this way. They are *post*modern. They are not individualistic. They are all about being in community. They want to huddle together, not travel alone like lone rangers.

I understand the yearning for community. Its loss has been one of the great casualties of the modern world. And the yearning for its recovery is very real and very deep. However, postmoderns are deceiving themselves if they think the autonomous self died with modernity. It did not. This is one of the threads that weaves its way, unbroken, from the old Enlightenment days into our newer postmodern disposition and explains an awful lot about the way truth is being understood.

Then it was that Enlightenment thinkers demanded to be freed from all external authority in order to make up their own minds. They demanded to be freed from God, religious authority, and the past. This, as Kant said, had been the ball and chain people had dragged along that had hindered their progress. Now they were casting it all off and were going to be free. More than that, once this ball and chain was gone, people could begin to mature. This attitude has come down to our own time in the form of secular humanism.

It is true, of course, that postmoderns, in and out of the church, despise this older rationalism. They reject its arrogance. They cannot accept its worldview — indeed, they think, any worldview — and they reject the false absolutes that these rationalists made.

There is much to be said for this rejection of Enlightenment rationalism with its false certainties and its ungrounded absolutes. However, the breach here with the past is not nearly as complete as postmoderns imagine. There is actually a thread of continuity that ties that age to ours, and this thread is quite unbroken.

This thread is our understanding about the self. Then, as now, it has become loosed from every external constraint, be it in God, the past, or religious authority. We *demand* to be free. We today, postmodern though we may be, are more unconstrained, more emancipated from everything except our own selves than were the proponents of the Enlightenment.

This, then, is a thread that actually connects how people have thought for a long time in the West. We will be picking up this motif at a number of places in our narrative. I will try to develop it a little further in each new context.

We meet this theme in this chapter because how people think about truth is deeply affected by how they think of themselves. We will meet it again in the next chapter when we look at how our understanding of God is affected by this sense of ourselves. In the chapter after that I will delve into its expression in the self movement and why this is actually hostile to evangelical faith. And we will find it again in the chapter that follows when we look at the new resurgent spiritualities. These are all an expression of this autonomous self, and we will be thinking about how they relate to Christ. It is quite an extraordinary, pervasive theme!

Our Modernized World

In this chapter we will lay the foundations. We need to think about the developments that began to break the links the self had to the external world because they carried the seeds of some of the later developments. After we see some of these developments, we will think about truth in this context.

What has happened to us as we have had to adjust to the world as it has become modernized? By that I mean, of course, that as capitalism took root, it required that the society reorganize itself around the processes of production and distribution of goods, services, and information. We moved during the nineteenth century, as we have seen, from being a predominantly agrarian society to being overwhelmingly urban, with 93 percent now living in our cities. What happens to us in this new context we have built for ourselves? We find ourselves dislodged from the world, cut loose from life, our connections becoming ever more fragile and tenuous. Let me try to explain how this has worked.

Craft

Many years ago Reinhold Niebuhr wrote that the self gains its substance through its connections to family, community, and craft. This is not of course the whole story, but the point he was making is surely correct and important.

These connections have not fared well in the modern world, and the self, as a result, is not doing well in the modern world. And that is where our problems begin. Let us walk down this road for just a few more steps.

Mechanization and industrialization largely destroyed workmanship as an expression of the person whose work it is. This connection now remains mainly in our hobbies. The connection of the person to his or her work in the workplace is, the polls tell us, now quite strained. Undoubtedly, competition has contributed to the extraordinary levels of stress and job insecurity. But factors like these are not entirely responsible for the sense of disengagement many people experience from their work. Manufacturing processes, or bureaucracies, or technologies now stand between the worker and his or her work as well. Survey after survey has found that work has become uneasy and unsatisfactory for many people.

Very few, in fact, have the satisfaction I have as an author in which very little comes between my ideas, the expression of what is important to me, and the product that results. When this connection is as close as it is for me, the level of both accountability for what is written and satisfaction in the writing is very high. Where the connections are diminished, however, both accountability and satisfaction correspondingly decline.

Community

What shall we say of community? It has, for most people, disappeared. The town, or even neighborhood, once provided this, and a person's private and public worlds overlapped. Today they do not. Then, people were known by others in both their worlds, both in their circle of friends and by those with whom they worked. Today these worlds are divided. We are known in the work world by those we work with and in our private world by those we associate with, such as friends and family. Two different worlds often coexist side by side in people's lives, the values and beliefs of the public world and those of their private world. We live in one world in one way and in the other world in a different way. It is a bit like telling different stories to different people and hoping they never meet up and compare notes! So it is that we live our lives. The deception, underhandedness, and ruthlessness the workplace seems to require of us are not things we would ever want to bring back into our relations with family and friends. In the end, what we typically do is cater to different constituencies. One is our private world. The other is the public world.

The real test of character, it has been said, is what a person does when alone. That is true. However, it also assumes that there is something to which a person is holding himself or herself accountable in anonymous situations. It is precisely this, of course, that has disappeared for many people. The loss of community that bound together public and private has played a role in our loss of accountability. But this is not all.

Family

And what shall we say of family? It is no secret that over the last century in the West, the family has suffered under the fearful strains that modernization has produced. An enormous literature has grown up around this theme. It is trying to explore and explain the decline of this most fundamental institution. But whatever are the reasons, the conclusion is unmistakable. Not only do half of the marriages fail, but even the families that remain intact find it hard, though not impossible, to function as actual families.

One of the most important consequences of this is that now the chief conduit for the transmission of values from generation to generation is blocked. Tradition, I know, is not a good word today. That itself is telling. It tells us that as the world becomes more and more modernized, the past recedes. The past becomes culturally passé. It has been superseded. It is outdated. It is irrelevant. What a previous generation believed, we can no longer believe today. Nor do we want to. Indeed, what was believed then needs to be avoided. So we think. And so we often are thinking in the church today.

That the past is gone is of course true in some ways. It is true in all the ways in which the world is modernizing, in the replacement of villages by towns, towns by cities, hand tools by machine tools, slow communication by lightning fast and technologically facilitated deliveries, and herbal cures by laser surgery and antibiotics. However, it is foolish to think that the human spirit is in the same category as these things, that what grandparents believed about right and wrong can no longer be believed today because we are now modern or postmodern. That is the conceit that is driving many in our current world as well as many in the church.

Tradition is the way one generation brings another into its understanding about life. It is the way knowledge, understanding, beliefs, and wisdom are handed on and inculcated. A person takes a journey from childhood to adulthood, and along the way is taught much about life. Although it is within the family that this transmission of understanding and lore has been accomplished, each nuclear family has typically been part of an extended family and has usually lived within a specific context, such as a neighborhood, a town, or a city. All of this has usually gone hand in hand with things that we think of as ethnic, such as language, food, dancing, dress, customs about weddings, family gatherings, and funerals. These are the very things that give individuals a sense of belonging, for they are living within a group. They think of themselves as part of the way the group sees and experiences life. This is how relationships are cemented, and cemented relationships are what gives a sense to individuals of being rooted and belonging.

Today, we are neither rooted nor do we have much sense of belonging. We are in fact the uprooted generations, the disconnected, the drifters, the alone. We are being blown around by the windstorms of modernity. Our roots in families, place, and work have all withered or been cut off.

Our families have sagged under the pressures of modern life. It is certainly an ominous sign when out-of-wedlock births exceed the number of children born within marriages, and that has been the case for some time, for example, in the black community. There the illegitimacy rate stands at 70 percent, and they are not alone in this. And what is the result?

The result is predictable poverty. But that is only part of the story. In some of our inner-city neighborhoods gangs have sprung up in place of families. They are surrogate families for what is not there. What happens, then, when this most fundamental of conduits for the transmission of belief and behavior from one generation to another lies broken as it does? Our children are being "raised" by other children, by television, by fading fads, by inner-city culture, and by the equivalent elsewhere, the affluent way of life. They are in effect being abandoned. In terms of enduring belief and behavior, they have little in their daily experience to offer them any direction.

This is what has happened. The beliefs of parents, or the ethnic group to which we belong, that once were embedded in a neighborhood or town now hold little power over us. We are, in this sense, disembodied. We float free of the past. We are cut loose. And this, remarkably, even happens in churches where the past is junked on the assumption that it is past. It is therefore obsolete and has no relevance at all to new generations.

Some years ago, in *Where the Wasteland Ends: Politics and Transcendence in Postindustrial Society,* Theodore Roszak observed of

American society that in the very moment when we have great technological mastery, we are also producing art and thought whose nihilism
is unparalleled. Our many-sided conquest is built around a withered
soul. Surely, he said aloud, we must be honest enough to confront this
fact about ourselves and ask why this is so.

In the last half-century, amidst our growing abundance, and the
multiplication of options and opportunities we have produced, our nihilism has deepened. The literature of the last half-century has been
filled by an unparalleled despair. Isn't this a strange juxtaposition: so
much and yet so little? So much in our world and so little in ourselves.
This, as David Myers avers in a book by the same name, is the "American paradox."

We have unparalleled abundance but, at the same time, are being hollowed out. Our culture smothers us in largesse, but now this
same culture comes in through the back door and holds out its hand
for payment. We can have everything in the world that we want. We
can have it now. We can have it all now on credit, but the far, far larger
payment we must make comes, not through the mail, but in our spirits. We are being consumed in the very moment when we are consuming. And this despite decades of the self movement and more than a
century of psychology.

If Niebuhr is right, then already we can see that the three fundamental ways in which people are rooted, from which they gain internal
substance, have been mostly cut. What, then, is going to happen to us?
The simple answer is that we will have to find in ourselves, entirely in
ourselves, what we once were given from outside of ourselves. But what
does this do for our understanding about truth and about God?

The Changing World Inside

We Live Alone

The changing fabric of the world outside of us, I am arguing, is what
greatly impacts our sense of ourselves and of life. It changes how we
think and what we want. The world we experience outside of ourselves,
in fact, is what makes some ideas seem plausible and others seem im-

plausible. Today, in our modernized world, what seems implausible is that there is a God who is objective to us, who stands outside of us, who is the measure of truth, and who holds us accountable. We simply do not experience this in the course of life, and our experience inclines us to think that it is probably not true.

Many years ago the Swiss theologian Emil Brunner made the argument in *Christianity and Civilization* that we are living at a unique moment in the West. Never before, he said, has a major civilization sought to build itself deliberately and self-consciously without religious foundations. Beneath other civilizations there have always been these foundations, whether they came from Islam, Buddhism, Hinduism, or Christianity itself. Such religious frameworks make the civilization more important than the individual. Beneath ours there are none. There is now nothing more important than the individual. There is, in fact, nothing but the private individual.

We are living in a civilization of the most marvelous intricacy and one of stunning brilliance, but it is built over a vacuum. The individual is therefore without accountability to anything or anyone higher than himself or herself. This is so because private interest has become the sole value. And when private interest is the only norm, the sole controlling value, then conflict in society, and its fragmentation, is simply inevitable.

This kind of attack on all religious authority has for several centuries been the central project of the Enlightenment. In the 1970s in America, it was carried forward in the name of secular humanism. The literature of that decade was filled with secular-humanistic optimism that its views would prevail.

Perhaps the nature of Christmas cards is a bit too wispy to support very many serious conclusions. Yet it was striking that in 2006, in Britain, 99 percent of the cards had no religious message. In America secular humanism is also surviving, but in pockets mainly of the cultural elite, such as Hollywood, the nation's leading newspapers, academia, and literary and artistic circles, not in the wider populace, at least not as the secular humanists would like. In a colorful image, Peter Berger remarked that America is like an India being presided over by a Sweden. It is like an India because it has now become so religious and spiritual; it is like a Sweden because its cultural elites are still so wedded to the old, rationalistic ways of the Enlightenment.

In an eye-catching reversal, however, by the 1990s, 78 percent of Americans were describing themselves as "spiritual." The problem with much of this spirituality, as we will see in a later chapter, is that so many of these "spiritual" people are stripped of any reference points outside of themselves, whether in the past, in the present, or in a God external to themselves. What is sacred is within and indistinguishable from the self. It arises within the self and is accessed from within the self and asks nothing the self is unwilling to give. This kind of spirituality really is a sanitized version of Hinduism, there for the taking in America by its affluent and self-indulgent. And it really does not change the fundamental inclination of Western postmodern societies to think that there is nothing that stands over against the self and calls it to account.

Postmodern Selves

Many writers have spoken of a new cultural type emerging in this context — modern, shallow, changing, hiding, and evading. To this list we must add another label, "spiritual." This new cultural type is the kind of person for whom the only reality that remains is inward. However, the self into which all reality has contracted is now empty and insubstantial but tinged with the sacred. Various writers have their own terms for this new kind of person. Their essential point, though, is that this modern personality is built around the idea that there is nothing fixed in life, nothing authoritative, and nothing absolute. All is in flux and movement. Gone is the preoccupation of earlier generations, certainly earlier Christian generations, with right belief, right behavior, and right values. This personality is built on the idea of freedom, of being liberated from all beliefs, from all expected behavior, from all ethical norms, from the past, and from God as something other than the self. This emancipated self is a law unto itself. Indeed, in the way it actually functions, this self assumes that it is authoritative over God and the church. This enthronement of the self, about which more later, is what has flowed into American individualism.

Earlier forms of individualism were built around two central ideas. First, they believed in the worth of the individual. Second, they believed that the individual was more important than society, and so anything that would interfere from the outside with our right to think for ourselves, our right to make decisions for ourselves, and our ability to live in ways that we ourselves had chosen was viewed as morally repugnant. These ideas were worked out differently in different forms of individualism. In our contemporary moment, though, we are especially concerned with expressive individualism, to use Robert Bellah's term from *Habits of the Heart*.

This kind of individualism, which has a special affinity for our therapeutic culture, assumes that all people have a unique core of intuitions and feelings that they are entitled to express. One only has to turn on television to see this in action! No matter how embarrassing the revelation may be, no matter how intimate it is, people want to talk about it. They want to tell the whole world! This being so, we might begin to think that the television studio has become the new confessional. This is the place, rather than the church, where people unburden themselves.

That is what we might think. The problem, though, is that now there is no burden to be unloaded, no guilt to be cleansed, nothing of which to be ashamed. All that remains is that each one of us has the right to "tell our own story," in our own way. And that is what people are doing with very little sense that they actually do inhabit a moral world where there are enduring rights and wrongs.

This emancipation from all authorities external to ourselves gives us the freedom to fashion our lives the way we want and develop our beliefs the way we want. Thoughts about a truth that might be objective to us have become quite remote.

Many other factors have no doubt affected our changing internal landscape. But the key factors are undoubtedly that we have been disconnected from place, from family, from the past, and from an external God who has the power to reach into our lives and pull them around. But consuming has affected us, too. What we do as practiced consumers is to make daily inventories of our needs and how they might have changed. As I will suggest, it is probably our constant consuming, with the constant choosing and reevaluating that it requires, that has strengthened the relativism that now ripples through all of our life making the very idea of a truth that is fixed and unchanging seem strange.

Power

What happens in a world where we can, in a way, make our own reality unhindered by a God or a truth that is external to us? One way to think of this is to see what has happened already in the West. Western cultures have all been held together by three sinews: tradition, authority, and power. Of these, only the third has survived.

This is what agitates so many postmoderns. They have come to think that everything in life, every word spoken, every action done, every posture, every word written, is either an overt or a covert attempt at hegemony, to use the going lingo. Everything is about power. Everything is about control, manipulation, domination, using or being used for someone else's purposes. While this has gone hand in hand with much cynicism, with suspicion about everyone's motives, with doubt about everything that is said, it is not illogical.

G. K. Chesterton once observed that when God and his truth vanish from a society, it would be natural to think that people would no longer believe in anything at all. That, however, turns out not to be the case. Now they believe in *everything*.

How else do we explain the remarkable circumstance of highly sophisticated people, secularized or postmodern, who can assault any and every religious belief but who, at the same time, can indulge fantasies about aliens? Or sightings of Elvis? Or the most far-fetched conspiracy theories, like that the Bush administration actually planned and carried out the attacks on the World Trade Center on September 11, 2001? Or, on a more mundane level, how can these highly sophisticated people also think that every religious belief, no matter how unlikely, has validity as long as someone holds it sincerely? However, in this atmosphere, where everything is believed and anything is believable, at least to someone, nothing can act as a norm. All that is left is power. And, in a fallen world, we do well to be cautious when all there is, is power.

The experience of living in a modernized society, with its (post)modern ethos, is now rubbing away so many of these religious notions in which authority is rooted. Once they were handed on in families. Once they were ensconced in neighborhoods and towns. To some extent this remains the case in the American South, but even there some of the lines are becoming blurred. And in Europe, Canada, Australia, and New Zealand, they have all but gone. Even Christian memory, those ideas that have lingered on about right and wrong, good and evil, long after their source in the Bible has been forgotten, is itself now disappearing. What remains is simply power. We might well sympathize with postmoderns in their deep suspicions about all of this.

What Is Truth?

If there is such a thing as truth, how are we going to define it? The classic definition that emerged in the Middle Ages is this: truth is the correspondence between an object and our knowledge of it *(veritas est adaequatio rei et intellectus)*. What is said about something must reflect exactly what that something is if that statement is to be true. This understanding of truth did not emerge out of the blue. It was picking up on something essential to the biblical understanding of truth, as we shall see.

Let me begin, though, with our common speech. What do we typically mean by "truth"? If I say, for example, that "this chain is made of pure gold," we can judge this as truthful or not simply by asking whether the metal is unalloyed gold. If it turns out that the chain is not gold but only coated steel, then the statement is false. In that case, there is no correspondence between the thing and my statement about it. The idea of correspondence decides whether or not deception has been attempted.

Here is another example. I might say that the ongoing strife created by the Islamic terrorists is "ghastly." If this is my assessment, then this statement is true and genuine. However, a contrary judgment might be equally true. These terrorists, looking at the same events, may speak truly when they express their jubilation at the West's discomfort. What the West sees as evil, they see as good. In this instance truthfulness is decided by the *intentions* of the speakers. We can speak truly and be completely wrong about the morality of an action. Truthfulness in these cases is decided by whether or not the statements intended to correspond to the actual judgments of the speakers, different as those may be.

So it is in our courts of law. Witnesses swear to tell the truth, the whole truth, and nothing but the truth. Oftentimes, though, there are inaccuracies in their recollections, sometimes even major inaccuracies. It is possible that witnesses might *think* they are telling the truth even when their witness is not fully in accord with the facts. By contrast, other witnesses know their testimony is not in accord with the facts but nevertheless attempt to pass it off as true. Their testimony is untrue despite the pretense of its truthfulness. Either the witness thought there was a correspondence between his or her knowledge and the circumstances being described, in which case the witness was speaking truly, or he or she was faking that correspondence, thereby giving untrue testimony.

This understanding of truth makes two assumptions. The first is the existence of an observable, objective world outside the human subject. This world is not the construction of the mind, as Eastern philosophy, and some Western philosophy, is inclined to think. Second, it is assumed that we can know the events of life in a way that corresponds to what happened, fallible though we are. Indeed, we need to go further and say that we can know the events of life truly even if not exhaustively, for then we could know nothing since only God knows everything exhaustively.

That we can know what is true, "the facts about a situation" as we might put it, used to be self-evident. Journalists believed that they could discover and report on the facts. Their readers and, later, in the format of television, their viewers did not question this. However, as early as the 1930s in establishment institutions like *Time* magazine, doubts began to be expressed about the ability of any reporter to be objective. What at first was just recognized as a difficulty has now, under the postmodern sun, developed into a full-scale posture. What initially passed as an attitude has now hardened into a politically correct position that everything is relative. We have our lenses of gender, social investment, religious outlook, and ideological commitment that necessarily blur how we understand what we see. Journalists, it is often said today, are therefore self-deceived if they say they can report on the world as it is; they report on the world only as *they see it*. They can see the world only as they see it and not as it actually is.

This distinction is easier to maintain in some areas of life than in others. If a journalist, a devoted Red Sox fan, were to report on the outcome of a game not as it actually happened, but as the reporter wished it had happened, there would be legitimate outrage. There would be thousands of witnesses to testify against this fabrication that had been reported as if it were the actual truth.

However, the emancipation of the journalist from the objective world is much easier to pull off when the world being reported on is far away and unfamiliar. How many of the accounts of the wars in Iraq and Afghanistan have actually corresponded to what happened? We obviously do not know, and that is the whole point. It is interesting to note that the view Americans have of these conflicts, gained through television and newspaper coverage, often appears to be a little different from the perceptions of many of the military who were actually present in these theaters of conflict and saw the events for themselves.

In an earlier generation this would not have been acceptable; today it is part of the "postmodern condition." Then, accounts such as these would have been viewed as prevarications and rank propaganda. Now they are viewed simply as the journalist honestly telling his or her own story. This is their "take" on things, but, of course, their "take" is assumed to be different from "spin."

Spin is a deliberate reconstruction of things. It is a deception. A journalist's "take" is just the story from the journalist's vantage point. The assumption is that there is no right and wrong way of doing this and that the overriding viewpoint being expressed is at least as important as the events being reported. Here is the nub of the issue. Can our posture in life, our sense of morality, or our political vision be allowed to dictate what we see as credible evidence? Or should we not at least search for solid evidence and allow it, however inconvenient it is, to trump our private disposition?

The Christian notion of truth is not unrelated to these other considerations. It assumes, given the revelation that God has provided in the biblical Word, that we can know his character and intentions in a way that corresponds to what is there. Undoubtedly the writers of Scripture, being human, were fallible. However, the Spirit's work in inspiration means that he has secured through their writing, despite their human fallibility, a correspondence between what they wrote and what was there.

The outcome is a revelation that is truthful. This revelation reflects who God is. Because he is utterly pure in character, it is impossible for him to lie (Heb. 6:18; cf. 2 Tim. 2:13; Titus 1:2; 1 John 1:5). We are sometimes deceitful and untruthful, but this is quite impossible with God. He cannot be other than what he is as holy. He cannot have given us "truth" that is untrue. And because he is all-knowing, and has known the end from the beginning, it is impossible for him to be mistaken as humans often are.

The fact of inspiration, then, means that whatever deficiencies the writers had as fallible human beings did not have any part in the revelation as given. Nor is it possible for God to give us a deliberately false "read" on reality. Nor can he be mistaken in the "read" he has given to us, however unintentionally, because his own knowledge is true, comprehensive, and complete.

What Scripture says, therefore, God says. That is the correlation that Scripture itself makes repeatedly. And what God says is the exact reflection of what is there, whether this is in his own character, plans, and intentions, or in the world, in the human heart, and in our human future.

Christian Truth

Biblical Baseline

It is not my purpose in this chapter to write about the "how" questions such as: How does the church evangelize postmoderns who are deeply suspicious of those who think they know truth? How do we commend this belief to those not disposed to believe in truth? How can such a belief live alongside postmodern habits of thought that are relativistic without itself becoming postmodern? If the church does not become postmodern to postmoderns, how will it ever reach them with its truth?

This, I believe, is a subsequent discussion. What needs to be established first is the position to which it is hoped postmoderns will come. In other words, what should the church believe about truth and why?

Is it possible for anyone to miss the clarion call that sounds forth in the words and gospel-actions of the apostles? Surely not! Although they were encircled by many superstitions, many religious claims, and were constantly under the gaze of a Roman power that demanded their total allegiance at pain of death, they nevertheless declared that truth, truth of an enduring and absolute kind, had been born. Christ was the culmination to the long history in which God's redemptive acts had occurred. Now these acts had reached their apex and culmination in Jesus Christ (Heb. 1:1-4; Gal. 4:4-6; John 1:14; 14:6). In him the revelation that had been partial had been completed, what had been fragmentary had now been brought to a final synthesis. It was this claim that rattled the bones of the Caesars and, in time, led to state-sponsored persecution.

The Christianity that grew from this moment, though, spread with astonishing speed through the apostles' declaration of the gospel and the simple witness of those who had come to know Christ. This proclamation was not simply a telling of their private experience, nor just their own personal opinion. It was not what had become truth for *them*. It was a proclamation about truth for *all*. The gospel, which is the same gospel for all people, in all ages, and at all times, is "the word of truth" (Eph. 1:13; see also Col. 1:5; 2 Thess. 2:13; Heb. 10:26). Faith is about "obeying the truth" (Gal. 5:7; 1 Pet. 1:22). Those who are condemned are condemned because they do not believe "the truth" (2 Thess. 2:12). Those who are depraved in mind are depraved because they are "deprived of the truth" (1 Tim. 6:5). This faith, which is all about the truth that God has given us, is delivered through his truth (2 Cor. 4:2) and is made effective by the Spirit who is the Spirit of truth (1 John 5:6). Christianity, in short, is from first to last all about *truth!* It is about he who is the Way, the *Truth,* and the Life.

In an earlier time it would have been unnecessary to make this argument. Surely, this is what all Christians thought, was it not? Furthermore, the language of truth had been a stock ingredient in all Western thought for a long time. It was not simply a Christian interest. Of course, people had for centuries debated about what was true and what was not. They had disagreed sharply on some specific issues, but the *notion* of truth was not itself in dispute. That, in a way, is what explains the fact that there was any debate at all. Those who do not believe that we can come to a knowledge of what is true waste no time in debating about it.

Christianity is supernatural religion. It is the exact opposite of all paganisms, ancient or (post)modern. It is about the one God who has made himself known, who has provided an objective truth through the inspired biblical writers, and who, in his grace, has provided the subjective conditions within the hearts of sinners whereby that truth can be received, understood, and obeyed. Those in the evangelical church today who are being lured by the siren call of postmodern relativism, who are increasingly uncertain that truth can be known, or that it matters all that much anyway, would do well to ponder the fact that this uncertainty goes to the very heart of what Christianity is all about.

Muddled Emergents

What has happened is that emergents, like the postmoderns they are mimicking, believe that the links between the truth statement and what that statement refers to have been broken or, at least, are obscure. The language we use in truth statements refers, not to the outside world, but simply to ourselves. It is self-referential. That means that the value of the words we use has been destroyed. Indeed, words themselves have no stable meanings.

What we hear from many of the emergent church leaders who are most aware of the (post)modern ethos, therefore, is a studied uncertainty: "We do not know." "We cannot know for sure." "No one can know certainly." "We should not make judgments." "Knowing beyond doubt is not what Christianity is about." "We need to be more modest." "We need to be more honest." "Christianity is about the search, not about the discovery." "Christianity is about the spiritual journey, not about arriving." They forget that Scripture is divine *revelation*. It is not a collection of opinions of how different people see things that tells us more about the people than the things. No. It gives us God's perfect knowledge of himself and of all reality. It is given to us in a form we can understand. The reason God gave it to us is that he wants us to know. Not to guess. Not to have vague impressions. And certainly not to be misled. He wants us to *know*. It is not immodest, nor arrogant, to claim that we know, when what we know is what God has given us to know through his Word.

Actually, speaking postmodern, as Stephen Katz has written amusingly in an article entitled "How to Speak and Write Postmodern," is usually a bit more complex than saying we cannot know anything for sure. Plain language and clear communication are not in vogue in postmodern circles. They reveal the speaker as too much of a realist, too obviously rational, too modern, too *unchic*. No, we can't have that! The required alternative speech is subtle parody, contradiction, being indeterminate, being ironic, being playful. But this is not as easy to do as it seems, and many postmoderns, lacking the skills, settle simply for being obscure.

There are tricks to this. A plain speaker might write of someone else's "view." A "view"? How flat-footed and prosaic! How about that person's "voice" or, better yet, different "vocality"? And prefixes are a treasure trove for those in search of depths beyond the grasp of the reader, prefixes such as "pre-," "hyper-," "post-," "de-," "ex-," and "counter-" — as in words like "de-confusing" and "reconstructing." These all open up new possibilities, as does a new constellation of suffixes to go with them. We today, you see, are living in a moment when the multi-vocalities of postcolonial others are entering our intra/post/spatialities and are exposing the antisociality concealed in the hegemony of our discourse and sensibilities.

This kind of empty obfuscation is what we hear all too often from the emergent church, though usually without the veneer of intellectual sophistication. In its place (and usually on the Internet) we hear the confidence of those who have a sense of being on the edge of what-is-happening-now but who, for that very reason, are diffident, unsure, tentative, and, more often than not, simply confused.

In the Wren Library in Cambridge, in early 2007, Ludwig Wittgenstein's handwritten philosophical reflections from 1914 were displayed in a glass case. I leaned over the case to read what the great philosopher had said. The person next to me was having trouble deciphering his writing. And, it is true, the writing was awful and the ink had faded. However, I observed, in a quiet whisper, that it all would have been a lot easier if Wittgenstein had not recorded these thoughts in German. Then, in an afterthought, I added, just as quietly, that per-

haps I was wrong. Perhaps he would have been no easier to compre-
hend in English!

Language sometimes is opaque because of the intellectual complexities behind it. Language sometimes is opaque because of the intellectual confusion behind it. And sometimes people pass off the latter
as if it were the former.

Listen to the New Testament, by contrast, and hear plain speaking and words that ring with conviction: "We know. . . . We know. . . .
We know." In the Johannine Epistles, for example, we are told that we
know the truth (1 John 2:21; 2 John 1; cf. John 8:32). And not only in the
Johannines. Paul speaks of coming to a "knowledge of the truth"
(2 Tim. 2:25; cf. 3:7-8; 4:4). The writer to the Hebrews speaks of a
"knowledge of the truth" (Heb. 10:26), and Peter speaks of "obedience
to the truth" (1 Pet. 1:22). If truth is uncertain, elusive, out-of-reach,
lost on us as we live in our own private worlds of (post)modern "reality," what on earth are the apostles talking about? What is it we are
supposed to know and what is it we are supposed to obey? Our own
reconstructions of reality? Our own "take" on what life means? Our
projections of our own experience?

How many self-respecting postmoderns would ever talk about
knowing truth in these biblical ways? None. How many emergents
would want to be heard using this kind of truth-talk in public? Very
few. Why not? Because truth, in the (post)modern view (or should we
say vocality?), is as shapeless as a wad of bubble gum — and as elastic.
Everything in life can be understood differently, all is contingent, all is
a matter of what construction we wish to place on it — or *need* to place
on it. And if this is not the view taken of truth by emergents, then why
are they so skittish about saying otherwise?

The (post)modern mentality mistakenly assumes that "truth" is
rather like the set of traffic rules our authorities have constructed. No
one really thinks a serious moral breach has occurred when a thirty-
five-mile-per-hour limit is exceeded by one mile per hour. The speed
limit was, in the first place, just an approximation devised by someone
who thought the posted speed would be safe. It is somewhat arbitrary.
There is no inherent reason why it should not have been forty miles per
hour, or thirty. So it is with all truth statements, they contend. These
statements are only approximations made up by someone else. They

are arbitrary rules that do not correspond to anything that is actually "there."

Biblical Heartbeat

The biblical writers take the opposing view. Truth statements do indeed correspond to what is out there. Biblical affirmations are neither arbitrary nor provisional but have all the weight of eternity behind them. And the biblical authors clearly assume that despite capacities for misreading our own desires into this truth, seeing only what we want to see, refusing to see what is actually there, we can still know this truth. And this is so despite the many innocent mistakes that we might also make in reading the Scriptures.

In the biblical view, we know the *truth* and not just arbitrary rules and approximations. This knowledge of what is "there" includes the truth about Christ (1 John 5:20), about God (2:13-14), his character (3:16), his redemptive purposes (3:5), our own nature (1:6, 8-11), and the (postmodern) "world" we inhabit that is filled with "the desires of the flesh and the desires of the eyes and pride in possessions" and is also "passing away along with its desires" (2:16-17). On all these matters we have God's truth, and for the church to be shy about saying "We know. . . . We know. . . . We know" is an act of self-betrayal. More than that, it allows the vacuum in our intra/post/spatialities to be filled with all those (post)modern multivocalities that are saying, "We are too modest to know. . . . No one needs to know. . . . Only the arrogant claim to know."

Scripture, by contrast, sees itself, and is seen, as the self-disclosure of God that is therefore unlike anything else on earth. It is *the* truth. What it says corresponds to what happened in the world of which it speaks. It really does reflect what is in the human heart. It is the measure of reality. It is the standard by which we are to judge life's religions and philosophies, its programs and values, its hopes and its fears.

Yet we must go further because Scripture itself goes further. Scripture is not only a measure, not only a standard, but it is also *truth*. What this means is that with respect to God, it is the sum and substance of what we know of him, his character, his will, and his redemp-tive acts. What he has given us to know of himself is what we are able to receive with the confidence that we know exactly who he is. With re-spect to the church, Scripture is God's all-sufficient, complete, and un-changeable guide and gift for the life of his people in this world. Paul speaks of "the faith that was once for all delivered to the saints" (Jude 3). There is a finality, a completeness, to what has been delivered, and Scripture is our only account of that teaching. It is a teaching that is not modified in every succeeding generation, otherwise it could not have been given "once for all." It is not so modified by our own social lo-cation so that we cannot get what God wants us to have.

Scripture is not a "vocality" that is just one stance among many. It is not making its voice known in a cacophony of other voices none of which will be authenticated until we accept them. It is not modified by how we "read" it unless we depart from how the authors wished to be read and how the Holy Spirit delivered God's truth through them. No. This is a voice unlike any other voice. It speaks unlike any other voice, and what it says is unlike anything else heard anywhere else in the world. It speaks across the ages, across the generations, across psycho-logical divides. And it accesses our very innermost being, even our very innermost (post)modern being, modest as we may wish to be in what we can receive from God. This is truth that is rudely and insistently "in our face." This "word of God is living and active, sharper than any two-edged sword, piercing to the division of soul and of spirit, of joints and of marrow, and discerning the thoughts and intentions of the heart" (Heb. 4:12). Can anyone really contend that this truth can be held at arm's length just because we are postmodern?

The Johannine writings offer us a special angle of vision on all of this. There are, first, the expected uses of the language of truth. For ex-ample, on one occasion Jesus' opponents sought to kill him because he claimed he was "equal with God" (John 5:18). In his reply to them Jesus laid out the argument for thinking that he was who he said he was and part of this was the testimony of John the Baptist: "he has borne witness to the truth" (5:33). Later, many people said "everything that John said about this man was true" (10:41). At the end of the Gospel, its author de-clares that in his account he has been giving witness to what happened, "and we know that his testimony is true" (21:24). So it is at the end of his third epistle, too. The apostle says in respect to what he had been teaching that "you know that our testimony is true" (3 John 12).

In each of these cases the meaning is unmistakable. There is a correspondence between what Jesus claimed about himself, or was said about him, and what was actually the case. There is a correspondence between everything John the Baptist said in his prophetic role of revealing the identity of Jesus and who Jesus actually was. There is a correspondence between what the apostle John recorded and what really happened. And there is a correspondence between what he had been teaching and what is actually the case.

Alongside these conventional uses of the word "truth," however, are others that are a little different. In the incarnation, for example, when the fullness of God in the second person of the Godhead became enfleshed through Mary, his divine glory still shone through so that John could say that Christ was "full of grace and truth" (John 1:14). Later, Jesus called himself "the way, and the truth, and the life" (14:6). He is spoken of as "the true light" (1:9), and after his resurrection John could say that "the true light is already shining" (1 John 2:8). Furthermore, Jesus called himself "the true bread from heaven" (John 6:32), the Father's gift to us, and "the true vine" (15:1).

In cases like these, truth language means something a little different because here what is represented by the "truth," "bread," and "light" is embodied in Christ. Scripture is true, but he *is* the truth. He does not merely speak about the truth. His words are not only true in that everything said corresponds exactly to what is there, but everything of which he speaks in relation to the glory, grace, and goodness of God we also see flawlessly, perfectly, and fully embodied in the Son. The reality of God and its representation to us in Christ coincide. "Whoever has seen me has seen the Father" (John 14:9). No one else can be said to embody the truth in this way because no one else has ever come from "above" to the human life "below" as John says over and over again of the Son. No one else preexisted in the Godhead. Never before had God been incarnated, and never again will it happen. We who are merely human can speak of the truth, preach the truth, point to the truth, believe the truth, and obey the truth, but only of Christ can it be said that he *is* the truth. Truth "came through Jesus Christ" (John 1:17), says John, and Paul can say that "the truth is in Jesus" (Eph. 4:21).

The Christian message, then, is very clear. It is not, as the neo-orthodox imagined, that the experience of the resurrected Christ, the living Word, happens apart from the written Word. This is a fallacious distinction. It produces a damaging dichotomy between truth in the pages of Scripture and truth in the person of Christ, between the historical Jesus and the Christ of faith. The gospel, in fact, is the gospel of both the historical Jesus and the Christ of faith at the same time. This proclamation was initially oral. Now it is found in the pages of Scripture. And this disclosure of God and his redemptive purposes in the Son is absolute. It will endure for all of time.

The apostles did not shrink, as we are prone to do, from the consequences of this fact. "Whoever has the Son has life; whoever does not have the Son of God does not have life" (1 John 5:12), declared John. And this life-giving knowledge, this knowledge of Christ as incarnate God and self-giving sacrifice in our place, is brought to us through the knowledge of his written Word. How are we to call upon him if we have not believed? And how are we to believe if we have not heard? "And how are they to hear without someone preaching? . . . 'How beautiful are the feet of those who preach the good news!'" (Rom. 10:14-15). The Holy Spirit first inspired this Word, whose principal work is now to point men and women to Christ and so to work in them that they are able to bow before him, accept him for who he is, and by faith receive his death in their place. The Holy Spirit, in doing this, uses this Word to glorify Christ. There is no saving knowledge of God except through the truth of Scripture, except as our trust is placed in Christ by its teaching, and except as the Spirit imparts to us the desire to trust Christ in this way. We cannot know God in any other way. Whoever "does not abide in the teaching of Christ, does not have God" (2 John 9).

Some may want to quarrel with the claims Scripture makes of itself, and how the apostles used it, and the place it has in bringing us the knowledge of God in Christ. But we should not be in doubt about what those claims are. Scripture does not merely contain truth. It is not a sublime statement of our understanding of God. It does not mark the forward progress that the human spirit has taken. It is not the result of the questing human spirit reaching out for something absolute. It is not a human guess. It is not just an approximation of what is there. No.

It is, instead, the result of the supernatural work of God in the human writers, and what we now have is "the truth." It is not partial truth, or incomplete truth. It is the full, accurate, and complete revelation of all that God wants the church to have. This written truth is fully sufficient for the church's life in this fallen world.

That being the case, is it any surprise to discover that apostolic Christianity was shaped into a set of clear teachings, now the doctrines of Scripture? Sometimes these are simply called "teaching" (Acts 2:42; 2 Tim. 3:10) or "the standard of teaching" (Rom. 6:17) or "doctrine" (1 Tim. 1:10): "watch out for those who cause divisions and create obstacles contrary to the doctrine that you have been taught," Paul says (Rom. 16:17; cf. Heb. 2:1; 1 John 2:24). In the Pastorals we find more varied language. Besides "teaching," we also have "the faith" (Titus 1:13; 1 Tim. 3:9), "the truth" (1 Tim. 2:4; 4:3), the "pattern of the sound words" (2 Tim. 1:13), or "the deposit" (1 Tim. 6:20; 2 Tim. 1:14).

Christianity, in these and texts like them, is described as the faith, the truth, the pattern of sound words, the traditions, the sound doctrine, and what was delivered in the beginning. This is what the apostles taught, it is what they believed, it is what they "delivered" to the church, it is what is "entrusted" to the church. Christians are those who "believe" this teaching, who "know" it, who "have" it, who "stand" in it, and who are "established" in it. The New Testament letters were written to remind believers about their responsibilities in relation to this teaching, this faith that has been delivered to the church in its final and completed form. The apostles, we read, write to "remind" them of it, urge them to "pay close attention" to it, to "stand firm" in it, to "follow" it, to "hold" onto it, to "guard" it as one might a precious jewel, and to "contend" earnestly for this truth.

Can we see the most basic point here? It is that the church in its earliest days was a learning community. What it was learning was the ways of God, his character, his acts, through the truth he had given and was giving them. This they knew was indispensable for a life of obedience in this world.

By contrast, all of this is conspicuous by its absence in much of the contemporary evangelical church. Knowledge of the Bible ranks low in how the born-again judge themselves. And the preaching of the Bible's truth has all but disappeared from many churches. We are today walking away from what we see modeled for us in the book of Acts as God's will for the church.

Evangelical Adventures

In recent years this understanding of biblical inspiration and its resulting authority in all of life has been undergoing a major revision among some evangelicals. The revision, on the high end, is evident in the work of N. T. Wright, for example, and I. Howard Marshall; it is evident on the low end in experimenters like Brian McLaren, Rob Bell, and a host of other cultural *fashionistas.*

Marshall, in his 2004 book *Beyond the Bible: Moving from Scripture to Theology,* was thinking about the ways Christian faith has "developed" across the ages. Much of what he says is unexceptional. However, he does say that some of the images Jesus used to speak of God in the parables are simply unacceptable today, such as God being compared to a jailer (Matt. 18:34) and presiding over a hell (Luke 16:25, 28), or killing people (Luke 19:27). These images are incredible to us now, even if Jesus did use them, and the reason is that the Spirit has been enlightening our minds since then. The Holy Spirit himself is liberating us from some of the very revelation he gave in the course of history! In this sense, under the Spirit's leading, biblical truth is evolving. We are, in some ways, moving beyond the New Testament, he argues. So much for the apostolic injunctions to stand firm and to follow, hold, and guard it!

Wright, more adventurous than Marshall, disengages the authority of God from the authority of Scripture rather more radically. In different ways and in different places he mocks the idea that Scripture contains timeless, unchanging truths or that it was ever meant to do so. The authority of God today is experienced as something other than the authority of Scripture. This was his thesis in *The Last Word: Beyond the Bible Wars to a New Understanding of the Authority of Scripture.* Wright offers a baffling illustration to make his point. Suppose a lost Shakespeare play were found today. Four of the acts have survived but we know that originally it had five acts. What would we do? Would we not try to create the fifth act as faithfully as we could so that the play could run its course? That is our situation in the church today. We do not have the fifth act of God's revelation, the one for our present moment.

The problem with this, of course, is that the fifth act to Shakespeare's play could be written in any number of ways with any number of outcomes. So it would be with Scripture had God left us to our own wits.

Among emergents, all of this subtle sophistication is largely passed up, but the same point is nevertheless made. Bell's *Velvet Elvis,* for example, distinguishes between Scripture as a trampoline and Scripture as a brick wall. The doctrines of Scripture are like the springs in a trampoline that propel us upward in our journey with God. However, as trampoline jumpers know, the direction in which they are propelled is a tad unpredictable. So it is in life. We can say only what "seems" to be right in terms of what we should believe and do. We have to make our way, in our own way, having been projected by Scripture.

Scripture, to change the image, is not about living in a brick world where nothing changes and where one brick dislodged in the doctrinal wall may threaten to bring down the whole edifice of Christian life. It is not about having one painting, to change the image again, that we carry all the time. No. It is, Bell says, about making our own paintings through our own explorations as we move along. So, to go back to trampolines, would it matter if we took one or more springs out? Such as the Trinity and the virgin birth of Christ, for example? Clearly not, he thinks, so long as there are still enough springs left to get us airborne.

Neo, the hipster in McLaren's *A New Kind of Christian,* indulges in the generational conceit that the world when it was modern in the 1960s was adolescent whereas by the 1990s it was all grown up. What evangelicals believed then, they can no longer believe now. This would be fine if the only thing that Neo, a McLaren look-alike in the book, was rejecting was Enlightenment rationalism. But it is not. Neo wants a whole new framework in which we ask, not which religion is true, but which religion is good. Elsewhere McLaren has said that theology is all about the searching, not about the finding. Once we understand, he says, that we cannot know truth in an objective way, our whole perspective on life changes.

Indeed. And, if I may say so, that is true. And it is not only true for me. It is true for everyone. However, I interrupt the argument.

A line connects Marshall and Wright to Bell and McLaren. It is that the authority of God functions separately from the written Scriptures. Marshall thinks the Spirit has liberated us from some of what is in Scripture; Wright thinks the Scriptures were never given to function as absolute truth in our world in the first place; Bell thinks the Scriptures simply send us on our way to do our own thing; McLaren thinks historic faith needs to be de-reconstructed for postmoderns so that the baggage of enduring truth can be dropped.

The common thread across this broad front is that Scripture cannot be fully authoritative at the level of its functioning in the life of the church today. We are in fact autonomous, freed from its language and constraints as we shape our own understanding, in our own way, in the postmodern world. At the end of the day Christianity is about filling out *my* story, being propelled on *my* journey by the Scripture or the Holy Spirit, and being propelled into the (post)modern world. It is not about our fitting into the *Bible's* narrative. It is not about seeing it as an objective framework of truth. Why not? Because that does not sit well either with the (post)modern autonomous self or with the (post)modern world. Here is the postmodern preoccupation with the self into which the whole of reality has been contracted, the self at the center of the universe and, despite all the Christian words that are spattered around, actually refusing to be part of God's (objective) narrative.

Everywhere, in fact, there is this airy dismissal of the importance of biblical doctrine and the assumption that it is neither central to nor important in the life of Christians and churches. Indeed, William M. Easum and Thomas G. Bandy's *Growing Spiritual Redwoods* says this explicitly. Growing and vibrant churches, they say, are those that have forged their own understanding of Christ. And this is exactly what McLaren does in *Generous Orthodoxy.* This book is neither generous to those who take a more traditional Christian position, nor is it orthodox. The author has apparently no respect for those who have gone before him and who contributed the classical understandings of Christian faith.

How could the apostles have gotten it so wrong, one wonders? Why were they at such pains to speak of Christianity in doctrinal ways, as the "teaching," "the pattern of the sound words," and the "tradition," if all of this was irrelevant to building successful, vibrant churches?

Would it be wrong to think that we (post)moderns have finally decided that we know better how to build the church because Paul is irrelevant and lags catastrophically far behind our times? It would seem so.

How amazed God must be by all of this since he took such pains to give the church his inspired Word for its instruction and nurture! He has told us what its function is to be. And here we are, at the beginning of the twenty-first century, writing our own script for our own private spiritual journeys!

In fact, when we listen to the church today, at least in the West, we are often left with the impression that Christianity actually has very little to do with truth. Christianity is only about feeling better about ourselves, about leaping over our difficulties, about being more satisfied, about having better relationships, about getting on with our mothers-in-law, about understanding teenage rebellion, about coping with our unreasonable bosses, about finding greater sexual satisfaction, about getting rich, about receiving our own private miracles, and much else besides. It is about everything except truth. And yet this truth, personally embodied in Christ, gives us a place to stand in order to deal with the complexities of life, such as broken relations, teenage rebellion, and job insecurities.

It is through Christ and by his Word that we once again begin to enter the paradise we lost and that has left us adrift in a sea of endless meaninglessness. It is by this truth, as it were, that we enter a port. To change the image, it is by this truth that we enter a realm where everything is real and nothing is fake. Should this not be the church's message? Then why are we hearing so much mumbling on truth issues and so much chatter on so many other subjects? The church is, to put it charitably, very distracted right now. This may well explain why it is struggling for its very life in the West.

Would this not be a great time for the Western church, with its vast material and educational resources, to put itself alongside the church in other parts of the world where God is working in remarkable ways in order to learn? Could it even serve in a backup role? Is this not a time for a little humility?

Truth Engagement

One of the most striking aspects of life in America today is that so many people have had an encounter with gospel truth at some point in their lives. This is a tribute to those who have so tirelessly, and in so many ways, made its truth known. In small churches and large, on street corners and in corner offices, in the workplace and in places of leisure, in magazines and on the airwaves, the gospel has been talked about and preached.

Yet what also stands out are the numbers of people who began with the gospel, apparently accepted these biblical truths, and yet somehow lost their way. They never matured into the fullness of biblical understanding.

It is true, of course, that we are to expect quite varied responses both to the gospel message and to the consequences of it in people's lives. How else are we to understand the parable of the sower (Matt. 13:3-8; Mark 4:3-8, 14-20; Luke 8:5-8; 11-15)?

In this parable Jesus speaks of three different kinds of responses we see in the church to the gospel seed. Some receive the Christian message in the shallow soil of their hearts, but beneath it there is only impenetrable rock. The plant dies as a result. Apparently in view are those whose minds actually repel the message despite their apparent acceptance of it. These recipients have no intention of paying the cost in self-commitment that is required if the message is in fact to be believed. Belief, after all, entails both the acceptance of the message and commitment to the one at the center of that message. These "converts" refuse to have their lives turned upside down in this way. They merely go through the motions of having done so. There are, apparently, many like this in America today.

There is a second kind of person in the parable who has brushed up against the gospel, and these people, too, are everywhere in American society today. They appear to be more serious than the first kind, whose momentary allegiance to Christ results in nothing. They are the ones who have heard the Word, who do not reject it, and in whom it apparently takes root. It does not strike rock. Nevertheless, "their fruit does not mature" (Luke 8:14). Why is this? The seed falls on ground that has not been cleared well. The weeds are not immediately evident, but soon they make their presence known. When they do, they kill off the small plant that is struggling for life. What are these weeds? They are "the cares and riches and pleasures of life" (8:14).

In the West we have not the slightest inkling that, in reveling in affluence as we do, we are playing with fire. This affluence so easily becomes an alternative Way, Truth, and Life, a counterfeit gospel in which to have is to be saved and to have not is to be damned. Unfortunately, *la dolce vita* is not itself satisfying, not in an enduring way. It tends to make us shallow, self-absorbed people who give ourselves to chasing what is superficial by way of styles, fads, and what is pleasurable provided there are no demands for commitments. The styles quickly become obsolete, the fads are forgotten, and the pleasures fade like the morning mist so that this kind of life constantly has to be reinventing itself. Those who fashion their lives around these things die of emptiness. The pains that linger in the soul like a bad headache stay a long, long time.

It is hard to know exactly how those who have received the Word stand in relation to Christ, but they show nothing of spiritual merit in their lives despite their hearing of the Word, their born-again professing, and maybe their churchgoing. They may show up in the born-again category in Barna's polls, but they are not in the right category in life.

There is a third category. It is made up of those who not only hear the Word but also "hold it fast in an honest and good heart, and bear fruit with patience" (Luke 8:15). Hearing the Word is not hard; holding it fast is a different matter. Here are the people who cut their lives to its truths, who hear in its words the voice of eternity, indeed the voice of their incarnate and resurrected Savior speaking.

In fact, there is nothing quite so cheering, so invigorating, as to be with people like this. They are people whose eyes are wide open to the shadows and pains of life, but they also live on another plane. They no longer stare in self-pity at their own pains, and no longer run from one preacher to another seeking some therapeutic release from anxiety, fear, confusion, and bewilderment. They are people who are tough-minded, morally sinewy, and infectiously joyful. They are the ones who have done what is necessary. The Word entered not only the surface of their lives but also the soil beneath it. The tangled roots of the weeds have been pulled out of this soil so that the seed grows into a strong plant.

There are examples of each of these categories of response all through America today. We expect this because Jesus led us to expect it. Has it been like this in every age? Jesus' parable certainly suggests that it has.

What appears to be different today, though, is that the first two categories — the stone in the heart and the weeds that choke the seed — are so abundant and so disproportionately represented. They are the exemplars of the "Christianity Lite" that so many evangelical churches are propagating. What catches our attention — and our breath — are the vast numbers of Christian misfires. Almost half of America is claiming to be born again, but fewer than one in ten has even the foggiest notion of what it means to be a disciple of Christ in biblical terms.

These misfires, these remnants of faded, tattered, undemanding faith, are found everywhere. One does not have to dig too deeply before discovering in the lives of many people a time when they had made a "decision" or had been part of an evangelical church. They stand out in colleges and universities and, not least, on college and university faculties. There one finds many disaffected evangelicals, people whose religious lives were started in a gospel crusade, or in hearing the testimony of another believer, or in a Christian organization on campus, but somewhere along the line things fell apart. Some of these retain a memory of the day Christ was "accepted," but it is overgrown by many other interests like getting tenure, or getting to the next level, or not being embarrassed culturally, or earning acceptance in the academic guild. They move on. Having done so, they are disinterested in, and disconnected from, the gospel. In some cases a remnant of sympathy toward Christian faith remains, but more typically, whatever else was there has long since gone and has been replaced by what is hard, resistant, and even hostile. Here, indeed, are the antagonisms of the disappointed and disaffected.

Does the church not bear considerable responsibility for this situation? I believe it does. The church has been like the shortsighted business CEO who goes for the quick profit and puts off the long-term considerations of these business decisions. The quick gains yield a good write-up in the *Wall Street Journal,* good PR, a good bonus, and the stockholders are held at bay. Then the chickens come home to roost.

The quick gains, it turns out, happened at the cost of the longer-range health of the enterprise. Soon the business is wheezing and struggling for breath. Its strength sapped, it cannot withstand competitors. It succumbs. The investors, quick to perceive their potential losses, move on to brighter prospects, the CEO takes his or her reward, the business closes its doors, and the employees are put out onto the street.

So it is in American evangelicalism today. Far too many leaders and churches are out for the quick kill, the instant success, the enviable limelight, the flattering numbers, the bulging auditoria, the numbers to be boasted about — "my church went from ten to ten thousand once I arrived!" — the filled parking lots, the success story all dolled up for the pages of *Christianity Today* or *Leadership*. All of this is about the short-term interest of the pastor(s), not the long-term health of the church. In Christianity, cut-rate products bring a cut-rate future.

A Better Way Forward

The desire of marketers and emergents to engage the culture is commendable. Engaging it, though, is not the same thing as capitulating to it. Missionaries know the difference. They know they can adapt to local dress and blend in by learning the language and by fitting in with the accepted rhythms of daily life. They can understand the fears and hopes of those they serve without actually embracing those hopes and fears themselves. However, the day they accept the worldview of those they work among, it is time to go home. They have nothing to say anymore.

If the evangelical church does not want to lose its voice, it will have to ensure that its engagement with postmodern culture is done biblically, thoughtfully, and conscientiously.

The church must remember two points in particular: first, that Christianity is about truth, and second, that those who say they are Christians must model this truth by their integrity. A world without truth, postmoderns know, is an empty and dangerous place. And in a world full of hype and spin, manipulation and posturing, personal integrity is like a precious jewel. Even a little integrity goes so much further than all the technology, the country-club churches, and the big performers that can be mustered in the propagation of the biblical gospel.

One Truth

What is truly remarkable about the born-againers in America is that only 32 percent believe in absolutes, either of truth or of morality. Two-thirds do not. It therefore follows that the uniqueness of Christ as God's self-disclosure to us, the uniqueness of his death in our place, and the uniqueness of his role in restoring fellowship with God have now fallen by the wayside. And all of this has occurred in that segment of the Protestant world that is formally committed to the principles of "Scripture alone" for its truth and "in Christ alone" for its salvation!

There is not a lot of difference between these attitudes of the born-again and those in the wider population. In America as a whole, 54 percent say the only way to find truth is through experience, rather than from a book such as the Bible.

Figures like these are not really surprising because our Western cultures are so rife with relativism. There are many reasons for this, but the most important one is that in our daily experience we are in constant contact, at least at the level of knowledge, with other worldviews, lifestyles, and beliefs, and they tend to negate each other. They rub the corners off each other and make it seem highly unlikely that any one view is uniquely true.

Globalization, we recall, is not simply about goods crossing national boundaries as if those boundaries were not there. It is also about many other things crossing those boundaries, and not least ideas, fashion, and knowledge of others. What are we likely to find as a result? A world full of seeming incongruities that, in every way, undermine claims to uniqueness.

One day in 2006, before the sun arose, I traveled briefly with some African game rangers who were tracking white rhino. These are animals that charge first and investigate afterward when they pick up an unfamiliar scent. So these rangers came armed with AK-47s. But they also carried cell phones (in a country whose per capita income that year was $398!). They were doing what everyone in the West does! That I had not expected. And at the end of the day, on their way home, they may well have stopped at the Coke stand I noticed.

This is the world we inhabit. On the one hand, it is full of the "other" — other products, cultures, religions, ways of looking at life, ways of believing. It is a world of exotic cuisine and eclectic style, of Italian silk ties sold in African airports and African carvings sold on the streets of Pisa. On the other hand, it is a world where everything is the same. Airports look the same all over the modernized world; Coke is in the poorest countries in the world; and everywhere one hears the same music and sees the same movies. There are the same credit cards, the same autos, the same advertisements, the same brand-name clothes, and the same . . . cell phones.

In our Western cities we come face-to-face with these incongruities on a daily basis. Everything that is the same and everything that is different — we find it all in one place, side by side. Because so much is the same, because we expect everything to be the same, it becomes hard to stand out. Christianity seems just like every other religion.

What is different — such as the claim that Christianity is about what is absolutely true — is therefore very hard to sustain in a culture like this. Nothing in the culture makes it likely that the claim is true, and everything in our experience seems to say that it is not. Those who want to maintain the position that Christianity is about truth have an uphill slog before them.

When diverse, even contradictory, ways of thinking, being, and behaving come together in close proximity with one another, relativism is the almost inevitable outcome. Worldviews and belief systems all get softened. And Christian faith is right in the middle of this mix today.

If the postmodern world is going to be engaged successfully, it will have to be at this point. A soft, shapeless Christianity ready to adapt to any worldview may enjoy initial success, but it will soon be overtaken and lose its interest. The problem with all such adaptations is that those outside the faith soon see that they can reap Christian benefits on purely secular grounds without paying whatever small price is being asked for the adapted version of this faith.

Christian truth simply is not amenable to adaptation. It requires application, but that is an entirely different matter. Apostolic Christianity was doctrinally shaped. The churches were instructed to guard and preserve that teaching.

This apostolic framework of belief is not something that many in the contemporary church want out in the open. So they hide it. The first Christians guarded it. We venture far beyond it. They treasured it and lived within it. We think it will get in the way of our church's success. They thought that without it, front and center, there could be no church. They were right and we are wrong.

Integrity

Truth and integrity lie very close to one another. In the absence of what is true, all that remains are power and manipulation. What takes the place once occupied by truth are private agendas, community ideals, rhetorical force, savage ad hominem attacks, fabrications, exaggerations, and power seeking. In the absence of truth, lying becomes the common coin of the realm. And this lying takes on especially virulent forms when it becomes religious. For then God is pressed into service for personal advantage. The stage is then set for terrible things to happen. We understand the dark side of this connection.

On the positive side, this connection between truth and integrity shows itself in that kind of ethical consistency that binds the whole of an individual's life together. To know God is to know him in every facet of our being. It is to know him in our mind, heart, and emotional life, in our private world at home and in our public world, in worship, in Christian service, in the arena of ideas, in the conflict of worldviews, in the competition between religions. Because it is the same God whom we know in each of these ways, through the same truth that he has given us, a person of integrity will be the same person in all these arenas. The point about hypocrisy is that a person is different in different contexts. The person creates a pose, or an image, to gain some advantage with some audience. The person and the pose, however, are two different things. The point about integrity is that a person is the same, even when audiences may not be pleased and when there is, as a result, some cost to pay.

What an extraordinary moment it would be if Americans — Americans of every kind, from secular humanists to Buddhists, from New Agers to old-fashioned liberals — had no option but to think of Protestants as people of truth, people who lived by that truth!

CHAPTER IV

God

—w—

The most painful experience of modern consciousness is the loss of center.

RICHARD WEAVER

For from him and through him and to him are all things. To him be glory forever. Amen.

ROMANS 11:36

In this chapter I am going to explore the fate of God. That, perhaps, sounds more dramatic than I intend. I am not actually worried about God. Not at all. The fate I am really talking about is in ourselves. What has happened to him in our minds? In our souls? In our society? That is rather different from asking what has happened to God himself.

Postmodern writers have been saying that the universe is empty. They say it has no center. It therefore has no overarching meaning(s). That is the world we inhabit, and this is part of what is fed daily into our experience. What happens to our understanding about God when we are constantly experiencing a world that seems centerless and chaotic?

Biblical writers, by contrast, declare that the only reason there is life and hope is that there is a center. It is in the triune God, the maker and sustainer of all things and the one in whom we find reconciliation through the Son. When we know him, life fits back into a meaningful pattern and we are filled with hope about its end.

It is these two perspectives that I explore in this chapter. However, in thinking about this, it is important to remember that culture does not give the church its agenda. All it gives the church is its context. The church's belief and mission come from the Word of God. They do not come from the culture either through attraction to it or in alienation from it. It is not the culture that determines the church's priorities. It is not the (post)modern culture that should be telling it what to think. The principle here is *sola Scriptura,* not *sola cultura.*

At least, that is what should be the case. But as I have been arguing, the church's practice has often departed from this principle. Too often what we see is *sola cultura* in place of *sola Scriptura.*

We see churches, particularly those of a marketing and emergent kind, that are rather blatantly adapting themselves to their own generational culture. They are taking it as a given that they cannot communicate to a (post)modern generation unless they adopt (post)modern ways of thinking. Yes, even in regard to God. Perhaps especially in regard to God.

I beg to differ.

What is of first importance to the church is not that it learn to mimic the culture but that it learn to think God's thoughts after him. The people of God are here on earth to learn how to recenter him, as it were, to see him in the place that he actually occupies, to worship him accordingly, and to live before him day after day. To live before him, not as we want to think about him because we are postmoderns, but before him as he really is. This is the way — indeed, the only way — the church can be faithful to him in its own time and context.

What, then, is this going to look like, given our postmodern context today? I need to begin by thinking about our context and trying to understand why the West has lost its center. That is my first question. My second is, what should life look like if we see its center in the creator-redeemer God who rules sovereignly over all of life?

The Lost Center

Why has life lost its center? There are actually two answers to this question. One is biblical and the other is cultural.

The biblical answer explains why all of life has become disordered. As the twenty-first century is beginning in the West, part of that disorder is the sense that life has no center, that it is adrift, and that it has no meaning. This answer, which explains all of this, is sin. And this is the normative answer. It does not change. This, in every age, is the answer that explains life's disorder.

The cultural answer, one being explored by many contemporary writers, simply looks within the modernized social life of the West to see what might explain the loss of meaning, the disappearance of the "centeredness" that so many are experiencing. Answers along these lines are always subject to change as the culture itself changes. They are, therefore, always provisional. And insofar as they are just our best thoughts on the subject, they are always subject to revision.

We need to think from both perspectives as we consider why life no longer seems centered. Of course, it is vital to know what God has revealed about fallen human life, which is one answer to this. In a different way, though, it is also helpful to see how that fallenness is actually working itself out in a particular cultural context, which is the other answer we are seeking. This is what contemporaries are experiencing. It is what they understand. Their understanding is of course quite incomplete and, at its heart, wrong. Nevertheless, it gives us a point of contact because we are all experiencing the same losses together. It is Christian faith that explains these losses.

Thinking Biblically

The biblical answer about why we have lost our center is rather straightforward. The center has not been lost. What has been lost is our ability to see it, to recognize it, to bow before it, to reorder our lives in light of it, to do what we should do as people who live in the presence of this center, this Other, this triune, holy-loving God of the Bible. For we start our life's journey on the alternative premise that he is not there, or that he has not spoken, or that he does not care. We do not reckon on his providential and moral presence. We begin as if life were empty and without a center and as if we were empowered by our choices to make of life what we will. And so we create our own center, we create our own rules, and we make our own meaning. All of this springs from an alternative center in the universe. It is ourselves.

Paul's statement is that, since the fall, we have "worshiped and served the creature rather than the Creator" (Rom. 1:25). We will not reckon with our internal sense that God does exist. We also try to ignore our own sense of the moral fabric of life (Rom. 1:18-20; 2:14-15). And we have also made some substitutions. We have replaced the actual center of life with one of our own making, substituting our interests for God's, our perspective for his, our norms for his, our meaning for his, and our privatized truths for his absolute truth. All of this is the essence of sin. And the result, Paul says, is that our minds are now "futile" and our hearts are now "darkened" (Rom. 1:21). This is the unvarying perspective, the insistent proclamation, of the Bible.

Is it a great surprise, then, that we now see our world as empty? We have wrenched ourselves free from the hand of God. We are in flight from him. We reject reality as he has defined it. We redefine our world and ourselves to accommodate our rebellion. That is why life has lost any center other than ourselves.

Evil

Let us pursue this a little further. The biblical understanding of sin is far deeper and far worse than our contemporary understanding of evil. The language of evil has largely vanished today. It made a brief comeback in America after the terrorist attacks on the World Trade Center in New York and on the Pentagon in Washington on September 11, 2001. It was a way for us to express our utter dismay at what had happened — and our moral outrage. The problem, though, is that when we do not live within a moral world — and most Americans do not in their minds — the language of evil has no referent. Evil in relation to what standard, we must ask? In our postmodern moment, we are leery of standards. If there is some standard, we want to know who erected it.

Whose truth is it? Who holds it as a standard? Why was it established? What do those who claim there is a standard get out of it?

That something could be so inherently wrong as to be called evil, not simply because we see it as evil but because it is evil in itself, makes no sense anymore. It withers under the (post)modern sun. It dies in the face of a thousand qualifications and a thousand cultural suspicions.

What this means is that evil has become purely privatized. It is simply what is bad for me. And what is bad is only the way things feel or look, not as they are in their own moral nature.

Secularists, with their low cognitive horizons, their tired agenda, their world with rooms that had only windows and no skylights, became thoroughly boring. They began as rebels and ended up as little-minded conformists. Postmoderns are not boring — at least not yet — but they are very trivial.

Let's get a bit more serious about this. Let's assume that there is a moral sphere. I know this is a huge assumption to make today. But unless this is the case, we won't be able to break out of the shallowness and triviality into which postmoderns have led us.

Given this assumption, we can say that evil is corruption within this moral world, the opposition to what is good, any grievous assault on human well-being, and all the acts of brutality, cruelty, oppression, and nastiness that fill the news every night. Evil is badness at a deep level, one that we intuitively feel demands reparations and penalties because it offends against an inviolable norm. It is always wrong. It is not only wrong to me. It is wrong everywhere.

Is this really so hard an assumption to make? How many postmoderns who say there are no moral absolutes would actually think the rape of a small, innocent girl is not morally wrong? That it is not a moral outrage? That it is not always and everywhere wrong? How many would brush off the Nazi concentration camps, or Pol Pot's killing fields in Cambodia, as just misdirected social policy that, unfortunately, didn't work out? How many would say that acts like these are not reprehensible? These acts of evil are surely wrong, are they not? Always wrong.

Here, though, is the difference between sin and evil (as we use this word today). Evil is simply badness. Sin, though, is altogether more serious because it sets up human badness in relation to *God*. It is not just the absence of good, or corruption, brutality, oppression, and nastiness, but it is all these things, and many more besides, as they are understood in relation to God. They are acts of moral defiance of him. They are a rejection of his authority over all of human life. That is the Bible's perspective.

Sin

Our perspective on sin in America is different. Only 17 percent of Americans define sin in relation to God, so for the overwhelming majority sin has become a trivial matter, no more serious than having violated some church rule about something quite inconsequential. For most Americans the more serious word by far is "evil," though when postmoderns lift it out of a moral world, it has no more than a passing emotional significance. I believe "sin" has far more gravity than "evil" because of the standard by which sinfulness is exposed.

Sin, biblically speaking, is not only the absence of good. It also entails our active opposition to God. It is, then, the defiance of his authority, the rejection of his truth, the challenge to his sovereignty in which we set ourselves up in life to live the way we want to live. It is the way we wrench ourselves free from obedience to him, cut ourselves off from his grasp, and refuse to let him be God. It is therefore all the ways we live life on our own terms, to our own ends, with accountability to no one but ourselves.

This really is the point of the biblical language. Sin is described as missing the target (Rom. 3:9; 7:5), falling short of a standard, or transgressing boundaries (Rom. 2:23; 5:20; Gal. 3:19). However, the target missed, the path abandoned, the authority defied, the law transgressed are in each and every case *God's*. Sin is all about taking issue with God, defying him, refusing to submit to him, and displacing him from the center of existence. We are now disaffected with his rule, resent his claims on our lives, are hostile to his truth in the biblical Word, and are determined to pursue our own values, goals, and pleasures in defiance of what he has said. This "freedom" from all that God is, and all that he has said, turns out to be an illusion. When we freed ourselves in these ways, beginning with the fall, we fell headlong into a dark captivity both to our own selves and, beyond that, to the powers of darkness.

This is wonderfully illustrated in Tolkien's *Lord of the Rings.* In a parallel universe the inhabitants of Middle-Earth are themselves struggling with evil in the form of the Dark Lord himself, Sauron. In a previous battle the One Ring was lost and then discovered by a strange little creature called Gollum. This Ring had terrible powers because it infected those who had it. This Ring was self-centeredness, fallenness, and corruption, and once these enter a soul, all freedom from what is dark is lost. So it was that Gollum, who found this Ring, came to love it. He both loved it and hated it, Tolkien tells us. He hated the darkness, but even more than that he hated the light. But even while he hated the Ring, and hated himself for loving it, he could not give it up. His love for it was too great. This Ring stole his will and made him its captive.

At the heart of this sin that holds us captive is pride. The essence of pride is finding in the self what in fact can be found only in God. So pride, as Cornelius Plantinga writes in *Not the Way It's Supposed to Be,* leads us to think much *about* the self and much *of* the self. We imagine that within ourselves we have power enough, wisdom enough, and strength enough to live in security, in the fullness of happiness, as we want to live, amidst all the conflicts and opportunities of life. Very finite preoccupations are therefore substituted for those that are eternal, and we then confidently take the place God once had. We therefore redefine reality. Is this not the ultimate explanation as to why life in the postmodern world has lost its center? What I am describing here, from within a biblical framework, is what others in the postmodern world are seeing without this framework. This is the "autonomous self."

It is not hard to see how the self movement — to which I will return in the next chapter — has tapped into this by offering self-mastery through the right technique. It encourages us to think much about the self and much of the self. It is an industry that in fact lives off of and for pride! As such, it offers a way to dissolve all our internal aches and heal all our internal wounds. Perhaps it can offer some amelioration along the way, a few coping skills against life's blows, but we might as well try to empty the ocean with a thimble than depend on these techniques to solve our deeper issues.

Nor is it hard to see that once the self has established itself at the center of reality, its own judgments, no matter how flawed, are seen as ultimate and unchallengeable. They stand as if they had been issued from God himself. And in a sense they have. They have been issued by his stand-in, the autonomous self.

This kind of pride refuses to accept limitations on its knowledge. Pride wants to make of private opinion something akin to a binding address. There are professors, Plantinga dryly notes, who have left faculty meetings more enlightened by what they said than by what they heard! Pride goes hand in hand with self-righteousness because it refuses to accept moral evaluations that are uncomplimentary. Pride will not acknowledge any flaws. Proud people are always right in their judgments as well as in their behavior. This same pride lies beneath so many other sins like indifference to others, injustice, and the many ways, some cruel and brutal, in which we live as if no one else counted for anything.

Sin, as Plantinga says, has many different ways of showing itself. It has a "thousand faces." But all expressions of sin break apart what God has put together. Sin began by breaking apart our relation to God, and from this followed every other breach that has left life in pain, confusion, and disarray. The environment is under siege, marriages are in pain, the workplace is rife with rivalries and deceit, nations are at war, and we ourselves, even if surrounded by all the fruits of affluence and living in the plush quiet of American suburbia, struggle with emptiness and having to settle for what is superficial and fading. One might say that sin is what has dissolved the center that holds all of life together, robbing it of its meaning.

The short answer, then, to the question why life has lost its center has a beguiling simplicity to it. The center has not been lost. It has only been lost to our view. And that is because our disposition, the orientation of our nature from birth, leads us inexorably to replace God with our own selves, to substitute our interests for his, and to redefine life around its new substitute center in ourselves.

The Culture's Answer

From ground level, however, the question of a lost center looks different. How are we to explain this? Since our postmodern culture refuses to do so in terms of a Christian doctrine of sin, it really is at a loss to explain why we have no center. But this inability is not without its benefits. In the absence of a center, we are free to define life as we will and we are accountable to no one but ourselves. That, of course, is exactly how the Enlightenment defined freedom. We may be in pain and confusion, but we are free!

Emptiness

All people bring sin into life. That is why God has, in our minds and hearts, been dislodged from the center of life. However, this displacement is given different cultural forms in different times and places. In ours it is the question of meaning — or, more precisely, of meaninglessness — that haunts us the most.

Why is meaninglessness the calling card of our time? Why does sin take this particular turn in the West? All I can do here is sketch broadly, and I need to begin a little before our own time to get some perspective on it.

The Gathering Storm

In America it was already clear midway through the nineteenth century that the world was losing its center. That life had a purpose that transcended it, one that was larger than simple survival, slowly disappeared. This disappearance was undoubtedly aided by Darwin's work. Natural selection did come to be seen as the alternative to God's providence. This displaced the biblical understanding of creation, too, and with it any thought about a meaning to life large enough to encompass it all. Once that happened, the idea of evolution migrated from biology into many other disciplines, such as history, politics, ethics, Old and New Testament studies, and theology. It became the dominant conceptual framework in the second half of the nineteenth century for understanding life as a whole.

It would be a mistake, though, to lay all the great cultural changes that rolled through that century at Darwin's doorstep. The truth is that as America became modernized, with all the attendant social reorganization, people who had never even heard the name

Darwin began to think differently about life. This had been a land where individualism flourished, but that had meant mostly that people took responsibility for themselves. They did so out of a sense of duty. They felt some accountability, if not to God, then at least to some moral principles or to their community, or their family. But this canopy of meaning began to cave in. Many of the writers in this century began instead to think more in terms of a void at the center of life. The idea of God's providence, of his control over life, of a meaning larger than any individual, began to collapse amidst all the gathering social complexity and, indeed, suffering.

The Civil War no doubt hastened this development. Why did one man die and not another? What possible purpose could be seen in these events? This human tragedy seemed, Andrew Delbanco argued in *The Death of Satan,* to force the idea of God's providence into retreat. He said it became more fashionable to hope for luck than to trust in God's providence. To see in any of the apparently random deaths any kind of divine purpose became embarrassing. And evil itself mutated and became simply bad luck. "Good luck!" became the new benediction.

What needs to be remembered, though, is that evil, so painfully evident in the Civil War, did not first appear in the nineteenth century. There has always been evil, and it has always raised questions about the providence and purposes of God. And not only do the evils of war raise such questions, but so do many of the perplexities of life that are present in every age. Why does one person who wants to work remain unemployed and another not? Why do some strike it rich and others remain paupers? Why does one person find the right spouse and another not? Why do some children, even with the best upbringing, become wayward and others do not? Why do some rise from the humble neighborhoods, from slums and chaotic barrios, to become great leaders while others, raised on the best in life, abandon it all for a life of dissolute living?

Life, it seems, is just a large, unpredictable accident that has neither rhyme nor reason to it. It is on this sense that the insurance companies have thrived, beginning in the nineteenth century. They developed actuarial charts in an attempt to handicap chance in life. In time, insurance became available for almost everything. It is also

true that insurance is a prudent preparation against the unseen calamities of the future. But for those with no sense of God's providence, and no belief in his ability to control life's events, it does function as a purely human offset against cruel, mindless events when
there is no other alternative.

Postmoderns Emerge

A revolution began in the 1960s, unnoticed though it was at the time. It
was a turn inward to the self. In addition, it was a turn away from all
that the Enlightenment had stood for: a rationalistic world, a naturalistic view of life, meaning that is universal, and moral norms that are embedded in the nature of things and can be discovered with just a little
effort, as can structure, order, and coherence.

This is the heart of the postmodern rebellion. It turned away from
meaning that is fixed and universal and turned toward meaning that is
private and subjective. It shifted from absolute moral norms to those
that are simply private. It rejected the Enlightenment's confidence in
(naturalistic) reason and began to think more in terms of intuitions
and to give greater weight to feelings. In this situation it is the self —
the empty, minimal, disintegrating, and autonomous (post)modern
self — that must assume the center in life. It is the self and its intuitions
from which we derive the only meaning we have in life. This means that
the transcendent from which we once took our bearings has been relocated within. The self must function as our transcendent norm. It is
from within that we are left to read our own meaning.

This meaning, though, is more sensed than reasoned. The life of
the mind now is denigrated and distrusted. We are skeptical of reason-
ing, imagining that it has been discredited by its misuse during the
long reign of the Enlightenment. Today we traffic in the illogical and ir-
rational without skipping a beat or wincing. We do not trust the mind.
We lean far more confidently on the emotions.

What made the Enlightenment ideology so enduring, I believe, is
that the view of life it produced found unwitting confirmation in the
modernized world. It was the soul of which the reorganization of life
that modernization requires was the body. It was a perfect fit. What the

Enlightenment ideology projected — a rationalistic order that was self-sufficient, and progressing — found confirmation in a world that was driven by technology, owed nothing to God apparently, and was improving every aspect of life by its own inherent capability. This was a marriage of supreme convenience. Once Enlightenment ideology and the modernized world discovered each other, they worked together so well that for two centuries at least it had been extremely difficult in the West to think about life in ways that were at odds with the Enlightenment and the secular humanism it spawned. The reason is, quite simply, that the modernized world gave great plausibility to the kind of idea the Enlightenment had advocated.

Now this is all coming down about our ears. It has finally dawned on us that the modern world, with its rationalistic philosophies, is profoundly inhospitable to the human spirit. We live amidst its bright splendor, basking in its plenty, but our souls are withering. The modernized world of the West is coldly impersonal and anonymous. And because it has been emancipated from the divine, it is a world in which dark human impulses have no restraints. We recognize no outside authorities as larger and more compelling than our inward desires. This gives us an enormous sense of exhilaration, but soon we also realize that without restraints, societies start to fall apart. And we fear those who desire to bring us harm and can do so because their powers have been magnified many times over by technology. Is this the end to which the Enlightenment claimed we were all progressing? What kind of progress is this?

It is a painful, difficult, threatening kind of world we inhabit now, although it is filled with options, opportunity, and plenty. It is both of these things at the same time. And yet, despite its plenty, it remains a place — at least in the West — where the human spirit is ill at ease. It is not at home. It is haunted by the sense that it was made for something more than buying and selling, television and sleek cars, vacation homes and investment accounts.

Our creation in the image of God makes the human spirit restive in the middle of this substitute paradise we call the West. Indeed, as Augustine once observed, it is restless until it finds its rest in God who made it. The story of the West, in many ways, is also the story of this restiveness.

Many consequences follow upon all of this. Our world, our resplendent culture, has been turned into a substitute for God. However, this substitute, we quickly discover, offers us no principles by which to live. Furthermore, we also find that the self that has to fill the void at the center of our lives is incapable of fulfilling this function.

These are consequences that many writers are observing, even some with little interest in a Christian worldview or the Scriptures. And, once again, the way these writers are describing the world and the way the Bible sees it are different, but not entirely different. Let us pursue this thought a little further.

Nothing Makes Sense

Our time has been called many things. But William Donnelly's description of it as the Autonomy Generation is quite apt. What he was seeing at work is what I have referred to as the autonomous self.

As he says in his book *The Confetti Generation,* since we are without any external center from which to take our bearings, life's experiences become like confetti. These experiences — a concert, a bank robbery, political defeats, Congressional scandals, terrorist threats, the stock market performance, interest rates — are separate, disconnected things that fall into our lives in a random way. There is no way to make sense of the whole picture. We cannot make an evaluation of it that is sweeping enough to take everything into account so that we know what is true and what is not, what is important and what is not, what is right and what is not. Ours is now a centerless universe. We have no map, and even if we did, we could not get our bearings. We have no purpose larger than ourselves.

In the absence of a compelling external authority that enables us to draw the line confidently between right and wrong, true and false, we are left to fumble about with only our feelings to guide us. And are these feelings not often driven by self-desire and self-justification? Feelings are notoriously unreliable as a guide to belief or behavior.

Postmoderns have attacked the idea that anyone can have a worldview. Actually, it is quite incorrect for them to say that they have no worldview. Everyone has a view of the world from their own place in it. This view comprises an understanding of what is ultimate (if anything is), how this might be discovered, whether there is such a thing as truth, how that truth might be found, what is the meaning of life, what is the explanation of what has gone wrong, and what are the end outcomes to life. The answers to these questions form a view of the world that can be called a worldview, however inconsistent and confused it might be.

What has changed in recent years is not that worldviews have disappeared, because they have not, but that worldviews that are comprehensive, that are true for all people, have become an impossibility. There can no longer be a *single* way of looking at reality, of evaluating it, of reading its meaning. Worldviews are as different as the people who hold them. And that means that there can be no comprehensive purpose to life nor any truth that is absolute and applicable to all in the same way.

It is true, of course, that not all people follow this logic to its final, devastating emptiness. How we think about this, how we live with it, varies greatly. European writers have generally expressed a more bleak, brooding, and despairing attitude than American writers have, though in some of the rock music that now fills the air in America one can hear expressions of despair as dark and unrelieved as in any café on the Left Bank in Paris. Perhaps more so since European intellectuals seem now to be trying to get away from the bleakness of existentialists from the 1960s.

However, American culture is by nature more upbeat, more optimistic than European culture, more about opportunity than about our lost philosophical bearings, so it tends to think differently about our lost center. It is naturally more hopeful. It therefore stares not so much at the void as at the prospect of a Caribbean vacation, at the high-end catalogues, the upward move, and the new Lexus. Europeans might still see themselves in Samuel Beckett's *Waiting for Godot.* Americans are more inclined to while away the time by watching something distracting or amusing. Maybe *Seinfeld.* This brilliantly acted television show was, by its own reckoning, a show about nothing. Beckett's world, too, was a world in which Nothing reigned. Here are two streets that end up at the same destination, one at a highbrow level and that other at, well, a lowbrow level. But Beckett's was nastier.

One consequence of this is that when there are no central principles, when culture has lost its center, we are stripped of our ability to
discriminate. This shows itself most importantly in the fact that for a
majority in America there is no enduring right and wrong. But we also
lose our ability to distinguish good from bad taste, good from bad behavior, worthy ideas from those that are unworthy. In this context all
ideas become equal, as do all religions, all lifestyles. Nothing is differ-
entiated from anything else. Nothing is better, truer, or more helpful. It
all sits on the shelf, all the same. It is there waiting to be validated by a
buyer. Only when we take something into our lives does it assume any
importance, and the only reason it has importance is because we have
chosen it. We bought into it. The value lies in the consumer's choice,
not in the idea itself.

An unholy alliance exists between the relativism that results from
having no center in culture and the habits that have been fashioned by
consumption. The one is a belief, the other is a habit. One comes from
our internal world, the other from the external world.

The marketplaces for products and for ideas are not as different
as they may seem. We are constantly choosing between new products
that are appearing on the market and old products that are passing
themselves off as new and improved. This unending choice wears on
the mind. Although manufacturers do their utmost to distinguish their
product from everything else that is available, so many products still
look the same. We, as consumers, carry this sense over into our "shopping" for ideas as well. There we are in the market for a religion, for ethical beliefs, for what will fit us personally. Religions, beliefs, lifestyles,
moral norms are all on the shelf, so to speak, ready to be picked out and
used. But until we actually choose one, it remains on the shelf as useless as the other products on the shelf. They are all products; none are
matters of truth. That is the sense into which, as I have suggested, the
church marketers are also tapping.

God Dies, We Die

Perhaps the most startling consequence of all of this is that our self begins to disintegrate. When the universe loses its center or, to be more

precise, when the center is lost to us as something outside us that has the authority to reach into our lives, we ourselves begin to disintegrate. The self that has been made to bear the weight of being the center of all reality, the source of all our meaning, mystery, and morality, finds that it has become empty and fragile. When God dies to us, we die in ourselves. That is the connection we need to see, and it has become especially aggravated in the context of our (post)modern world.

Many modern writers have pondered the emptying out of the (post)modern self. This was certainly evident in the 1960s, and it has continued down to the present time. Their language is sometimes different, but what they have in mind is much the same. Christopher Lasch spoke of the "minimal self," Lauren Langman of "decentered selfhood" and "an enfeebled self," Philip Cushman of "the empty self," and Donald Capps of "the depleted self." Their analyses came at it from different angles, but all saw a constant erosion of our internal substance in the modern world. And whatever else we wish to say about it, it does seem clear that this is related to our experience of being uprooted, of not belonging, of drifting, of being homeless. It is also related to our being constantly bombarded by images, ideas, demands, products, and options that wear down our inward substance. But, most importantly I believe, it is related to the fact that there is no one before whom we are summoned, no one outside our experience before whom we are accountable, none in whose light we measure who we are and where we are heading. It is this last point that many (post)modern writers do not understand. Their analyses, though, are often very accurate so far as they go.

Reinvented Selves

They all see that our Western societies are made up of complex, interdependent systems — capitalism, democracy, cities, communications systems, transportation systems, state bureaucracies, and corporate structures — that, as they work together, create a context in which the soul withers. This is correct and we need to reckon with it, for this is, in biblical language, "the course of this world" (Eph. 2:2) from which we also need to be redeemed. There is, though, something at work in this complex that many contemporary writers are missing but that the biblical writers know about.

What our contemporary writers often do not understand is why our Western experience washes away at our own personal reality. Of course, our Western societies are consumer-driven, suffused with change, large and anonymous in how they work. They favor — indeed, almost demand — a self that is flexible, malleable, light, and free, that can move when movement is called for and adapt when adaptation is called for. A flexible biography, a self that can remake itself, shift and change, refurbish itself, reinvent itself, reimagine itself, is the counterpart to our market-driven economy with its constantly changing conditions, demands, and opportunities. This, of course, makes a mockery of what was once thought to be a virtue — the idea of personal consistency.

Consistency was most commonly met in the thought that a person's word was his or her bond. A promise made was a promise kept, even if the circumstances had changed and it was no longer advantageous to honor the commitment.

A good illustration of this is marriage. On the day someone promises to be a "loving and faithful husband, for better or for worse, in plenty and in want, in joy and in sorrow, in sickness and in health," that person has not the faintest idea of what will be involved in keeping that promise. The future lies unopened and unread. As days follow each other, and the years unfold, it becomes clearer what is being demanded of him as he is called upon to be a loving and faithful husband. The same goes for the wife. The marriage starts out with mutually given promises, but after that, day by day, life throws up its difficulties, heartaches, and challenges. The commitment to love each other now becomes very specific. What this means becomes inescapable.

What the promise meant was that the husband would be the same person in the future as he was the day of the marriage in his exclusive, loving commitment, as would the wife. The passing of the years would not change that commitment. That is what was promised, the one to the other.

That promise, though, is tested over time by misunderstandings, illnesses, moral failings, temptations, and the unrelenting pressure that modern life brings. What sustains the continuity of the person across the years, what underwrites a sense of identity, is the very thing most imperiled in the (post)modern world: moral principle.

Keeping this kind of commitment becomes a matter of character because, by one means or another, it is always being tested. How will such a promise be kept? Promises of this kind are not kept in the absence of character, because they are not kept easily.

Character makes habitual the ultimate Good. What is ultimate — and for a Christian it is the character of God as revealed in Scripture — never changes. That being so, character always has a consistency to it. People of character act in the same way even when it is difficult or not to their advantage to do so. However, when (post)modern relativism took root, everything changed.

With respect to the person, we immediately encounter this cruel irony that has followed this (post)modern mood. It is that personal identity is eroding. This is what many contemporary writers simply do not understand.

The reason we think we can manufacture our identities through a flexible biography (read: one that is not always truthful), project new images of ourselves, stage a different character as new situations seem to call for that, and by fashion put together new "looks" that hint at different people within, is that no unchanging "I" tethers who we are. We are like boats that are not tied to any dock. We move with the tides, in and out, and there is nothing to which we are held. So it is with the (post)modern self. Increasingly there is nothing there, so the self becomes what it presents itself as being. Image is reality. Appearance is the substance. Is it any surprise, then, that marriage as an institution is on the rocks? It can be sustained only by the very thing now being most eroded. That is, personal, moral consistency.

Even as we have been so busy making ourselves, and projecting ourselves, we have been falling apart within. Who are we? This question lies behind the many answers that we hear in contemporary anthropologies today: "I am my genes," "I am my past," "I am my sexual orientation," "I am my body," "I am what I do," "I am what I have," "I am who I know," and many others like these. The emptiness of the self is signaled in every one of these identifications. We say we are our genes, past, sexuality, body, occupation, accumulation, or social circle because we have become nothing in ourselves. We are profoundly disoriented as postmoderns because what orients us to reality, the capacities of human nature, has been under severe, unrelenting assault.

This is brilliantly illustrated in Milan Kundera's 1980s novel *The Unbearable Lightness of Being*. He explores the many ambiguities we encounter in living in an empty universe. His novel is the story of random sexual liaisons in the overlapping relationships between five people. He uses their relationships to illuminate the difference between what is weighty and what is light in life. He is preoccupied with the passing, transient quality of life. The passage of life's events — its torments, its passions, its laughter, all that happens — takes place, unfortunately, within a blank universe. That means that verdicts about right and wrong, significant and insignificant, cannot be made because everything, all the time, is in the "sunset of dissolution." Nothing ever returns, nothing can be retrieved. Everything disappears. All is lost. So at the end of the day, if everything is gone, what point is there in passing judgment on it when nothing remains to be judged? It has all gone.

This sense that everything is passing gives to all of life, including our own being, its sense of "lightness." Where everything vanishes, we are without responsibility. Only if we were to be nailed to eternity, he says, would things be changed, and that is a "terrifying prospect" because we would be accountable. Nothing we said or did would ever finally disappear. So which is better: to be light and free, or to be weighty and accountable?

The choice, in fact, is not ours to make. So we carry around with us this burden that we have become as light as a feather in our random freedom. In an empty universe we lose all our weight, all our reality. But this is a painful way to be!

Indeed, everywhere today we are seeing this same terrifying sense. Now that we have contracted all of reality into the self, making that self life's center, we are face-to-face with this awful fact. The self is disintegrating under its impossible burden. Kundera simply put words to this sense.

The passion of believing, of believing in the greatness and goodness of God, is therefore replaced in the (post)modern world by the blank stare, the ironic posture. In its postmodern incarnation, this attitude says it is not chic to care anymore, except of course about ourselves. The sense of meaninglessness is the signature of the minimal, depleted, empty (post)modern self. Where we differ is how we handle this inward ache. Are we more European? Do we stand on the edge of the precipice and gaze down into the darkness below? Or do we simply shake it all off with a sly joke?

God and Modernity

My focus here is not apologetic or evangelistic. We could indeed explore the cultural context I have been sketching. Given postmodern sensibilities, we could ask how best to commend belief in the Christian God. Along with that, we could ask how best to make known his gospel, the gospel of Christ's saving work on our behalf. These are worthy tasks, but they are not my focus here.

My focus is the church. It is on what happens after the apologetic questions have been resolved and the gospel has been believed. It is not on the terrain that has to be crossed before belief happens. My focus here is what happens afterward.

Being Recentered

It is by believing the gospel of Christ's saving death that sinners are reconciled to the Father. Those who were far off have been brought near. Those who were "enemies" have been "reconciled" (Rom. 5:10). Those who were rebels have been pardoned, cleansed, and blessed in Christ (Eph. 1:5-9). They are the ones who have been called "out of darkness into his marvelous light" (1 Pet. 2:9). And they are the ones who, in the light of their knowledge of the Father through the Son, must rethink the meaning of their lives.

They had once substituted themselves for him. They had been life's center and he had not been. They now know what it means to feel their own inward world disintegrating. They were trying to stand in a swiftly flowing river but their feet found nothing on which to stand. However, all that has now changed. Yes, they live in a (post)modern context — at least here in the West — but what should (post)modern life look like from within the circle of biblical light in which they now also live? That is my question.

This question has an almost endless number of parts to it, for it asks us to think about the engagement of Christian faith with our contemporary cultural context along the entire front. There is not in fact any part of our lives that is not touched in some way by the world in which we live. This external world, therefore, should be encountering in us a knowledge of God and of his truth at every point where its information, opportunities, threats, anxieties, hopes, techniques, beliefs, and moral expectations enter our inner world. Trying to describe this nexus, this shifting, changing engagement between what is internal and what is external, is of course quite impossible.

But we can think about one part of it in more detail. It is our understanding of God in this contemporary context because this was the center we had lost, both because of sin and because of our cultural experience, and it is the center we have found again through Christ. It is from the triune God that all life came into existence and by him that it is all sustained. He is also the one who sustains the moral world that is as enduring as is his character. All of us are in fact nailed to this kind of eternity as surely as Christ was nailed to the cross.

This may create great discomfort to those who live for their own autonomous selves, but the apostles' joy arose from the fact that they had been freed from themselves to serve the glorious God of the Bible. Here was to be found the ultimate meaning of life, the source of grace, and the boundless wonder of glory. "Oh, the depth of the riches and wisdom and knowledge of God!" cried Paul. "How unsearchable are his judgments and how inscrutable his ways!" (Rom. 11:33). And since Paul was always God-centered in his thought, in the nature of the case, he was always Christ-centered as well. It was in Christ that God took human flesh, revealed his character, and conquered sin, death, and the devil. It was in Christ that Paul saw "the light of the knowledge of the glory of God" (2 Cor. 4:6). Paul's thought therefore ran from God, to Christ, to the church, to the world, and then back to God again as triune and holy-loving, the center and focal point of all reality, and all of this in a never ending cycle. How is this active believing affected in the (post)modern world?

Being Private

For a long time we in the West thought the main cultural pressure came at the point of confessing a belief in God. Secular humanism seemed to be demanding that the slate be wiped clean, that all religious belief be banned. Religious belief, Enlightenment ideologues said, was a relic from the past that was doomed to rapid extinction. This turned out not to be the case, and it is now clear that the explanation of how secularism actually works was too rough-and-ready.

In fact, what the secularization of life does is to demand that all belief in a God or the sacred be kept *private* and not appear in the public square. That was all. It does not demand that all belief be abandoned, and this is the nuance that has come into our understanding of how secularism is to be defined.

In the United States this was then hitched up to the thought that the framers of the Constitution, in separating church and state, had intended to exclude all religious belief from public life, rather than thinking of this notion the other way around, as limiting the state's power to meddle in the life of the church.

This is where the matter stands today. People can believe whatever they want, ground it in God or the sacred, and can practice those beliefs in any way they choose — as long as they do it privately. How we order our life collectively is to be decided nonreligiously. It is this separation of private life from public that coalesces with the way our modernized world forces us to see things. And this is what has given this Enlightenment ideology such staying power in the West.

Modernization, if I may say this again, has meant that our world has been reorganized. We have moved from a world where family and community defined work to one in which communities have disappeared for the most part, families are often dispersed, and the workplace is dominated by impersonal bureaucracies, structures, and global forces. This really does change the way we experience life, how we see the world, and how we think about work. The main consequence is that our lives are now sharply compartmentalized. We have two kinds of life, one private and one public.

Private life is made up of our circle of friends and family, our social associations, and perhaps our neighborhood. This is the realm of personal relations, and it has a built-in accountability in terms of behavior.

In our public world we are mostly cogs in a machine, parts of a working order where accountability is in functional terms, rather than those of personal ethics. God can be part of the picture in private, but he is not to be a player in the public square, in the corporation, or in how the workplace functions in general.

Public life is the life of the commercialized world. It is what has come about through the capitalism we have developed, the systems of law, transportation, and information we have created to make all of this work. The public environment goes hand in hand with this reorganized world, one that is large, anonymous, globally conscious, suffused with constant change, a world of competition, striving, danger, and abundance. Here our relations are those of profit and loss, and here accountability is less personal than it is business-oriented. This world offers no supporting structures, no plausibility for an understanding of God as the center of life from whom meaning and morality are derived. These become alien intruders into the public square where we live much of our lives.

We live in both of these worlds, though rarely at the same time. In fact, we have had to adapt to this circumstance. We have had to become amphibious creatures. We have had to learn to swim in both worlds, to live by the rules that each has, and that often means operating with different worldviews. We learn to adjust our worldview according to the world we inhabit. Study after study has shown that in the modernized world, many people live by different moral standards depending upon whether they are in their private or their public world. In that sense they become different people, adjusting where adjustment seems to be called for and adapting where adaptation seems necessary. They cannot function as if they had a consistent core. This is, of course, how postmoderns have learned to survive in our contemporary world. When this strategy of survival is carried over into our understanding of God, however, something catastrophic happens to Christian faith.

Pressure is applied along a seam that has often proved to be a weakness in the life of the church. It is the seam that divides the transcendence of God from his immanence, his otherness from his relatedness, so that we are inclined to have the one set of truths but not the other. What our experience in this modernized, postmodern world does is to incline us to tilt to the one side and to ignore the other. We put all our eggs, so to speak, in the basket of God's nearness, his relatedness, and we lose everything related to his otherness and transcendence. This yields a God who is familiar, safe, accommodating, but also very small. This is the "god" who is accessed through the self, who showers us with therapeutic benefits, and whom we intuitively hear "speaking" in this or that event of life. But it loses the God of the Bible who, in addition to being near, is also elevated over all of life and who summons us to see him, not just as our psychological aid, but as he is in himself, in his glorious beauty and power, to be in awe before him, worship him as something other than ourselves, and to hear in his Word something other than what we naturally sense within ourselves. Let me now explore this distinction a little further.

The Inside God

Rather than speaking of God's transcendence and his immanence, or his nearness and his otherness, I am going to invent some new language. It is that of the inside and the outside God. This, I believe, will get to the heart of our central issue today.

The argument is that our experience in the modern world inclines us to think of God solely as the inside God and to lose sight of him as the outside God. This certainly fits in with how our society and our experience of a modernized world incline us to think. For those reasons it seems very "natural" to us to think of God only as the inside God.

But Scripture does not offer the truths about God on the "inside" and the "outside" as options. We lose something essential to who God is, essential to what Christian faith is, and essential to our understanding of ourselves if we lose either side of this equation. And when we do, the side we retain always becomes perverted and dangerous because of the side we have lost.

What Does Nearness Mean?

When Paul spoke on Mars Hill and told his hearers that God is "not far from each one of us" (Acts 17:27), confirming this fact through the words of a Greek poet that "in him we live and move and have our being" (17:28), he could easily have been misunderstood. Pagans in his audience would have been very inclined to hear in these words the pantheism that is at the heart of all paganism, their own included. This paganism thought that Creator and creation were infused in each other, that the access to God was through the creation. More than that, they believed, for example, that the gods were affected by human activity because they were bound to the created order. This was the theory behind cult prostitution. Sex in the pagan temples meant fertility in the fields.

It is important, though, that we not miss what Paul had been doing up to this point in his address. By this time he had already deconstructed the pagan worldview and put in its place the biblical way of looking at life. Creation does indeed come from the hand of God. It is sustained by him in providence. However, it is separate from him and is not self-sufficient, or self-sustaining, and it cannot act on him. It is finite whereas God is infinite. That is why it has to *be* sustained and God is sovereign over all of it.

This is the viewpoint consistently maintained in Scripture, and not least in its confrontation with the paganism of its day. If creation came about because of a sovereign act of God's creative will bringing something out of nothing (Gen. 1:1), then the meaning of creation can be found only in relation to its creator who is its center. Meaning is no more self-contained within the creation than the creation is self-sustaining. It is sustained by the God who first created it, and its meaning is found only in relation to him. It is because of this divine preservation that the heavens are as secure as God's faithfulness (Ps. 89:2). He is the one who established "the moon and the stars" (Ps. 8:3; cf. 33:8-9). And everywhere "he looks out on all the inhabitants of the earth . . . and observes all their deeds" (33:14-15).

No pious Israelite in the Old Testament, or believer in the New, ever doubted that God is everywhere present in the world and is able to bring about his will as he sees fit. Indeed, Psalm 139 joyfully celebrates

God's omnipresence and his omnipotence as if they were inseparable from each other. God is everywhere and he is all-powerful. It is these truths that guarantee human existence. It is sustained because God sustains it and not simply because we have learned the arts of survival. God declared as much to Noah when he announced his gracious intention that while "the earth remains, seedtime and harvest, cold and heat, summer and winter, day and night, shall not cease" (Gen. 8:22). And Paul, much later, would see in the preservation and consistency of nature a "witness" to this divine goodness. God, Paul said to his listeners, "did good by giving you rains from heaven and fruitful seasons, satisfying your hearts with food and gladness" (Acts 14:17).

God is not only near to us and related to us through creation and his preservation of it, but he also rules over all of life, guides it to the end he has in mind for it, and holds all people accountable for their lives. The fact that he has in mind nations other than Israel came into view only later in the Old Testament, but it is unmistakably there. We need look no further than Isaiah's vision, which makes the point, against its pagan backdrop in which gods and goddesses all had local and small-sphere rule, that the creator God's power is universal. This is seen in creation (Isa. 40:15-20) itself, in his sovereign rule over the nations (40:22-26), and in individual life (40:21-26). The nations may puff and bluff, swagger and threaten, oppress and destroy, but they "are as nothing before him, they are accounted by him as less than nothing and emptiness" (40:17).

It is not necessary to belabor this point. The sustaining and ruling presence of God in all of life has a clear and secure place in the biblical outlook, and it has subsequently had a sustained place in Christian consciousness. Of much larger interest here, given the modern habits of thought that we bring to Scripture, is what we do with all of this. In our postmodern world we are seizing on his creational relatedness and turning it into a spirituality of our own making. And what we are doing in the church is not much better for evangelical faith and is often little different from this cultural spirituality.

Misunderstanding God's Nearness

What we are doing, in the face of our own disintegrating center in ourselves, is reaching out to create a center that will give us more internal
stability. That, I think, is the most plausible explanation of the rather
startling emergence of a deeply privatized spirituality evident throughout the West, to which I will return in a later chapter.

This spirituality is our way of trying to find a center in life, trying
to connect with Something larger than ourselves that will be more sub-
stantial than our experience, which in itself is often very shallow and
always ephemeral. But why is this spiritual search taking the form it is
today? Why do we not seek objects of worship in nature, or in something other than ourselves, as human beings have so often done in the
past? The answer, quite simply, is that we are postmoderns. Our experience in the modern world leads us to think that all reality has been relocated internally, that our access to everything of importance is
through the self, and that like any other consumer product, our spirituality should be tailored to our needs, time, and availability.

The important assumption here is that the "revelation" in this
spirituality and its "salvation" are alike unmediated. They come by creation alone, through our experience alone, accessed by the self alone.
They require no supernatural intervention in our lives to effect them.
They require no Bible, no incarnation of the second person of the Godhead, no substitutionary death, no resurrection, no gospel to be believed, no faith, no necessary regeneration, no superintending work of
the Holy Spirit. Indeed, this is all part of the religion that many people
who are spiritual reject as a condition of their spirituality.

This spirituality has all the marks of the postmodern disposition
upon it. It is deeply subjective, nonmoral in its understanding, highly
individualistic, completely relativistic, and insistently therapeutic. It
has seized on some truths about the nearness of God, but it has done
so on its own terms and in its own way. These truths then become perverted and misused and, in the absence of the balancing truths about
God's otherness, quite damaging.

The Bible, then, speaks about God's nearness, his immanence. Indeed, this is an important truth that we must hold. But we also need to
be on guard against its corruption. What is corrupting it is our modern

disposition to contract all of reality into the self, to think that God is found in the self, and that the only important things we know about God are known through the self. This gives us a sense of the nearness of God, but it is a corrupted sense. God is not what we find of him through our self because our self is corrupted.

Along with the nearness of God, we need to find those truths that speak of his otherness. We need the biblical knowledge of the outside God to complete our knowledge of who God is, and we will find that this knowledge often serves as a corrective to the corruptions to which our sense of the inside God is often prone.

The Outside God

God Above

What does it mean to think of God as the outside God? I begin with the Bible's own language. In many passages it speaks of God as being exalted, as being "high" and "above" all of life. They celebrate the fact that his being, character, and will are not subject to the flow, the limitations, the actions, or the relativities of life. God is not impacted by postmodern life. He does not have to change his mind as its complexities unfold. We are overwhelmed by life with all its options, pains, and ambiguities, but he is not.

Indeed, such is God's power that he can bring about his will even amidst life's complexities and evil. This sovereign rule may appear dark and mysterious to us. God is not under any obligation to explain all of this to us. What we need to know he has given us normatively through Scripture.

Although we do not know everything about God, and his rule over life sometimes confounds us, we ignore the teaching about his otherness at our peril. We note those texts that speak of God being over this world and above it.

He dwells "on high," says the psalmist (Ps. 113:5; cf. 99:2-3), and so his "greatness is unsearchable" and he is "greatly to be praised" (145:3). In Isaiah's vision God was "high and lifted up" (Isa. 6:1). It was this confidence in God's ability to stand outside all of life and to act in it be-

cause of the greatness of his being that Stephen expressed in the clos-
ing moments of his life. God, he said, is the one who is "Most High"
(Acts 7:48).

God as Holy

However, these rather general statements of God's greatness are also explained more specifically. God is great in his being, in the fact that he is
everywhere, is all-powerful, and knows everything, but he is also great
in his *character*. This gives us an important interpretation of the more
general statements that simply state his elevation, that he is above all
and over all. Part of the reason for his elevation is his holy love. Isaiah
saw that in his vision and immediately declared, in the light of who God
is, "Woe is me! For I am lost; for I am a man of unclean lips, and I dwell in
the midst of a people of unclean lips; for my eyes have seen the King, the
LORD of hosts!" (Isa. 6:5). This is just one of many texts that speak of the
painful and terrifying reality of God's utter purity.

The prophet became horribly aware of the peril in which God's
character places people. No one can stand in his light. Everyone is destroyed by it because it is the kind of light that asserts itself against all
that is wrong, perverted, selfish, unbelieving, ungrateful, and disobedi-
ent. And yet, a little later he says, "I will wait for the LORD, who is hiding
his face from the house of Jacob" (Isa. 8:17). Later still he says, "Truly,
you are a God who hides himself" (45:15). Why would the God who had
so awed Isaiah disappear? Why did God seem to leave the prophet out
on the end of a limb?

Sometimes God's "hiding" — the fact that he is "above" and inac-
cessible to us — is an expression of his judgment, and judgment is
nothing but his holiness in action. He judges his people by withdrawing
the blessing of his presence from them. More than this was at stake in
Christ's cry of dereliction on the cross: "My God, my God, why have you
forsaken me?" (Mark 15:34). Yet it is unmistakable that his abandon-
ment in this moment because of our sin that he had taken upon himself was an expression of the judgment of God. At other times, though,
his judgment is expressed in his actions against the proud and oppres-
sors. As Mary sang in the Magnificat, "he has scattered the proud in the

thoughts of their hearts; he has brought down the mighty from their thrones" (Luke 1:51-52). And always it is a reminder to us that God cannot be had on our terms. He cannot be manipulated. He cannot be bought. He is never subject to our will. If we know him, it is only on his terms. And the result often is that much of what he does by way of his providential rule is hidden from us. Even God's way of working with and through Israel, Paul says, is "unsearchable," and his ways "inscrutable" (Rom. 11:33).

His apparent absence from our lives, then, may not be a sign of his judgment. It may simply be an indication that his ways are beyond us, that he has not felt obliged to explain himself to us in every detail. This is often baffling, especially to those in moments of deep suffering. "Why, O LORD, do you stand far away?" asked the pained psalmist. "Why do you hide yourself in times of trouble?" (Ps. 10:1). And the book of Job is the chronicle of one man's deep and excruciating wrestling with the fact that God seemed both silent and absent.

He is, however, neither silent nor absent. His silence has been broken by his revelation in Scripture, which culminated in the birth, death, and resurrection of Christ. He is not silent and has indeed spoken. What he has given in the pages of Scripture, under the inspiration of the Holy Spirit, is everything that the church needs for its instruction, nurture, and life in this fallen world. Nor can it ever be said that he is absent to those in Christ to whom he is bound, by oath and by covenant, for all eternity. This is the truth. It is our experience that says otherwise, partly because we struggle with sin in our own selves, and partly because God has not explained everything to us that we might like to know about his dealings with the church and with the fallen world. "The secret things belong to the LORD our God," we are reminded, "but the things that are revealed belong to us and to our children forever, that we may do all the words of this law" (Deut. 29:29).

And So . . . ?

Here I want to explore a few of the consequences that follow from the fact that God is outside us, that he is objective to us, that he summons us to a knowledge of himself that is not something we have or find in ourselves, and that he summons us to be like him in his holiness. This summons, this calling to stand before God in his awesome moral purity, is not something we would ever hear within our fallen selves, nor from our fallen world or our postmodern experience. It is a call that, as it were, is wholly alien to us. It is other than what we are in ourselves. It comes from the outside.

God's holiness is part of the explanation of the biblical language of God being "above" and being "high." It is why God is Other, why he is the outside God. This translates itself, though, into very practical realities. That God is the outside God means at least five important things.

There Is a Law

It means, first, that there is a moral law. Indeed, without the holiness of God, his character as morally pure, there would be no moral law in the world. Our conscience reflects the moral nature of things (Rom. 2:14-15), however imperfectly, and in God's self-revelation in Scripture we have our full, objectively given instructions on how to live. The "law," Paul says, "is holy, and the commandment is holy and righteous and good" (Rom. 7:12). These are the moral norms for life that reflect the holy character of God. What would we lose if we had neither this law nor human conscience?

We would lose all knowledge of the difference between good and evil, and in fact, we would do evil in complete innocence. We could not appeal to conscience, as Martin Luther King did when he asked Americans to treat people fairly without respect to the color of their skin. Indeed, there would be no morality at all. Is this not a picture of what hell will be like?

Now let us think of the reverse side of this coin. God has not abdicated his rule. His character of holiness has not been eliminated from the world. He still sustains the difference between right and wrong. And knowing that difference, being helped to work it out in practice, is what gives our first moments of recovery a sense of what it is to live in God's world on his terms. It steers us away from what is dark and destructive and into what is right and healthful. Satisfaction, protection, and joy result from following God's law. All of this is a consequence of God being the "outside" God.

There Is Sin

The second consequence is that without the holiness of God, sin loses all its meaning. Sin, as I have argued, is not simply the breaking of some church rule but is every act that is an affront to the character and will of God. It is true that only 17 percent of Americans define sin in relation to God, but their mistake in no way diminishes the nature of what their sin is.

What has been lost is not the sin itself but its *culpability.* Sin in all its forms is still present in life. It is still trailed by all the pain and confusion that always attend it, but it is not being understood in relation to *God.* It thus loses its depth, character, and culpability because we have lost our internal compass. That compass lines up our sinning, not merely horizontally, but also vertically. Sin brings not only shame but also guilt when we understand it in relation to God's holiness. "Against you, you only, have I sinned and done what is evil in your sight" (Ps. 51:4), cried David after the calamity he brought upon himself by his sexual affair. Only then do we understand its nature. When we lose the holiness of God we have sin's pains and calamities, but we do not understand it any more.

But if we begin to see the nature of sin, we are on the road back into reality. We are on our way back into the presence of God through Christ. It is not that the knowledge of sin alone suffices, but rather that it pushes us to seek our deliverance from it. Knowing about sin is therefore vital knowledge. There are none quite so lost as those who know little or nothing of their sin. Knowing about our sin, therefore, is something for which we should be deeply grateful. This is why it is so important for us to be able to understand that God is not simply the inside God but he is the outside God as well.

There Is a Cross

Third, without the holiness of God the cross would be emptied of all meaning. Christ was not a social reformer, or a do-gooder for whom things got out of hand. These are the old liberal ideas, but they are not biblical thoughts. The cross was not an accident. It was planned in eternity, and it was for this, Jesus said, that he had come. He had come to die. And in his moment of death the holiness of God and our sin collided. This is what called forth his cry of dereliction. It is an impertinence, at the very least, to say, as Steve Chalke and Alan Mann do in *The Lost Message of Jesus,* that this view makes God guilty of "cosmic child abuse," that the cross needs to be purified of its violent images. This may appeal to a postmodern constituency, and to its Arminian counterpart, but it is remote from the way the Bible thinks about Christ's death and distant from the way the church, down through the ages, has thought about it. The truth is that Christ's death is simply incomprehensible if we do not start with the demands of God's holiness, which cannot tolerate sin's violations.

Without the holiness of God, then, there is no cross. Without the cross there is no gospel. Without the gospel there is no Christianity. Without Christianity there is no church. And without echoes of the holiness of God in those who are Christ's, there is no recognizable church. What is it about this chain of connections that the evangelical church today is not understanding that is leading it to soft-pedal, overlook, or ignore the holiness of God?

Let me now say this positively. What we see at the cross is the white-hot revelation of the character of God, of his love providing the price that his holiness requires. The cross was his means of redeeming lost sinners and reconciling them to himself, but it was also a profound disclosure of his mercy. It is, in Paul's words, an "inexpressible gift" that leads us to wonder and worship, to praise and adore the God who has given himself to us in this way. This is what has led people to give themselves away, too, to give of themselves in service to others, to go to the mission field. It is what has impelled Christian believers to give of their substance, and to reach out in acts of mercy to those who need it, and in acts of courage against the injustices in society.

There Is Conquest

Fourth, without his holiness God is reduced to being kind, amiable, approachable, and harmless, but for all his likability he is incapable of dealing with evil in the world. The perspective of the Bible, by contrast, is that God's patience and forbearance will one day run out. The time will come when he acts in judgment because of his holiness. And when he does, he will place truth forever on the throne and evil forever on the scaffold. All that has broken and defiled life will be finally, and irrevocably, overthrown.

This doctrine of God's judgment should not be an embarrassment to the church. It is not simply a negative doctrine. It is profoundly positive.

It is this doctrine that carries in it the church's hope. For in this world evil often triumphs, often goes unpunished, and what is good and righteous is often dismissed or even penalized. However, this applies only to this interim period. In the end evil is judged, the world is cleansed, and the church is finally redeemed. This is why Christians have hope. All the injustices, the upside-down nature of things morally will be set right. God's holiness will descend upon the rebel creation. And then, as John saw, the "night will be no more." And God's people "will need no light of lamp or sun, for the Lord God will be their light, and they will reign forever and ever" (Rev. 22:5). This vision of the end of time now throws back its clarifying light into the muddled present.

Sin, grace, love, and faith, P. T. Forsyth said, have nothing but a superficial meaning until we see them in relation to the Holy, arising from it, and setting it forth. God's love is his holiness reaching out to sinners; grace is but the price that his love pays to his holiness; the cross is but its victory over sin and death; and faith is but the way in which we bring our worship to him who is holy.

There Is Obligation

Such is the holiness of God. What would the church be like if it saw this more clearly? What would it be like if its preachers and teachers took the Word of God more seriously so that God's holiness could be understood more fully? What would it be like if individual Christians took more seriously their study of Scripture's truth for their homes and places of work?

We may never know, for holiness is slipping from the grasp of American born-againers today! The evangelical movement is simply at sea when it comes to matters of holiness. In fact, according to a Barna study in 2006, there is very little difference between the born-again and the non-born-again in understanding what holiness is. Of the wider American public, only 35 percent believes that God expects people to be holy, and within this category young people are less well represented than those who are older. As we think about the future, this is indeed a straw blowing in the wind.

But even among the born-again, fewer than half have any idea what holiness means. This ignorance, from among those who should know what Christianity is all about, no doubt has many causes. It certainly is related to what churches are — or, more accurately, are not — teaching. It is certainly an outcome of the cut-rate Christianity now being marketed by the seeker-sensitives. It is an inevitable outcome of the emergents' disposition not to think in terms of absolutes and not to be "judgmental" about the lifestyles and behavior of people. And by whatever route we have reached this point, it is also related to the fact that when it comes to spirituality, knowledge of the Bible ranks at the bottom of the list. So goes our knowledge of God as holy. So goes our understanding of holiness.

The truth is, the importance of holiness to Christian life is not something we come to understand naturally. It is not something we naturally desire. It is something we discover through God's *revelation*. But if that revelation is shelved and closed, if those who go to church rarely hear any sustained discussion of its truth, what should we expect other than this dismal misunderstanding?

When asked to describe what holiness is, only 7 percent of Americans rooted this in the character of God. Although 72 percent said they had made a commitment to Christ, and 71 percent said their faith was "very important" to them, and 60 percent said they were "deeply spiritual," only 16 percent said their faith was the highest priority in their lives. Barna's conclusion was that most Americans like the security of being able to think of themselves as "Christian," but most also resist the

biblical responsibilities that go along with that claim. For the great majority, he says, being identified as a Christian is more about image than
about substance. It is a cultural thing. It is all about creating a pleasing
self-image.

We probably did not need Barna to roll out this revelation. It is
there to be seen everywhere in America today. But where this state of
affairs is most scandalous is in the churches that imagine themselves
on the cutting edge of advancing Christian faith. What many of them
are producing are so-called followers of Christ who are in it for their
own spiritual comfort but who are at sea when it comes to understanding the significance of God's holiness for their Christian lives. And the
reason for that, quite simply, is that many churches, obsessed with
their own success, have made Christianity light and easy so that they
can market it successfully. What are the consequences, then, of losing
sight of the holiness of God, this aspect of the outside God? And, just as
important, what are the consequences of seeing the holiness of God?

Our situation today is not that different from what pertained in
much of Israel's history. The Old Testament people of God were religious, but often their religion made little difference. This, apparently, is
exactly what we have in the born-again sector in America today. The
ancient Israelites' religion was not an impediment to idol worship or to
a whole assortment of pagan practices. They had the written law and
the temple worship. They had the prophets. They had all they needed
to please God, but so often they would not listen. They would not
reckon with his holy will. They became careless, living as if he were not
there, living as if their ways were nothing more than a lifestyle choice,
always hearing but never understanding, seeing but remaining blind —
hearts hard, ears deaf, eyes blind. And the problem? The problem was
that again and again, with monotonous repetition, they lost sight of the
holiness of God. And they paid the painful consequences for this, again
and again.

Is this really so different from what we have now in the West? We
have enough Bibles for every household in America a couple of times
over. We have churches galore; religious organizations; educational institutions; religious presses that never stop pouring forth books,
Sunday school materials, and religious curricula; and unparalleled financial resources. What don't we have? All too often we don't have

what the Old Testament people didn't have. A due and weighty sense of the greatness and holiness of God, a sense that will reach into our lives, wrench them around, lift our vision, fill our hearts, make us courageous for what is right, and over time leave behind its beautiful residue of Christlike character.

Is this a matter so impractical that we can claim that it has nothing to do with our lives? Is this really so abstract that we can dismiss it as not being "practical" and therefore as irrelevant to what is important to us on a day-to-day basis? We may claim that, and indeed, many in the evangelical church are doing so.

Let us not mince words. If we could see more clearly God in the full blaze of his burning purity, we would not be on easy terms with all the sins that now infect our souls and breed easy compromises with the spirit of the postmodern age. This is what leads to the casual ways in which we live our lives with their blatantly wrong priorities. If we could see this more clearly, the church would be filled with much more repentance and, in consequence, much more joy, and much more authenticity.

So what do we need to do? Quite simply, we need to find again the outside God. We have been busy fashioning evangelical faith mostly in terms of the inside God. Why have we done this? Because it has been in our interests to do so. God has been squeezed into the nooks and crannies of life that are private and where we feel the strains of life, where we feel the need for his therapy. This is where consumers are in the hunt for Something. Pastors know that. Everyone knows that. And so, hungering for success and acceptance, the church has adapted itself to its context. When this happens, the church is reduced to being just another organization trying to perpetuate itself for its own reasons. It loses its seriousness. It loses its God-given purpose. It loses its way.

The reverse side of this is that as long as we are on this side of heaven, we can always find again what we have lost. We can always rejoin a path off which we have wandered. We can always find our way back into the blessing of God because God is more willing to bless us through Christ than we are to be blessed. We can always find again the outside God because this is how he has revealed himself in Scripture. It is this about himself he wants us to know, for without it we will be adrift on a sea of meaninglessness.

CHAPTER V

Self

—m—

Selves as possessors of real and identifiable characteristics —
such as rationality, emotion, inspiration, and will — are
dismantled.

Kenneth Gergen

So we do not lose heart. Though our outer self is wasting
away, our inner self is being renewed day by day.

2 Corinthians 4:16

Sometime in the 1960s, Daniel Yankelovich has written, something decisive happened in American culture. Along with the social upheavals, the antiwar sentiment, and the student revolts, a
new way of looking at life emerged. At the time most people did not understand this. They confused it with all the social turbulence that was
going on, but it was in fact something different. It lay beneath all the
surface unrest. And it was by no means limited to those protesting the
war. It was reshaping the worlds of very ordinary people who, even if
they opposed the Vietnam War, would never have placed daisies in the
gun barrels of national guardsmen as some of the protesters did.

In a nutshell, what happened was that our individualism, which had always been a potent factor in American life, turned inward in this decade. It withdrew from the outside world. And during the 1960s a new worldview emerged. To a great majority of Americans, it now became clear that the self had become the source of all values. The pursuit of the self was what life was all about. That was one of the themes of the last chapter, but now we need to follow this out in some new directions.

In Pursuit of the Self

That a new cultural direction was in the making was becoming evident in many ways. By the 1980s, for example, a large majority had begun to think that what was worthwhile in life had nothing to do with its normal routines such as getting up each day and going to work. Nor with the traditional responsibilities of marriage and the raising of children. Rather, life is about its more exotic moments. It is not about what happens on Monday through Friday, but what happens on the weekends. Its real meaning, and its real rewards, are found when the self, unencumbered by routine and responsibility, can be found, nurtured, and satisfied. Two-thirds of Americans began to think a lot about their selves. A great majority, 80 percent, forsook the older traditional ways of looking at life, certainly the older ethical norms, and began to search for new rules by which to live. About half wanted new experiences. They also wanted new freedoms, even trivial ones, like being able to dress the way they wished, unrestrained by convention. They also were looking for more excitement and new sensations.

Thus it was that the individualism in which you should think for yourself, decide for yourself, provide for yourself, and work to serve others in personal or civic ways has ended up as something rather different. This older individualism has turned inward. Now it is about finding the self for yourself, discovering your inner potential for your own benefit, esteeming your self, and developing new ethical rules that serve the discovery of . . . the self.

It is not unreasonable to think that this turn in our culture would have found resistance among the religious. And it did at the more liberal end of Protestantism, ironically enough, but evangelicals fell head-long into this new way of seeing life.

It could be heard, in the 1980s and 1990s, every time Robert Schuller's cherubic countenance appeared on television. He was moving in a new direction, though he also claimed to be traditionally Protestant. He announced that this new self-focused preoccupation was nothing less than a new Reformation. He went on to construct the whole of Christian faith around the self and its discovery.

In 1983 James Hunter discovered that of evangelical books published in that year, almost nine out of ten dealt with matters of the self. In 1989 Lyman Coleman spoke of the assumptions beneath the widely used *Serendipity Bible for Groups,* which he edited. The principal one was that all people were made in the image of God. There was nothing novel about that. However, this old truth was being understood in new ways. He understood it to mean that all people have unlimited potential. Sadly, he went on to say, only a handful, 5 percent to 10 percent, are ever able to tap into all of this potential. What is there for the great majority lies buried beneath mountains piled high with painful memories from childhood, fears, broken dreams, and shame. It is, of course, Bible study that unlocks all of this hidden potential.

And so it came into our pulpits. In sermon after sermon over the last two or three decades, preachers of an evangelical kind have latched onto this cultural way of thinking. Self-talk, it seemed, would be a natural springboard into salvation talk. Even if it never actually got to salvation, there was enormous benefit to be had along the way. So, why not venture along this path? Imagining themselves to be speaking the language of their congregations, and being quite au courant, these preachers actually ended up buying into a worldview that is deeply hostile to Christian faith. They seemed not to notice that feeling good about yourself is not the same thing as actually being good. In fact, people often feel good about themselves in moments when they should not. Some feel good about themselves in moments of great self-indulgence, of revenge, and certainly in moments of inebriation. Is this not the warning that we should have heeded? Should we not have noticed this?

When evangelical churches entered this new universe of the self, they left the moral world behind. The evangelical church, which takes seriously its responsibility to steward the gospel, should have been the first to see this because the gospel makes sense only in a moral world. Sin, after all, is not simply feeling bad about ourselves. It is violating what is right in God's law and character. Those who inhabit this self-world look only for therapy, not for forgiveness and regeneration. Recovery, in fact, is their way of speaking about regeneration. It is all about human technique and not about miraculous intervention. All of this was apparently lost on evangelicals who stumbled after one another in their earnest pursuit to recast their faith in this new language from the culture.

Some in the church are nominal and some are true believers. So it is in the culture with respect to the self. The true "believers" are to be found in those who have read the older theorists like Abraham Maslow and Carl Rogers or their disciples. These theorists left us with a way of thinking that is still on the ascendancy in our culture, even though, in professional circles, they themselves have faded into oblivion.

Today, "nominal believers" in this way of thinking fill our streets, our schools, and our churches. We all want to think like this now. The language of the self, of self-actualization, of self-fulfillment, of self-esteem, and all the other kinds of self-action has taken up residence in our minds. It is an essential part of the furniture of the mind. It gets reflected in our most earnest conversations like a little glistening pearl drop.

The Nation Signs On

When we all latched onto this self-talk, sometime in the 1980s, it was as if we had suddenly found the answer to the gigantic puzzle of life. And by the time Christina Hoff Sommers and Sally Satel wrote their *One Nation under Therapy* in 2005, the conquest had been completed. The true believers at the center were leading virtually the whole culture in thinking of all of life in terms of the self.

Sommers and Satel recognize, of course, that there are people who are mentally ill, that there are situations that really do require counseling, and that there are experiences in life that are harsh and hard to bear, and it is not wrong to seek help when we find ourselves beset in these ways.

However, what we have here is the entire nation putting itself on the psychiatrist's couch. And not just when devastation strikes but also when we are simply unhappy with ourselves, bored, empty, or frustrated. Or when we are not adequately appreciated.

As it turns out, we are a nation, frankly, in which we are all underappreciated. Even worse, we have all been victimized by someone. And worse yet, we are all about to collapse unless we get in touch with our feelings by getting entirely naked. Or, as those in the know say, by becoming "vulnerable." Beneath the surface of normality, you see, is a car wreck about to happen. Everywhere. In everyone. That is what we are all assuming. And that is how we are now looking at every aspect of life.

Psychologist William Pollack, for example, the author of *Real Boys: Rescuing Our Sons from the Myths of Boyhood,* argued that adolescent boys who appear happy enough, even while coping with bouts of hormones, are actually all incipient replicas of the murderers who shot their classmates at Columbine High School.

Actually, most parents have had those same thoughts about their own children at one time or another, but they are probably not true!

The Girl Scouts in 2001 introduced a new badge that could be earned by lighting candles whose smell was reminiscent of nature. They also have to keep a diary of their feelings. This reduces the stress that is destroying these psychologically endangered eight- to eleven-year-olds.

Quite a few public schools have banned competitive games because they dent the self-esteem of those who do not win. Most schools have so elevated self-esteem over performance, feeling good over doing well, that we have produced a nation of children whose estimate of themselves is sky-high but whose academic performance lags ever further behind that in many other nations. Indeed, it lags behind the performance of many who are our economic competitors. In one College Board survey of almost a million high school children in America, only 2 percent rated themselves below average in leadership ability. When it came to getting along with others, 0 percent rated themselves below average, 60 percent rated themselves in the top 10 percent, and 25 percent in the top 1 percent! Whatever happened to all the crippling inferiority complexes that once ruined our lives? They are gone! Years of careful nurture have brought triumph, and now our children are really feeling good about themselves!

And it is not only the children. Apparently we all think rather well of ourselves. In 2007, for example, 82 percent of American drivers rated themselves among the top 30 percent in terms of safety. The survey does not reveal what the car insurance companies thought, but we can assume, without fear of contradiction, that they thought otherwise! And if any Boston drivers rated themselves with the safest 30 percent, I can vouch personally for how disconnected from reality humans can be and how shameless our capacities for self-deception have become!

Susan Faludi, the feminist and author of *Stiffed: The Betrayal of the American Male,* has written about the awful predicament in which men find themselves. The internal anguish that all men experience is rooted in the fact that it is impossible for them any longer to be manly. They have been raised to be stoical, but, in today's world, what are they doing? They have been reduced to hugging and weeping. Their sense of self, as a result, is conflicted, confused, and evaporating.

These are just a few illustrations of an important fact. It is that America has become a very sensitive nation. There is always someone here who can be offended, if not by what is said, then by what is not said. Or by what could potentially be intended in what was said. Or by what could be read into what was not said. This has created a flock of national censors, most of whom are functioning in a purely unofficial role. Indeed, they are mostly self-appointed. And some have become so vigilant that one suspects they might have attained positions of some prominence in the Middle Ages! Too bad for them that they were born in the wrong century.

From all of this has arisen a busy and very profitable industry of healers, consultants, grief counselors, writers, and various other purveyors of comfort to the fragile and afflicted. In America, we have one-third of the world's psychiatrists, two psychotherapists for every dentist, and more counselors than librarians.

But what is even more important is that this is not simply the preoccupation of professionals. The truth is that, as the twenty-first century begins, we have all become adept at being our own healers and our own counselors, dispensing wisdom and comfort to ourselves. This is the important point. Not many can afford an ongoing relationship with a psychotherapist or psychologist. For those in serious need, a couple of weeks or, perhaps, months are about all that is usually possible. But if the circle of "competence" is widened, if we can become our own counselors, then the problem has been solved.

What happened, therefore, was that people learned to think in the language of the therapists. Language that had once belonged in a tiny circle of theorists of the self movement migrated into books, newspapers, schools, and then into common speech. Who has not thought about self-esteem? Who has not imagined that being authentic meant disclosing feelings, that reality was actually accessed through our feelings? That feeling was far more real and important than thinking?

So it was that we all became our own therapists. Our small group has become our own private workshop, our private narrative is our own textbook, and our internal struggles are our microcosm of the entire world's struggles. For what is reality except what *I* have experienced? What matters except what matters to me? What could be as important as what is feeling important to me right now? I am the mirror in which reality is reflected. All of it. At least all of it that is important to me.

None of this would be plausible had not the modern world made life very difficult. We do not usually think of it in this way. We think about the benefits the modern world brings us, and these benefits are genuine and numerous. But we have not always connected to these benefits the costs that have to be paid for them. There are, in fact, no free lunches. There is only the appearance of there being free lunches.

I have been writing about these costs for years: our sense of being disconnected, our loneliness, our loss of relational webs, the strains placed on families, the blank anonymity of much of our modern experience, the stresses that so much knowledge places on our frail psyches, the heightened internal tempo of too much change at too great a pace, the future that has become so threatening, and the elevated levels of anxiety everywhere.

In the United States, a Senate subcommittee reported in 1967 that by 1985 the average workweek would be down to twenty-two hours and people would be retiring at the ripe old age of thirty-eight. Mercifully, the prophets' names have now been forgotten. We can say for sure that these prophets should have been told to go and stand in the corner and have dunce caps put on their heads. Our world has turned out to be the exact opposite! The workweek is now much longer. People want to retire earlier but cannot afford to. And all of us, like it or not, find ourselves on a treadmill.

Not only so, but people living in our modernized world find themselves uprooted. We spoke about this in the previous chapter. They are "homeless," in Berger's language. The past is irrelevant, so they cannot look back for meaning as they would have in a traditional society. Nor can they find it in the present. It is shot through with so much impermanence and they have so little connectedness to it that it offers no foothold. Given the rapidity of change and the awesome power of technology, for both good and ill, the future is a strange mixture of bright prospects and dark potential. People look to the future to capitalize on its benefits and, if possible, avoid its dangers. But as it is riddled with the unpredictable, we cannot look to it for meaning. We can look only within, to the self, to find meaning, rules, and fulfillment. This is, to say the least, leaning on the proverbial weak reed, is it not? The fact is that being part of the modernized world is a two-edged sword. With the material benefits we enjoy there are painful psychological costs to be paid. This, as I noted, is the "American paradox."

The argument I will make in this chapter is that today we are at the convergence of three lines of thought. These are cultural, psychological, and theological in nature. What has made the psychological developments that have come into bloom in the self movement so powerful is that they have coincided with some deep cultural shifts that have been long in the making. Indeed, one might almost say that the self movement was the internal counterpart to the external changes that were happening as the world modernized. Our internal life, with its disconnects, loss of roots, moral ambivalence, and psychological confusion, is really just a mirror of the external world we inhabit with all its change, anonymity, ruthless competition, and loss of transcendence. What is outside us shapes what is inside us; what is inside us gives us a framework for understanding the external world that is outside us. In combination these two streams have produced the (post)modern self.

When the (post)modern self becomes religious, it may become liberal, emergent, or loosely evangelical. But when it becomes (post)modern in these ways, it will no longer be historically Protestant. It will not be biblical. It will not be apostolic. It will be Christian in name but not in thought. Sorting out these connections between what is psychological, cultural, and theological is what we now need to do.

Although Yankelovich only noticed these changes beginning in the 1960s, they were actually rooted in developments that had been long in the making. In America they have taken their own distinctive path, but the pattern has in fact been replicated all over the West. It involves four fundamental changes: first, the change from virtues to values; second, the change from character to personality; third, the change from nature to self; finally, the change from guilt to shame. These changes tell part of the story of the emerging autonomous self. These we now need to explore.

Virtues to Values

The shift from virtues to values may not be as apparent as it should be because of our language. For we use these two words interchangeably. We sometimes speak of "moral values" and have in mind what I have in view here by virtues. Let me clarify.

Virtues

Virtues, as I am thinking of them here, are aspects of the Good, or of Virtue. They are the moral norms that are enduringly right for all people, in all places, and in all times. It is true, of course, that there has been debate about what these virtues are.

In the Middle Ages they were classified into two sets. The natural virtues were wisdom, courage, temperance, and justice while the supernatural virtues were faith, hope, and love. That makes seven virtues, which paralleled the seven deadly sins.

The Protestant Reformation rejected this classification because it offered a basis of natural merit in four of the virtues that was simply upgraded by an infusion of grace. In fact, Scripture is more or less silent about virtue (cf. Phil. 4:8; 1 Pet. 2:9; 2 Pet. 1:3), but it clearly speaks of moral excellence and goodness in connection with the character of God. And not only in God's character but also as reflected in the creation (Rom. 1:18-20) and in conscience (Rom. 2:14-15).

However we understand this matter, it is inescapable that ours is a moral universe. It is one in which God still sustains what is right, still abhors what is wrong, and still demands that we be accountable for knowing the difference.

We can therefore say with confidence that there are moral excellencies that are always right because they make up who God is in his character. What Scripture speaks about in its narratives, psalms, and didactic sections is God's holiness, justice, mercy, love, and truthfulness. And each of these has multiple variations in its application to human life. That these are the norms by which we should live is rather clear; how we might actually do so is a different matter.

Across the ages people have tried to emulate these virtues. This has been true in Roman Catholicism, as it was in the liberal Protestantism of the nineteenth century. In their slightly different ways, they made the argument, one which has always appealed to the most morally earnest, that people should aim to be virtuous and that by practice they can become virtuous. Luther attacked this notion that, he said, came from Aristotle. It was the thought that just as a natural talent can be improved by practice, so can our own inherent virtue. This, needless to say, takes too little account of the way sin has intruded into all our virtue, perverting it. It is not practice that we need, but radical, supernatural transformation. That has always been the Protestant understanding of Scripture, and we will have occasion to return to it in due course.

This brings us to the heart of a conundrum: Does "I ought" mean "I can"? Does God still require of us obedience to what is morally normative even though in sin we cannot give that full obedience? Does he modify his demands to fit our abilities?

The answer, of course, is that God cannot modify his demands because he cannot modify his character. His moral demands, therefore, were the same before the fall as they have been after it. What changed was our moral ability to obey what God demanded. Yet, being unable to live as God demands in no way changes how we should live. God does not tailor his moral demands to our ability to fulfill them, otherwise the most degraded and scurrilous miscreants would have the smallest expectations to reach! No, his moral norms are the same for all people, in all places, and in all times. It is these norms that I have in mind as virtues, and when we put them all together they make up Virtue. His grace that we encounter in Christ so takes us into itself that God is able to see us just as if we had never violated a single norm and had always given him his full due.

To speak of Virtue, then, is to speak of the moral structure of the world God has made. Rebellious though we are, we have not broken down this structure, nor dislodged God from maintaining it. It stands there, over against us, whether we recognize it or not. We bump up against it in the course of life and we encounter its reflection in our own moral makeup. And from all sides a message is conveyed to our consciousness: "Beware! This is a moral world that you inhabit!"

Character is about the way this moral world becomes embedded in our nature. This does not mean that those who are honest, truthful, compassionate, and considerate are, for those reasons, providing a basis of their acceptance before God, because they are not. However, in the eyes of God it is surely better to be honest than to be dishonest, to be truthful than to be a liar, to be compassionate than merciless and considerate than thoughtless. And it is certainly better for societies when people behave morally than when immorality and what is unethical triumph. That is why society had placed a premium on good character until relatively recently. Whatever else might be said about it, it is a society's means of self-defense.

Indeed, in the nineteenth century letters of recommendation were typically *character* references and were carried around by the recipients and read with satisfaction. Letters of this kind today, especially if they make unhappy observations on the person's character, might invite a lawsuit. Today, though, we are less interested in a potential employee's character than we are in his or her competence. In a complex, highly competitive, technological, bottom-line-driven world, competence trumps character. Character is nice but competence is profitable. That, at least, is what we think.

The passing of this interest in character in our contemporary world, and its replacement by competence, has taken its toll across the board. Many people who are immensely competent in their areas of expertise turn out not to be people of integrity. Unhappy consequences invariably follow. We need look no further than our colleges and universities to see this. Faculties have among them the most inventive, brilliant, and creative people in the nation. Some of these same people, at the same time, have been known to be among the most cynical, perverse, adversarial, underhanded, deviant, destructive, cranky, and peevish.

This loss of moral character has become so large an issue in our nation that many business schools and medical schools have hurriedly had to reintroduce courses in ethics. However, courses in ethics, even if well taught, are but Band-Aids to those who, in their inner lives, no longer inhabit a moral universe. And that is where the vast number of people in the West are. They have vacated that older moral world. The great majority, two-thirds, say they do not believe in moral absolutes, that moral decisions are a matter of negotiation in each given set of circumstances.

Values

This is the context in which virtues have been converted into values. Values, as we speak of them today, are a relatively new idea. In 1928 the multivolume *Oxford English Dictionary,* which had been under construction since 1882 and had accumulated the meanings of close to half a million words, had no entry for "values." "Values" is a word in later twentieth-century talk in the West.

Indeed, values represent the moral talk of a relativistic world and one that is clearly quite novel in some ways. It is true that in the past, free thinkers, novelists, artists, and other avant-gardists have dispensed with any kind of moral world. But never before have we seen an experiment on so large a scale as we are seeing in the West today. Everyone is now avant-garde, not just the cultural elite. Everyone is experimenting with how it feels to live in a world without moral form, one that is devoid of objective ethical norms.

Once we left behind a moral world, we had no option but to treat values in a value-free way because what is right for one is not necessarily right for another. As the older moral world has faded, then, its virtues have faded with it. In the twilight of its dissolution, we are left with values.

Character to Personality

What we think of today as the self, a kind of internal center into which all our experiences flow and get sorted out, has been thought about as something separate from character only quite recently. Actually, the self came into prominence only in the twentieth century. Before that time people would have been quite baffled by all of this talk about finding the self, cultivating it, esteeming it, realizing it, and all the other things we think we are doing to it.

For centuries we in the West have thought about our consciousness — the self, in contemporary parlance — only in conjunction with nature and, indeed, with character. This center was thought about in terms of virtues to be learned and desires to be denied. These virtues were all sustained by a belief in moral law, be it natural, or revealed in Scripture, or perhaps just generally assumed.

Personality Emerges

As the twentieth century dawned, Warren Susman observed in his work *Culture as History,* the great change was under way. The words that had peppered the advice manuals of an earlier generation, words that came out of a moral world, were disappearing. These were words like "duty," "golden deeds," "morals," "manners," "honor," "citizenship," and "reputation." But as the new century began, a different set of interests came into view. These were signaled by the prominence in the advice manuals of words like "fascinating," "stunning," "attractive," "glowing," "masterful," "creative," "dominant," "forceful." The words most common earlier had been the words of *character;* these new words were those of *personality.* Character is not fascinating, glowing, or masterful. By the same token, personality is not dutiful, honorable, or full of golden deeds. Character is good or bad; personality is attractive, forceful, or magnetic.

Here was a move out of the older moral world, where our internal moral intentions were important, to a different world. This is a psychological world. It is a shift from what is important in itself to how it appears to others. God may judge the heart, but our preoccupation is with the outward appearance that, after all, is what others see. In a society where affluence is important and ethical norms are disappearing, success is paramount and character is not. Our preoccupation, therefore, is how we "come off" before others.

Self-Marketing

The result of this shift is that today people engage in selling themselves. Personalities are marketable commodities but character is not. People who pitch products on television are pitching their personalities, not their character. Image is reality. Impressions are as important as achievements.

And appearance is about performance. If the byword of the older world was self-sacrifice for moral reasons, that of this emerging world is self-realization for success. The point now is to stand out in the crowd, to be unique, to project oneself, to catch people's attention, to assert oneself. Indeed, late in the twentieth century, a whole industry had emerged to help people stage themselves as if the connections between the "person" who is public and out front and the person who is hidden and within were irrelevant.

These strained connections have come to light again and again. For example, we now have an epidemic of résumés being, as we say, "puffed." Perhaps even more amazing has been the research at universities that, again and again, could not be duplicated by other researchers and was then found to have been doctored up in the first place. These have been particularly egregious instances, but in more benign ways many people have worked at making themselves seem more important or more accomplished than they actually were.

Indeed, a whole literature has emerged about how one makes the best impression. Dressing to convey a sense of power, the importance of body language, positioning oneself in the office strategically. The appearance of success is more important than good character.

148

In these and many other ways people sought to create impressions of themselves for reasons of personal gain, false as they might be. In the older moral world that was fast receding, these would have been seen as lies. In this new, therapeutic world they are more likely seen as strategies than as lies. If things go wrong, if things don't "add up," the shame is not in the attempt at creating a false impression but in being caught.

In our commercialized world, we rarely believe sales pitches, so why would we feel outraged when people exaggerate accomplishments, falsify claims, puff and project themselves personally? An overwhelming proportion of Americans, 70 percent, believe they have been lied to consistently by politicians. Britons feel the same way. So, is this not something we are accustomed to and automatically discount?

Perhaps. But the art of lying has been taken to such a high level, is being done so proficiently, and with such extraordinary sophistication, that it has become virtually impossible to separate the truth from the lies in politics, the news, or the marketplace. We have come to expect no other world than one of grays, a world where there are no whites and no blacks, ethically speaking. We have learned to discount every claim and to distrust every assertion. We do this automatically, without even thinking. However, our coping mechanism, in this case, also covers over important character issues that are lost in the cloud of impressions that are not believed.

The tip of this spear, oddly enough, was the "traveling salesman." This figure became a byword for what was slick, clever, and so skilled in persuasion that buyers needed to beware. Dale Carnegie wrote his *How to Win Friends and Influence People* in 1935, and it became the most widely purchased nonfiction book of the twentieth century. When Carnegie died in 1955, he had become the leading figure in the world of personality cultivation. He was on the front end of what has become a massive, diversified, and flourishing self-help literature. All Carnegie did, though, was transform the tricks salesmen used on the road into techniques for selling ourselves. But along the way, more momentous things had happened. The cultivation of the good life had now been replaced by the cultivation of the self, with the result that today we think happiness has nothing to do whatsoever with our moral character.

The Commerce of Images

Television, which has transformed our world in the last half-century, was the perfect tool for this shift, and not only television but movies as well. Television accentuates personality. It is all about the projection of personality. The character of the person behind the image is hidden and irrelevant. As newsman Daniel Schorr once remarked, it's all about sincerity, and if one can fake that, one has it made! Here is the potential for a complete disengagement between the person who projects himself or herself as likable on the screen and who, off camera, may well be arrogant and thoroughly unlikable. Television dissolves the link, at least for its stars, between character and personality.

This has carried over into some of our marketing megachurches and more generally into how churches look at their pastors. Especially in megachurches of the seeker-sensitive kind, the pastor is preeminently a personality on the big screen up front, a performer, who seems close to everyone in the church but in fact is quite remote in most cases. The personality profiles of many of these pastors show them to be loners. The heavy lifting for the day-by-day pastoral care of the church therefore falls to a circle of trusted assistants. How very different this is from the older model, in which the pastor was not so much a performer as a shepherd who knew the flock and whose relations with the people in the church were the very means of fulfilling pastoral calling. To have been solely a performer in the pulpit would have spelled disaster.

This chasm between character and personality also explains why, in our culture, celebrities have replaced heroes and heroines. A hero is a person who has acted on some internal virtue. This has to do with *character.* Soldiers in war display great courage when they rescue wounded friends as bullets whistle all around; firemen enter buildings at their own peril to rescue those who would otherwise be lost; corporate whistle-blowers bring out company wrongdoing at personal cost; sometimes people show great heroism by their fortitude and good cheer in the face of crippling illnesses.

Celebrities, by contrast, are not about character but about *personality.* A celebrity is someone who is known for being known. In the commercial world in which we live, a world of images, fame can be manufactured quite easily. Most celebrities are not known for anything in particular, and many have had few real achievements, at least of a moral kind. But they know how to manipulate the world of images and image making. For what will future generations remember Madonna and Britney Spears? And yet, in our world today, they are far better known than the individual heroes in the armed forces who are putting themselves at risk in Iraq, the firemen who go about their work of rescue every day, and those who, in a multitude of different ways in the marketplace, do what is right, often at cost to themselves. The truth of the matter is that today personality trumps character and celebrities trump heroes.

The Fallout

With this shift have come many consequences, probably few of which were foreseen as these great changes began to unroll. The older vision in which character was paramount produced an understanding of the self that was quite different from what we have now. Then the thought was that personal growth comes about through cultivating the virtues and restraining the vices. Moral limitation through self-control and self-sacrifice was the key to satisfaction and happiness.

By contrast, the vision that grows with the new preoccupation with personality is one of unlimited self-expression, self-gratification, and self-fulfillment. The pursuit of pleasure has taken the place of moral nurture, the expression of emotion that of moral reticence. What is remarkable about this is that people now think happiness has nothing to do with the moral texture of a person's life and can be pursued as an end in itself. Indeed, many think it can simply be bought. That is what living in our consumer paradise has done to us now that we have vacated the older moral world.

This shift from character to personality has also changed our ideas about success. An earlier generation thought about success in terms of hard work. But not hard work by itself. It was work that was also done well, work that reflected moral virtues like diligence, integrity, conscientiousness, and standards of fairness. People who worked well tended to live more circumspectly. They were more likely to restrain self-indulgence, refuse to make their consumption conspicuous, and express civic virtues in their town and neighborhood. Success in these ways was something that all could attain regardless of what kind of work they did.

When it came to money, our grandparents, Christopher Lasch observed in *The Culture of Narcissism,* believed in saving for a rainy day. They looked askance at self-indulgence. They believed in patient accumulation. They thought this to be prudent, but they also considered it a duty to be fulfilled for the sake of their children.

We think differently. Plastic money, inflation, and advertising have combined to assure us that it is smarter to buy now and pay later. We do not believe in deferring gratification. We think pleasure is not simply a desirable by-product of life. We think it is a necessity.

When our focus changed from character to personality, so, too, did our understanding of what success is. Success was not about living the good life but about living well, high on the hog, as Americans say. Once others approved of us because of our character and the quality of our work. In this new world we have entered, these qualities have lost their shine. Now it is far more important to stand out simply for what we have and how we can impress others.

Today we may well prefer to be envied rather than to be admired. Whereas the older kind of success was durable, this is not. This is fleeting. It is dependent not on its own quality but on the perceptions of others. Perceptions, however, are fickle, changing, quickly superseded, quickly forgotten. Success today, therefore, has to be constantly renewed, burnished, updated, recast, reinvigorated, made even more current, made freshly appealing, dressed up afresh, and reasserted. This is an ongoing project, and if it does not go on, our success begins to evaporate.

These changes have brought us into some interesting contradictions. For example, this shift now encourages us all, if we are to be successful, to become "personalities." We need to stand apart, to stand out, to be unique, uniquely expressing who we are. We are to value ourselves and our feelings that are unique to us as people. So we stand apart if we are being genuine. We are to be "individuals," as we say.

At the same time, though, we have to be likable, pleasing, and connected to others. How do we pull this off? How do we both stand apart and yet make connections? How do we express who we are without violating the interests of others who are in our path? How do we pursue our own self-interest without obliterating the self-interest of others?

When the self began to be experienced through personality rather than within the framework of character, moral obligations that were common broke down. There was no longer a moral world outside each individual that restrained and directed that individual. Now, we have become self-directing, each in his or her own way. The obligation of one is quite different from the obligation of another. With no moral order to regulate private behavior, society begins to fragment because it cannot sustain a world of unregulated, competing egos. The higher law is replaced by the demands of the higher self. And when this happens, the self begins to be radically reconfigured into something it has never been before.

Nature to Self

Nature

For centuries in the West we have believed in human nature. We have thought that beneath all the differences on the surface — gender, ethnicity, age, language — was something common to all human beings. In its Christian form we speak of this in terms of the image of God. It is true that there has been debate over exactly what this is and how we should think about it, but this is partly because Scripture does not specifically define it in any one place. However, the possession of this image is the ground on which murder is prohibited (Gen. 9:6; cf. James 3:9), and from this we deduce that this image confers on people their extraordinary value before God as those who are at the peak of his creation.

The prohibition against murder arises from who we are by creation, not who we are from circumstances. We cannot murder those of another race because we do not like them, for they, too, are in the image of God. We cannot murder the elderly because they have become useless to society. The issue is who they are and not their utility. And, by extension, we cannot murder the unborn because they cannot defend themselves and would be an inconvenience to us. The image of God is common to all people.

Likewise, this image, which was tarnished but not totally destroyed by the fall, is being restored in all who are in Christ (Eph. 4:24; Col. 3:10). This is the nature of God's redemptive work in his people, and it goes along regardless of their gender, ethnicity, generation, class, or age. This is something that is common to all of God's people in all ages, places, and cultures.

It has always been believed, then, that there is this substratum to life that is common to all. Even those who have simply spoken of nature, and not thought of it in terms of the image of God, still less of his redemption, nevertheless have seen human beings as being identifiable as human, as belonging to a common species. It is their nature that they have in common and that defines them as being human. Thus it is that we have generalized about human nature. We have said, in reflecting on someone's behavior, that human nature is of course fickle, or crooked, or perverse, or good, depending on what our assessment is.

Nature Dies

No longer. Over the last two centuries, bit by bit, this understanding has come tumbling down. The Darwinian revolution led us to think that the human being is simply an animal like any other animal; nineteenth-century philosophers attacked the notion that there is an internal substance called nature; others, like the existentialists, thought such a notion would be derogatory to our personal choices and existence since all we would be doing was simply working out the "nature" within us; and many in assorted fields of science have come to see the human being as nothing more than a set of complex chemical reactions and electrical discharges. There is no "ghost" in the machine.

Today, many people, as a result, live in an amoral world, one with no moral structure, no norms, and where preferences and power alone decide what happens. Some act this out; some just watch it being acted out in the movies.

Hollywood, as the twenty-first century began, was raking in huge profits by churning out more and more splatter movies, those in which terror reigns. Limbs of captives are sawed off as the viewers watch, ears are sliced off, faces disfigured, acid dripped on bodies, and people — often women — are brutalized in unspeakable ways. In these horror movies, there is no right and wrong. All there is, is power, the power to do whatever a person wants. This is a mirror, however grotesque, being held up to our postmodern world. And the powerless, the empty, those drifting aimlessly in an indifferent society, can find in these moments of viewing, as they identify with the villains, what they do not have in life: unchallenged power over someone.

The dissolution of a moral world has also come about through the accumulation of the changes already mentioned in this chapter. A line of inevitable logic leads us away from the moral world of virtues, away from framing our lives in terms of character, and away from thinking about nature to thinking about self, about personality, and about value-free values. These things are all linked. They are a set of dominoes. When one begins to fall, it topples on the next, and on the next, until the collapse is across a broad front. At the end of this line, all that is left is power, power to be used in any way that anyone wants or enjoys. This development is especially dangerous to the weak, disabled, elderly, unborn, minorities, and any who, for whatever reason, are unable to defend themselves.

Self Emerges

The change, then, has been from nature to self. It is from what we all have in common to what is unique to each individual. The self is our interior world, made up of our own thoughts, private intuitions, desires, yearnings, springs of creativity, particularities, all that makes us distinct from every other person. My self is what in fact is unique about me. I have a body like that of others, the same legs and arms, but my self is unlike what anyone else has.

The self is simply our interior world made up of thoughts, intuitions, feelings, intentions, capacities (and not least of self-healing), and aptitudes. All people have within them what makes up their self configured in a unique combination. Their self is the place where the distinctives of gender, ethnicity, age, generation, culture, personal biography, internal psychological makeup, and all the other things that contribute to make us distinctive come together. Put it all together in one package, and we are all unique. No one else has exactly the same set of distinctives, in the same combination, yielding the same perceptions and insights as do I. Or you.

This is the message our schools have been delivering to our children for the last few decades. As he or she grows up, each child is to be distinctive, unique, each with his or her own values, private meaning, and place, and each is to be respected for this. And each is entitled to express who he or she is.

When we fail to understand this, promote it, allow for it, things go awry. That has been the theory. Since the 1960s, virtually all educators and psychologists appear to have agreed with this. Not only so, but there is now widespread public support of the myth that poor self-esteem explains bad behavior, failing academic work, acting up, anti-social attitudes, violence, divorce, racism, and the entire drug culture. All of this is rooted in a loss of self-esteem. Indeed, so pervasive is this myth, so impervious is it to the facts, that much educational policy has been confidently funded, at both the federal and state level in the United States, to address this matter.

The problem is that study after study over the last four decades has been unable to show any correlation between low self-esteem and all the social maladies that have supposedly followed it. Nevertheless, the myth is now so well established, preserved in place by so great a public desire to keep it there, by so large an industry with an interest in its preservation, that it borders on heresy to question it.

The truth, of course, is that Western societies *want* to think only in terms of the self, and they *want* to use this psychological world as an alternative to the older religious world. These desires to see reality in this way have proved quite invincible.

Rights

It is true that Western societies have shown different levels of tolerance for, and in the practice of, this kind of self-expression. That was the inescapable conclusion to the massive, European-based study that appeared in 2003 called *World Values Survey.* Its analysis encompassed 80 percent of the world's population. It identified the trademark of modernity as an attitude that defies tradition, traditional authority, and insists on free self-expression. The most advanced and pronounced expressions of these attitudes, it found, are in the old Protestant countries of Sweden, Norway, and the Netherlands. But the United States, Britain, and Ireland are not far behind. This kind of self-expression coalesces most often with what is secular and rationalistic. In other words, it partners with the older Enlightenment attitudes that were always resistant to religious restraints because they were always resistant to any authority outside the self. Interestingly enough, the older Catholic countries like France, Portugal, and Mexico are showing more resistance to this new ethic of the self, this new Western individualism. These attitudes, however, are close to absent in Islamic countries like Indonesia, in traditional societies such as are found in much of Africa, and in old Marxist countries like those of the former Soviet Union.

Despite some variations, the bottom line to this massive study is that the self and its expression over against all external restraints of a religious or moral kind is what characterizes Western cultures. It is also, we should note, what makes for such a hostile environment for Christian faith. It is not surprising that Christian faith is fleeing the West. What is a surprise is how readily evangelical churches have taken on board what is essentially an enemy of what they believe.

This pursuit of the self, as traced in the *World Values Survey,* was not expressly set in opposition to older ideas about human nature. That, though, is the reality. The one waxes as the other wanes. Throughout the West today it is unacceptable to speak of "human nature." Indeed, it is often heard as a put-down because it seems to diminish the significance of the individual's own experience. The idea of human nature seems to make war on the idea of uniqueness, of being an "individual." It seems to suggest that we are limited in the ways we can express ourselves because we can never get outside our "nature." Human nature sounds like an iron cage that contains us. We, though, insist on being able to define ourselves and shape ourselves in a way that is always free from all such impediments. That is where we have arrived today throughout the West.

This, too, has produced some interesting dynamics in our society. The Marxists and existentialists may have overdone it a bit when they spoke so disparagingly about "mass society." They had their own reasons for not liking the emerging, world-dominating commercial cultures of the West. However, it is our reality today, and it does profoundly impact our sense of ourselves.

Anonymity, for example, is an inescapable part of living in our highly complex, technologically driven, competitive Western societies. We live overwhelmingly in cities, many of them large, where we are mostly unknown to those we rub shoulders with on the street. We are lost in our governmental bureaucracies where we are only a social security number. We are lost in the corporation whose upper reaches are oblivious to us except as a name to whom a paycheck is sent. We buy from people across the counter who do not know who we are. We call plumbers and electricians to our homes for repairs and they have no idea who we are, nor do we know who they are. We share the highway with strangers. We are called at night by telemarketers who feign familiarity with us by using our first names but in fact are just reading off a list, or maybe having a computer do it for them. We read the newspaper and know personally not a single one of the people mentioned. In these and thousands of other ways, every day, we are reminded that we live anonymous lives. We are known to very few of those with whom we come in daily contact. From that angle this is a cold, inhospitable world that is totally, entirely oblivious to our uniqueness.

We all struggle with the consequences of being selves in a world that is, at best, indifferent to us and sometimes even hostile. This is what has incited us to assert ourselves in terms of our rights.

Over the last three or four decades the number of personal rights has exploded. The rights secured by the law are one thing; the rights people claim for themselves are altogether another. They are nourished in this internal bias we have for self-interest, but in the absence of any external moral law to curtail their demands, these rights have grown exponentially. We have the right to be treated as we expect, the right to health care, the right to affluence, the right to be left alone, the right to do our own thing, the right to behave as we want, the right to say what we want, and so it goes. As we left behind the moral world, as we entered the world of the individual self, rights proliferated and responsibilities disappeared. What we want is seldom matched by any-thing we will forgo. What we want is rarely sifted to judge its rightful-ness. That happens in a moral world, but that is not the world in which our rights and self-interests are asserting themselves today.

Few limits of any kind are imposed on the expression of these rights. As a matter of fact, everyone else appears as a threat to their ex-pression, and this is resented. This includes spouses and children, even friends, and certainly those we meet in the workplace, at the club, on the tennis court, or in the mall. The self has turned itself into its own central moral authority. Its needs have priority over all else, from family to government. Private choice has a privileged position, and anything that limits that choice is a violation of individual freedom. It becomes an act of self-violation, an assault, a mutilation.

These personal rights are then hitched up to the language of the civil rights movement. Wants morph into needs, needs into rights, and rights are all about justice for which we can seek redress through the courts. In 2006 *The Adventures of Huckleberry Finn,* which has been de-scribed as America's first great novel, was taken to court. The charge brought against the book was that it is racially insensitive.

This infatuation with our own rights is one of the lines pursued in Charles Sykes's *A Nation of Victims.* He illustrates this with the case of the man who belonged to the National Association to Advance Fat Ac-ceptance. It bills itself as a "human rights" organization. In Chicago one of its members brought a suit against McDonald's because he could not quite fit into one of its seats. His argument was that since 20 percent of Americans are seriously obese, at least 20 percent of the ta-bles in McDonald's should be designed to accommodate those with large girths. It is their right. The case may seem absurd, but this kind of story is being repeated all over America every day.

As the sense of responsibility for personal behavior has shrunk, the need for litigation has increased. America has more lawyers than the rest of the world combined. In his famous Harvard address, Aleksander Solzhenitsyn observed that it is a terrible thing to live in a country, like the former Soviet Union, where there are no laws. But, he went on to say, it is also a terrible thing to live in a country where there are only lawyers. That is what we have in America. Only lawyers.

No society can satisfy so many people who have so many rights of so many different kinds as we have today. Especially when we are all anonymous, working in daily contexts in which we are unknown to those around us. They owe us nothing. Often not even their time. How, then, can the world around me satisfy my desire to have my needs met, my wants satisfied, my rights honored, especially when these are not really matters of law? How very frustrating all of this is! The result is that we are now seeing the full-grown embodiment of a very common cultural type. This is the Annoyed or Aggrieved Person, one whose personal rights are not being honored and who sees the obstructors to those rights as perverse and even evil.

Loss

Certainly life today is chaotic, disordered, painful, jarring, and emotionally difficult. It is rather striking to remember, as Kenneth Gergen noted in his book *The Saturated Self,* that so many of the words in our common parlance that relate to this situation came to life only in the twentieth century, and many only in the last few decades: "repressed," "burned out," "paranoid," "bulimic," "midlife crisis," "anxious," "voyeur." This is, as he says, the language of human deficit. It is the language of loss, emptiness, and disorder, of things that have gone awry internally. This language has undergone enormous expansion in our time.

The transition to the new therapeutic world we inhabit is built on this sense of loss and misdirection. It makes the assumption that since we cannot find adequate satisfaction of our needs, we are all basically wrecks, emotionally speaking, all in free fall, all spiraling out of control. It assumes that we are all anguished, fragile, confused, and diminished. Our self-esteem is falling apart or is already shattered and desperately needs to be built up. All is in a state of damage and disrepair.

This assessment is not totally implausible. Life in every modernized society is complex, demanding, stressful, and frustrating in some ways. The problem is that the wrong tools of diagnosis are being employed on this situation and the wrong prescription is being offered.

The prescription offered for this malady is that we should be emotionally open about our grievances, about all the things that aggravate us and leave us in a state of frustration. We need to learn to be transparent and to bring into the open all the secrets, tensions, loathings, hatreds, lusts, and confusions that lie buried deep within the self in an unsatisfied tangle. Only the release of these internal energies by verbalizing them will help us to identify them, name them, and find some consolation from them.

The downside to this self-worked therapy, of course, is that this constant taking of internal inventory only reinforces our natural self-centeredness and self-absorption. That, at least, is my view.

But it is not the view of those who inhabit this therapeutic universe, which seems to be almost everybody else, even in the evangelical church. As they see it, if we are not being vulnerable to one another, we will be unhealthy people. Being vulnerable, of course, means being willing to be naked, emotionally speaking, to give vent to our feelings, no matter how private, destructive, self-pitying, or even vile they may be. Is it not a remarkable thing to behold those on television talk shows engaging in this public undressing? Until, at the end, if we have had the fortitude to watch and listen, every thought, every feeling, every perception, every experience has been laid out on the table. It is all there: look! It is the emotional equivalent of President Clinton talking about his underwear on MTV.

What it also shows us is how very diminished we have become in our ability to cope with adversity. All we can do is "vent" about it.

In the older world we left behind, people thought of adversity as inevitable. Adversity was a consequence of the fall for those of a Christian outlook. But even for non-Christians it was never seen as an unexpected intruder in life. It was never thought that life should be without pain. Pain, disease, setbacks, disappointments, and wrong done to us were all seen as part of our life in this world, part of its texture, a thread woven with all the other threads through the fabric of our daily experience. Adversity was seen, even, as a necessary component in life.

Today we resent adversity as an interruption in our pleasure seeking, a rude disruption of our opportunities and our sense of calm. It is a gross injustice. Why should bad things happen to good people? Where is the justice of that? We are entitled to better. Indeed, we are demanding better! Adversity of any kind is unacceptable.

Guilt to Shame

It is true that we often use the words "guilt" and "shame" interchangeably. We tend to mean the same thing by them. However, in recent years, especially in psychiatric literature, a clear difference has emerged between them. I am going to be following this distinction.

Shame

Shame is the sense of awkwardness a person feels when seen doing something, or heard saying something, he or she does not want others to know about. Shame is not necessarily "moral" in nature. A person may be ashamed about parents who come off sounding ignorant, or do not speak English, or are poor. A person may be ashamed of where he or she lives because it is in the wrong part of town. These are not moral matters, but they are still capable of making a person feel ashamed.

This same sense, though, carries through into more clearly moral matters. A person, for example, may feel quite awkward about being caught shoplifting by a video camera, or that news somehow got out that the IRS was pursuing him or her for evading payment of taxes. The dynamic in each case, however, is the same. A person feels awkward when others know something personal he or she wished to keep hidden.

Guilt

Guilt, by contrast, happens when an external standard has been violated. In our courts each day juries pronounce defendants either innocent of the charges brought against them or guilty. In the latter case, the defendants are judged to have broken the law even though virtually all defendants deny that and plead innocent. The person who hears this verdict may not feel guilty, though many do and hide their faces. The court, however, has no interest at all in how the defendant feels. It takes no account of how ashamed the defendant may or may not be before others. The sole point in dispute is whether that person did or did not break the law as charged.

It is the same in Christian faith. The guilt the gospel addresses is also objective in nature. It is our guilt before God's law. It is the result of our violating the standards of his character. It is all about our blameworthiness before *God,* not about how we feel or do not feel or whether, in the contemporary sense, we feel shame. Indeed, in America so many people think of themselves as essentially good that, from that angle, there is very little to be ashamed about.

Shame today is what lines up our actions *horizontally.* Guilt is what lines them up *vertically.* Shame is what we feel subjectively and guilty is what we are objectively. Shame is what we feel before others. Guilty is what we are before God. Shame belongs in a psychological world and guilt belongs in a moral world.

If shame is simply about how we see ourselves and how we feel, it is not hard to see why many psychiatrists and psychologists think of shame as a crippling, unhealthy emotion that needs to be healed. This is undoubtedly true of false shame — the unnecessary sense of embarrassment people might have about their lips, or nose, or ears, or parents, or where they live — but this new approach to shame forgets that lying in the midst of many of our feelings of awkwardness are real moral perceptions. This is not false shame. This is shame for real moral reasons. To feel embarrassed because we were caught embezzling, or deceiving, or (shamelessly) self-promoting is an entirely good and healthy emotion! To argue, then, that we need to be liberated from these uncomfortable feelings, that the ultimate liberation is to become entirely shameless, is to sever our connections to the moral world entirely.

Healing Ourselves

In a famous book he wrote in the 1970s, Karl Menninger asked, *Whatever Became of Sin?* The answer is that some of our sins simply became crimes and most of the rest became diseases. Today a flourishing set of organizations, and an industry to go with them, has been established to treat almost any malady. Identify one's disease and there is a twelve-step program to address it. Is the problem food? Then try Overeaters Anonymous. Is it work? Try Workaholics Anonymous. Is it sex? Well, there are many options here. Try Incest Survivors Anonymous or Sex Addicts Anonymous or Sex and Love Addicts Anonymous or Impotents Anonymous. Is it drugs? How about Cocaine Anonymous or Drugs Anonymous? Is it marriage? There are groups for you, too, such as Families Anonymous, Parents Anonymous, and even Grandparents Anonymous. And those who are tidiness-challenged have help as well. It is Messies Anonymous. And so it goes across the entire front of human maladies, foibles, failures, and difficulties. For every one there is an organization. All our weaknesses and failures can be healed by the right application of technique.

Only the hard-hearted would scorn the wounded and mock their efforts at finding comfort in this world. The maladies that have called into life these programs, and hundreds more like them, are indeed grievous. They inflict on us confusion and pain, and very often bring disorder and even destruction in their path.

Nevertheless, we should not pass this by without seeing its single most important assumption. It is that the self contains its own healing mechanisms. Just as the body participates in its own recovery following injury or illness, so too does the self. The trick in life is to be able to tap into those natural, inner springs from whence healing flows and recovery results. Sins of all kinds, what were once moral breaches, are now just emotional deficits. These deficits, we have come to believe, are as treatable as a cut or a bout of pneumonia.

One of the signs that we turned a corner came in the proliferation of health clubs. That, at least, has been suggested with some plausibility. Health clubs have increased as churches have declined in the West. It is not just a case of people being more health-conscious. It is the recognition that signs of aging betray us as becoming useless in a modernized world. That has to be avoided at all costs. And, perhaps more deeply, it is a case of people searching for a kind of secularized eternal life.

The older sense of inner pollution that belonged in the moral world has been relocated to the body. The distress, even shame, of the self, we now think, can best be treated by being dissolved in the body. The workout has become our secular worship. The treadmill is our path to eternal life. Or, at least, a way of beating back the aging process. The pounding of the sole, we think, just may save the soul. At least, in

164

the short run, so to speak. Our self-pollution will evaporate in our sweat.

Here is salvation without sin, recovery without a gospel. All of it is, of course, humanism. Is this so surprising? After all, the theorists of the self movement, like Rogers, Fromm, May, and Maslow, were all self-confessed humanists. What is amazing, though, is that the American public, which overwhelmingly thinks of itself as spiritual and a great many also as religious, has jumped into this therapeutic world like a frog into water. Should we not have wondered what we were actually getting into? And should not evangelicals have paused on the edge of this pond and asked themselves a couple of theological questions before taking the leap so enthusiastically into water so seriously polluted? One would have thought so!

A Different Universe

It will now be no great surprise to hear my gentle suggestion that it is time for evangelicals to alight from this train. Or, if I may change the image, it is time for them to recover their lost universe. And it really is a different universe. What we need to do is to think, once again, with an entirely different set of connections. The connections are not primarily in reference to self, but to God. They are the connections that have to be reforged in the moral world we actually inhabit rather than the artificial world of appearances we have manufactured. It is about making connections into the world of reality that endures rather than the one that does not.

My suggestion may seem to have little attraction to the evangelical world that imagines it is reaping great success from its foray into self-talk. It is worth pondering, though, that sometimes the children of our world are much wiser than the children of light. And in this case the children of our world have produced a literature of great abundance that the children of light would do well to heed. What is this literature saying?

The most startling consequence of this therapeutic turn, many authors are observing, is that our self begins to disintegrate. When the universe loses its center or, to be more precise, when the center is lost to us as something outside ourselves that has the authority to reach into our lives, we ourselves begin to disintegrate. Many of these writers have not seen this connection, but they do see the disintegration of the self. The self that has been made to bear the weight of being the center of all reality, the source of all our meaning, mystery, and morality, finds that it has become empty and fragile. When God dies to us, we die in ourselves. That is the connection we need to see, and it has become especially aggravated in the context of our (post)modern world. So many modern writers are seeing, as I have noted, that the postmodern self has become "minimal," "decentered," "enfeebled," "empty," and "depleted."

It is a curious thing that the evangelical church in the West has been willing to follow the self movement down this path so uncritically. The self movement, after all, is the very symbol of our collective emptiness and insecurity. Only the hungry, after all, are always thinking about food. Those who are not deprived think about other things. Only the unhappy are constantly preoccupied with happiness, only those haunted by their own self-emptiness are always searching for something to fill the self. Redefining evangelicalism in terms of the self, in terms of the self having spiritual experiences, finding itself, satisfying itself, fulfilling itself, has everything to do with culture and nothing to do with Christ. Here let me ponder, with you, some of the tensions along this seam between Christ and culture.

Rupture

First, the self movement assumes, in a way biblical faith cannot, that human beings are essentially innocent. That in fact is what a great majority of Americans believe. In 2002 a national survey by Barna discovered that despite all the moral chaos evident in our postmodern world, 74 percent did not believe in original sin and 52 percent of the born again concurred. These high percentages responded positively to the statement that "when people are born they are neither good nor evil — they make a choice between the two as they mature." This goes to the heart of American individualism, which believes that one's self-definition is a matter of private choice and, it turns out, this choice is unencumbered by the gravitational pull, and misdirection, of sin. It is all a matter of choice and not of nature.

This is the heart of the self movement, and it is anathema to biblical faith. The majesty of God's forgiveness is lost entirely when we lose what has to be forgiven. What has to be forgiven is not just what we do but who we *are,* not just our sinning but our sinfulness, not just our choices but what we have chosen in place of God. This belief in our inherent innocence is belied by the kind of life we all experience, and, more importantly, it is also contradicted by Scripture. When we miss the biblical teaching, we also miss the nature of God's grace in all its height and depth. In biblical faith it is God's grace through Christ that does for us what we cannot do for ourselves. In this kind of psychologized evangelicalism, grace works only around the margins of our self. It completes the bit that we cannot quite get done by ourselves.

It is, of course, quite pointless to mention that this whole movement is based on a new Pelagianism. This is the heresy that denied original sin. Pelagianism? Who cares? That is the response of a church now disconnected from the past and no longer thinking in doctrinal categories. Yet it is precisely the category of a full doctrine of sin that runs from one end of Scripture to the other. That is what explains God's redemptive incursions into this world and why we are drifting along on our high seas of modernity with very little inkling as to what it means to know God.

The language of the self is not interchangeable with that of human nature. They are two entirely different things. The self is the way we think about ourselves when we are inhabiting a psychological universe. Human nature is how we think of ourselves in a moral universe, and, as understood in the *imago Dei,* it is how we think of ourselves in God's universe. This is our entry into a Christian worldview. The components of this worldview are our views of God, of ourselves, and of the world. Together they form a web of understanding that gives us a place to stand amidst all the falling debris in the postmodern world. This substitute language of the self, with the whole overlay of techniques that goes with it, is a false trail, a dead end.

Why is this? May I gently suggest that the reason is that the essence of pride is finding in the self what in fact can only be found in

God. So pride leads us to think much *about* the self and much *of* the self. We imagine that within ourselves we have power enough, wisdom enough, and strength enough to find our way out of our own painful realities. Inevitably, though, very finite preoccupations are substituted for those that are eternal. Here is the "autonomous self" at work.

The self movement has tapped into this by offering self-mastery through the right technique. It encourages us to think much about the self and much of the self. It is an industry that lives off of and for pride. As such, it offers a way to dissolve all the internal aches and heal all the internal wounds that life inflicts as we try to do for ourselves what in fact only God can do.

Reconciliation

Second, the self movement in its spiritual dimension assumes that God is accessed through the self. This follows from the first assumption that the self is essentially innocent. Indeed, the sense that God stands over against us, that we are in jeopardy before him as sinners, is almost entirely lost. Only 17 percent of Americans understand sin in relation to God because the language of sin is not a part of the way people think of themselves. If the language is used at all, it is used trivially, perhaps of breaking some inconsequential church rule. Even the language of "living in sin," which usually was said with a wink, has gone. Certainly, few today hear in the language of sin the gravity it has in the Bible. There it speaks of our wrongdoing in relation to *God*. Today, though, no rupture has taken place between our self and God — they stand in relation to and in continuity with one another.

Postmoderns of a spiritual kind do not see themselves in need of reconciliation to God because they do not believe that any rupture in relationship has occurred. The biblical way of thinking is today a foreign language. This asserts that we have been alienated from God by our sin and he from us by his wrath so that, if reconciliation is to happen, he must be able to look on us without displeasure and we on him without fear. And that transformation, that transaction, happens in Christ as God's wrath is turned away from us on the cross and our sin is canceled as it is imputed to him.

The assumption that we have direct access to the sacred through the self rests on a pagan assumption: that the Creator and the creation are related to one another pantheistically. God, it is assumed, is found within the self. He is naturally discovered in the depths of our being. This speaks both to our understanding of sin — that no rupture has taken place — and to our thought about creation, that he who makes and that which is made are the two parts of one reality. No wonder Eastern thought has made great inroads into the West! I will need to return to this in the next chapter.

The appeal of this to evangelicals is many-sided. By speaking about faith in terms that are familiar in our world of self-fulfillment, self-esteem, and the whole many-sided self movement, the gospel suddenly is on the cutting edge of where-we-are. By assuming access to God that is as swift and certain as the swipe of a credit card, a spiritual purchase without waiting, the gospel makes itself appealing to consumers. They are getting it when they want and how they want it. By speaking of the gospel in terms not of truth but of feelings, evangelicals of this stripe guarantee for themselves instant success. Feelings are easy to arouse while thought is hard and slow. Without thought, however, the gospel dissolves away and leaves believers without a worldview in which to think about all of life.

Down this road there is supposedly access, but there is in fact no reconciliation. There is no reconciliation because there has been no estrangement. The glory of Christian faith is the grace that has bridged the chasm sin has created, the heights and depths of God's saving love expressed in the person of Christ. This new spirituality claims access but has none of the grace and power of the gospel.

It's Not Just about Me

Third, when the whole of reality contracts into the self, which is what the self movement builds upon, then engagement with the outside world is diminished. Is it so surprising, then, that evangelical faith, which has lamely followed along this cultural path, has lost its integrity in the world? In a therapeutic world we are preoccupied only with ourselves, and nothing is as compelling to us as our own self. An evangelicalism that enters this world, and leaves behind the moral world that alone makes sense of life and of the gospel, has lost the means to restrain the self. In the therapeutic world, it is all about self-fulfillment. It is not about self-sacrifice and self-discipline, self-restraint and self-abasement, which is what Christianity is about. These words, in fact, are obscenities in our world today — indeed, the only obscenities we have. The self movement is all about feeling good about ourselves, not about being good. It is therapeutic, not moral. Is it a great surprise to learn, then, that the born-again experience that happens along this path makes virtually no moral difference in people's lives? Are we surprised to see that many of the largest churches are oblivious to everyone around them — except, of course, as a source of converts?

This, in fact, is one of the great tragedies of our time, that evangelicals have lost their spiritual status as outsiders to the culture, those who march to a different drummer and have the capacity to think about their world in ways that are completely different from what is taken as normative in it. So many consequences derive from all of this, but I am able to pursue only one here: the matter of being salt and light in society.

Vice might be restrained and virtue promoted in a society in many ways. The one I ponder here is by way of example. My question, then, is how does a society hang together, ethically speaking?

About the Salt

Perhaps the simplest way to see the role the moral world has played is to think about some of the dilemmas our Western societies now face. Lord Moulton, an English jurist of the last century, proposed that for any society to be healthy and productive three domains had to be preserved: the domain of law, the domain of freedom, and the internal domain of "obedience to the unenforceable." Two of these domains are rather obvious.

Every society needs law as well as the machinery to enforce it, from police to courts to prisons. This is because every society includes those who rob, rape, steal, and in a multitude of other ways do harm to their fellow human beings. This machinery may cure no one, but it discourages antisocial action and protects those who might otherwise become prey to various kinds of predators.

Equally important is a second domain. It is the preservation of freedom. It is in the soil of freedom that invention, creativity, entrepreneurial work, philanthropy, and Christian believing all grow. Both law and freedom have to be preserved.

Lying between law and freedom is the domain of "obedience to the unenforceable." This is where restraint is self-imposed rather than imposed from the outside. It is where moral imperatives flourish, not because the law demands that they do, nor even that this is what others expect, but simply because they are seen to be right.

Many things are unethical but not illegal. Lying is unethical, but most lying is not illegal. Many acts of unkindness, many of the destructive rumors we are constantly hearing, character assassinations, acts of thoughtlessness, crude behavior, pornography, and homosexuality are unethical, but most are not illegal. In these and many other areas restraint should come from within, and very often the law is simply incapable of making illegal the offensive behavior. How could we pass laws against cutting remarks or demeaning and rude gestures?

Our society's law is both negative and positive. In prohibiting certain behavior, it is also requiring the opposite. It is illegal to cheat on one's taxes, so, by the same token, the law commands citizens to be honest in paying their taxes. However, law cannot command many things that are highly desirable to life. It cannot command us to be compassionate or benevolent, to care for each other, to be gentle, or to live out any of the other virtues. It can command only that we do not kill, defraud, or assault others.

The virtues cannot be matters of government policy, or of the law's requirement in any country. They have to emerge freely from within us as an expression of what we want to do. Similarly, it is we who have to restrain our own vices, many of which are not illegal. Gambling, for example, is regulated by the state, but we need to have the self-discipline to avoid it entirely by staying away from casinos and online betting.

From whence, then, comes this moral directive, this inward discipline, that produces this "obedience to the unenforceable," obedience to what our law, civil or criminal, often cannot require of its citizens? It comes from the moral world that citizens inhabit in their own minds and souls. What happens when that world disappears?

What happens is this. Freedom, cut loose from all inward, moral restraint, degenerates. It is reduced to meaning nothing more than that as free people we can do, say, or see anything we want, provided it is not illegal. We are free to do what we want all the way up to the line of illegality because once the moral world has disappeared, the only restraint that remains is a country's laws. This, though, is a recipe for unending social strife because people playing fast and loose, but living just within the boundaries of the law, create enormous damage. Our social life cannot survive so many people who are so free of any inward restraint. What is the answer?

The only answer we have been able to find is litigation, litigation in place of morality. It is litigation, or the fear of litigation, that must restrain the expression of inward vices and all self-serving behavior. To be successful, though, laws must be greatly multiplied to cover every situation where morality once ruled.

This, in a mild form, is also what political correctness seeks to do by creating rules that are a substitute for morality. These are then backed by social punishment for offenders of those rules. The illustrations of this dynamic are almost endless. As our moral world has died, freedom from the one side and law from the other have both rushed in to occupy the middle territory of "obedience to the unenforceable." And the options have now dwindled down to an aggressive legalism on the one side or a rampant, libertarian individualism on the other.

Where We Stand

Litigation and libertarian freedom are not the only two options. They are the two options struggling for supremacy in our culture in America, but there is a third possibility. It is the power of personal sanctity, integrity, and authenticity. This is not the whole answer to the Christian engagement with society, but, in its absence, every other kind of engagement comes off as empty, "political," and maybe hypocritical.

This third option is not seen much in the evangelical world today. At least that is what Barna found, since born-againers live no differently, at an ethical level, than plain secularists. Clearly, in the churches from which these born-againers come, there is abysmal ignorance about the Bible, about its central vision of the greatness of God's holiness, and about the consequent need for our own authenticity before him. In the evangelical world that Barna surveys, it is almost as if the prodigal, who had once returned to his father's waiting arms, has become beset by lingering doubts. Does he *have* to be so far from those pigsties? Is *everything* bad in the far-off country? Are the riotous parties *entirely* off-limits? Why can't he be in touch with the world he left behind? If he retains his place at home, can't he also become "all things to all men" and identify with that far-off country? Would that not secure for him more friends? How will they hear his story of having been welcomed back if he refuses to go to their parties?

There is no doubt that we are now having to come back to some very basic Christian questions. Those who pursue their selves, with all their worldly and self-serving interests, lose their selves. Those who become like the world, and live for the world, end up like the world, but they are not liked by the world. Because they are hypocrites. Those who become poor in their own eyes, and before God, become rich. Those who forsake all things for Christ's sake are given all things. Those who want to have a foot in both worlds lose their place in both.

As baffling as all of this may seem, as wrongheaded as it may seem, the fact is that there is no personal, Christian authenticity if we are playing the game by two sets of rules, one set from the Bible we claim to believe and the other set from the strategies we have devised for ourselves. We cannot claim to know God and not know that he is holy. We cannot say we know his truth and not know that we must forsake ourselves to be accepted by Christ. We cannot say we are born again and yet show no signs of regeneration. We cannot run with the hares and yet imagine that we are hunting with the hounds.

The fact that the modern self is empty and disintegrating, that our (post)modern society is fragmented and fragile, presents biblical faith with a truly golden moment. A deep longing exists in our society to see the real thing, to see lives lived out that have authenticity, that have substance. This authenticity, however, has nothing to do with following the broken promises of the self movement, which is now simply bankrupt. It has everything to do with taking our place before a holy

God, through Christ, in such a way that his character, as it were, reaches into our lives with both the restraint and the direction we need if we are to be restored. It is when this kind of thing happens that integrity is born. And with integrity come the salt and light of which our society stands in such great need.

Much in the world of our daily experience is not enduring. Its experiences are real, but their deepest reality is what parts good from what is bad. That adjudication is made in eternity, and so we live in the postmodern world not just as postmoderns, consumed by the present age, but as those who are of eternity and whose eyes are on the "age to come." We live not simply as those born again, but as those who belong in *God's* world, those who are learning to think their thoughts after him. We are those who, by his grace, are to be a reminder in this fallen world that there is another world that will be there long after all the ravages of time have done their work and all that we now see in our world has passed away.

Does it really demand that much courage for us to be countercultural enough to live this out? Or are we just so muddled, so besotted by the thought of our own success, so fearful of offending others, that we just cannot bring ourselves to say what is true? Looking at the evangelical church today, one really does wonder, does one not?

A renewed Protestantism, one that looks like it has in its high moments in the past, will have about it a joyous sense of knowing God, of knowing him through his Son, of being able to live in his world on his terms and celebrating his sovereign rule over all of it. Those are the terms of his truth, but they are also the terms of fullness, of a growing completeness, of wisdom, and of life. It will be sinewy and tough. It will not cave in intellectually to all the fads and rackets of our time. It will have an infectious joy in doing what is right. There will be a sense of awe in God's creation presence, of gratitude in being able to serve him in all the callings he gives. And here some of the things that have been torn apart by life and by its disarray will begin to be put back together.

This is something the self movement can only dream about.

CHAPTER VI

Christ

I believe that spirituality is a feeling of connection with a force that is greater than ourselves. Personally, I believe deep in my soul that there is an energy that connects all life on earth. Some bonds are obviously stronger than others, but the ability to feel these connections — this is what I consider spirituality.

SPIRITUALEXPERTS.COM

And you were dead in the trespasses and sins in which you once walked, following the course of this world, following the prince of the power of the air, the spirit that is now at work in the sons of disobedience. . . . But God, being rich in mercy . . . even when we were dead in our trespasses, made us alive together with Christ — by grace you have been saved.

EPHESIANS 2:1-5

The simplest way to understand what is happening in our cultures in the West is to see that we have brought upon ourselves a strange contradiction. It is a contradiction that has run all

175

through these pages, and I have had occasion to mention it several times.

On the one hand, we have built an outward world of great magnificence, with its cities and commerce, a world of brilliant technology and corporate structures, all laced together by instantaneous information. Western economies are spreading their influence and products far and wide, indeed, across the whole globe.

On the other hand, this world we are making for ourselves, though filled with abundance, opportunities, and exotic products, is also quite inhospitable to the human spirit. We want the abundance, the surfeit of affluence, but we find the cost to our spirits difficult, even unbearable. In this world, this artificial world, we have all become psychological vagrants. We are the homeless. We have no place to stay. Furthermore, our uniqueness is being swallowed up by all the indifference around us, by the mass marketing, mass culture, mass this and mass that.

This is part of the "American paradox." And this is what holds the answer, I believe, to the question of why, out of the blue, the West is suddenly turning spiritual. This is a truly astounding development that very few saw coming. This spirituality, and its biblical alternative, is the subject of this chapter.

However, before getting down to business, we must distinguish among the many kinds of spirituality afoot in our society.

Christian and Pagan Paths

There are two families of spirituality in life. Within each are many differences, much as there are within human family members. But what distinguishes them most importantly is that one begins above and moves down whereas the other begins below and tries to move up (or perhaps in). One starts with God and reaches into sinful life whereas the other starts in human consciousness and tries to reach above to make connections in the divine. One is Christian and the other is pagan. These are the two fundamental spiritualities in the West today.

Throughout the Old Testament this earthy, pagan spirituality was constantly being engaged both outside and inside Israel. Readers today associate this paganism mostly with its more vivid, reprehensible episodes such as sacrificing children to Molech, or Jezebel's flock of priests who tried to keep Baal content and whom Elijah faced off against. But beneath it all were assumptions of a spiritual kind that are often missed. These spiritual assumptions have persisted across the ages, coming down into our present moment, even though today the barbaric practices that went hand in glove with this ancient paganism in the Old Testament period have passed away.

These spiritual assumptions were present in the New Testament period, too. The apostles confronted them. Yet the church did not really enter into a life-and-death struggle until the centuries that followed immediately on the patristic period. At stake was its very existence. Would it think of its faith as the grace of God coming from "above," being incarnate in the Son, and conquering sin and death on the cross? And would it insist, against great cultural pressure, that there is absolutely nothing sinners can do to reach upward to God, to connect with him or to influence him, that he has had to reach down to us through his Son? Or would it allow for the possibility that sinners can reach down into themselves and find solace there in the sacred? Can they make this connection by their own religious effort? The apostles had made their argument that the real and saving spirituality was from above and not, in these ways, from below. The early church, for the most part, followed.

This life-and-death struggle was therefore won, for the moment, by upholding the New Testament's doctrines of incarnation, grace, atonement, and resurrection. However, this message was soon lost in the Middle Ages. Luther in the sixteenth century, followed by Calvin and the other Reformers, once again returned to Scripture and once again resounded the notes of God's undeserved grace, coming from above, which alone enables sinners to know him. Christianity is not about sinners lifting themselves up to God but about God coming down in condescension and grace to them.

Biblical spirituality and our contemporary spirituality are not two variations on the same theme. They are stark alternatives to each other. In the one, God reaches down in grace; in the other, the sinner reaches up (or in) in self-sufficiency. These spiritualities belong in different worlds, one moral in its fabric and the other psychological. One thinks in terms of salvation, the other of healing. One results in holiness, the other looks for wholeness. In the one, God's sovereignty is seen in the establishment of what is spiritual; in the other, a human-seized sovereignty is at work to create its own spirituality. Between these two kinds of spirituality there can be no accord, no peace, no cooperation. The one excludes the other. This is the message we have heard from the apostles. This is the message that was recovered at the time of the Reformation. And this is the message that should be resounding in the church today.

The church, however, is courted in every age by the alternative, counterfeit spirituality, first in one form and then in another. Today the evangelical church is in a life-and-death struggle with this spiritual alternative, even as the apostles were in the New Testament period and the prophets were in the Old Testament. Today this pagan spirituality comes, not in barbaric forms of child sacrifice — assuming that abortion is more about convenience than spirituality — but in the innocent tones of popular culture. We meet it everywhere.

Sometimes it is dressed up in sophisticated psychological language. More commonly we hear it in the everyday self-talk of our therapeutic culture. It is there in the television chatter, in the magazines near the checkout counter at the supermarket, and it is mentioned between neighbors. This understanding of being spiritual sounds plausible, compelling, innocent, and even commendable, but, let us make no mistake about it, it is *lethal* to biblical Christianity. That is why the biggest enigma we face today is the fact that its chief enablers are evangelical churches, especially those who are seeker-sensitive and emergent who, for different reasons, are selling spirituality disconnected from biblical truth.

The seeker-sensitive are adapting their product to a spiritual market that believes it can have spiritual comfort with very little truth. The emergents are adapting their product to a spiritual market that is younger, postmodern, and leery about truth. But in both cases we see this strange anomaly. Here are those who think of themselves as being biblical, as being the children of the New Testament, the followers of Jesus and the apostles, embracing an alternative spirituality in order either to be successful or to be culturally cutting-edge.

We now need to discuss further these two kinds of spirituality, since so much rides on understanding the differences between them. We will look first at the spirituality that emerges from below and that has burst upon our Western cultures. We will then look at its alternative, the spirituality that begins above in the counsels of God, in eternity, and is defined from first to last by his grace, his unmerited favor reaching out to sinners who, within themselves, are unable to surrender themselves, or to give up their hostility to his truth and his moral will. It is he who both secures their salvation and ensures their belief in Christ in whom that salvation is found.

From Below

The Facts

Let us begin with the facts. The most basic of these is that in America, 78 percent of people say they are spiritual. When solving life's dilemmas, 56 percent say they are more likely to rely on themselves than on an outside power like the God of the Bible. And 40 percent claim specifically to be spiritual but not religious. The same change has occurred in Britain. A study looking at the decade from 1990 to 2000 found that during this time weekly church attendance dropped from 28 percent to 8 percent but those who said they had spiritual experiences rose from 48 percent to 76 percent. There clearly has been a surge in spiritual appetite that is either hostile to religion or, at least, has lost confidence in institutionalized religion.

Religion as we typically understand it is a *publicly* practiced matter. It is about attendance in a church, synagogue, or mosque; about public praying and teaching; about accepting the disciplines of the believing community; and about respecting the boundaries of its belief. This new spirituality is about the *private* search for meaning, a search for connection to something larger than the self. It is in fact a self-constructed spirituality.

Why is that? The answer, quite simply, is that postmoderns trust direct experience but distrust what is mediated. What comes through others is subject to all the suspicions that are activated the moment they start to speak to us. What are their motives for speaking to me?

What's in it for them? Are they using words to manipulate me? These are the thoughts that arise in the cloud of doubt and distrust when postmoderns engage religious matters. By contrast, spirituality that is inward, rising within the self, arising from the perceptions of our own selves, is not something coming to us secondhand from others. It is innocent, untouched, unscathed, unpolluted. It is real. We can trust ourselves but we cannot trust others! We are unsuspicious about ourselves but highly suspicious of others!

In the United States, 80 percent believe that a person should arrive at his or her own beliefs independent of any external authority such as a church. Indeed, 60 percent say that since we all have God within us, churches are unnecessary. And in a generational slice that was made, 53 percent of boomers think it is more important to be alone and meditate than to worship with others.

The Church's Failure

The church's perceived failure is a large contributing factor to this emerging, new, spiritual direction. At the end of 2006, Barna singled this out as one of the most significant things he had discovered. Of those who regularly attend church, only 15 percent say their relationship to God is their first priority. This dismal figure is made even more dismal when put alongside another, this one relating to pastors. This situation should be giving them nightmares, but instead we find that 70 percent of pastors are camped out in Alice's Wonderland assuring themselves that all is well in their churches and that their people love God first and foremost. Clearly, congregations and pastors are thinking along rather different lines!

As they stand, these numbers are rather too general to be helpful. What exactly is meant by "first priority"? And what percentage of those surveyed would consider themselves born again? What percentage would, additionally, be evangelical? Although these numbers are still a bit raw and incomplete, it is not unreasonable to observe that since so many regular church attendees do fall into the two categories of born again and evangelical, and since "first priority" is so close to Jesus' commandment that we are to love God with all of our being, and that this is the "great" commandment (Matt. 22:38), we do need to pay heed to these findings.

In early 2007 I attended Evensong in one of the Cambridge Colleges. This particular college had been founded in the early sixteenth century. I sat that evening in its magnificent chapel, caught up in the majestic swells of the organ whose notes rumbled and reverberated around this ancient place of worship. The choir's performance was exquisitely rich and beautiful, so delicate, and almost fragrant. It was as if the angels had descended for this brief moment and lifted the congregation up in their praise. My eye, however, suddenly caught sight of something I had not expected to see. The choirmaster was resplendent in scarlet and white robes, but protruding beneath these robes were his blue jeans. Blue jeans?

I confess that I do not know what choirmasters should wear beneath their robes, but this did strike me as downright incongruous. Blue jeans in this formal, and breathtakingly beautiful, place?

As I pondered this anomaly, it occurred to me that this is how many people think of religion. It is something resplendent put on just for the occasion. But it is just as easily taken off. And beneath it are the same old street clothes that have been there all along. These are the clothes of the everyday world, the clothes that go with us everywhere we go. They have nothing to do with the robes that belong in church. Or, to put it the other way around, religion has nothing to do with our everyday world. That is how many people are seeing religion.

Indeed, they are seeing evangelical religion in this light, too. It has nothing to do with the real world. I actually share their skepticism. Not because I share their unbelief but because I share their yearning for honesty. It is rather clear, is it not, that evangelicalism, at least in America, is often not true to itself today as a revealed faith? It dresses for the occasion, but underneath are the same old street clothes. We know that because, as a faith, it is not very serious about life. And the reason is that it is not very serious about God.

What tips me off that we are looking at this sort of faith is that we see all the signs of self-construction. Self-made faith does not have in itself the power to remake human nature. So much evangelical church practice, so much of its preaching, so much of what people have come to think of as being evangelical, is actually self-oriented, not God-centered. It is about what we do, about what we get, not about what God has done or about what he gives in Christ. It is about getting what we want as religious consumers, not about receiving what God has given us in Christ's death in our place and in his written Word.

Our lives, though, are nourished not by spiritual experiences we can seek, but by God applying to us the truth of his Word. If it is true that all our experimenting with "doing church," all our marketing, all our cultural adaptation, has produced nothing but the sickly results Barna keeps reporting, then it should be no surprise that people are going off looking for some other kind of spirituality that will be more authentic. Many say explicitly that they are spiritual but not religious. And why not? Why not tune in to some other spirituality from "below" and see if it may not work better or be easier than what the churches have to offer since the latter are making little difference in people's lives?

Beyond these bare numbers, descriptions of this new spirituality become difficult. There are as many spiritualities as there are spiritual seekers. It is nevertheless the case that here, too, is an inner core whose ideas are crisp and clear, and circles of influence that move away from the center where the clarity dissipates.

The New Journey

The center of this kind of spirituality was conceived in the counterculture of the 1960s. It was carried by hippies, flower-power children, LSD experimenters, radical feminists who worshiped the goddess within, as well as New Agers. The Beatles sang about it. And it has worked itself out in an agenda of opposition to the traditional family, support of homosexuality, radical environmentalism, and often a radically libertarian attitude to the rest of life.

However, away from this hard-core center, ideas are hazier and less radical. Here we move from the encounter groups of the 1960s, through the self-help books prominent in the 1970s, to the vague spirituality of the 1990s. It is at the end of this development that we find the 56 percent of Americans who say that in life's crises they look to the god within rather than some outside source like the God of the Bible. They may not be radical feminists, may not be into New Age, may not meditate, may not use a mantra, may be averse to channeling, and may well keep the occult at arm's length. And yet, in ways that are ill defined and often unformulated, they are still part of this extraordinary search for what is spiritual. And that is what is noteworthy. These are not exotic types living on society's fringes. They are not in communes. They are not dressed in saffron robes and they do not have shaved heads. These are ordinary people doing ordinary things in life: living in the suburbs, going to the supermarket, reading *Time* magazine, watching CNN, and even voting in political elections.

Traditional Christian faith holds to the outside God who stands over against us. He is known not because we have discovered him, but because he has made himself known in Scripture and in Christ. We are not left to piece together our understanding of him. He has unveiled and defined himself for us. He has broken his concealment. He has come into view and has told us who he is and how we are to live.

The inside god of this contemporary spirituality is different. He emerges out of the psychology, the inner depths, of the seeker. He is known through and within the self, and we piece together our knowledge of him (or her, or it) from the fragments of our experience coupled with our intuitions. In so many ways this god, this sacred reality, is indistinguishable from how we experience ourselves.

The key difference between spirituality and religion is this. Religion that is about the outside God — whether in Christianity, Judaism, or Islam — is religion that makes truth claims about that God. Spirituality in this contemporary, cultural sense does not. Its "truth" is private, not public. It is individualistic, not absolute. It is about what I perceive, about what works for me, not about what anyone else should believe. And this "truth" is verified psychologically and therapeutically. The test of its truthfulness is simply pragmatic.

Those who are on this spiritual journey — and that is the most popular metaphor — have no destination in mind. This is the exact opposite of the way the Bible pictures the Christian journey. This journey, biblically speaking, has a clear destination. It is, in Bunyan's language in *Pilgrim's Progress,* the Celestial City.

The journey in contemporary spiritualities, by contrast, is about what people today have to do to experience the sacred or to increase that experience. There are no doctrines to be believed, no rules to be obeyed, and no practices to be followed. There is no worldview to which seekers must commit themselves. Nothing is fixed in eternity or by eternity, but all is in motion, everything is provisional, all is subject to ongoing experimental confirmation, all is adaptable to our internal needs.

This spiritual surge, happening throughout the West, eerily reflects our more general experience of the modernized world. Living in the modernized world means living like the homeless, not rooted anywhere, not in place or in family, but living as perpetual migrants. The migration, though, is not just around the many facets of postmodern experience. When this aspect of modern experience, this uprootedness, gets replicated in the spiritual realm, it means that people also keep moving from spiritual idea to spiritual idea, from religion to religion, in an endless search for the sacred. There is no fixed address here, either. No framework of belief in which one lives. No fixed points for the journey. No norms.

That means that *experimentation* constantly lubricates this search. It is a search for that mix of ideas and practices that will heighten the sense of the sacred or of what is spiritual. This may be a spirituality that is not religious, but that does not mean religions cannot be raided for ideas. A liturgy may be lifted from ancient Catholicism, a litany borrowed from some Buddhist monks, and New Age habits of meditation incorporated. The point is that there is no clear destination; this is a search in which one never arrives. One is always looking, always feeling out the path ahead, always searching but never finally finding. What is appealing about this kind of spiritual search is that it is always interesting. Just like the world in which we live, this spirituality is always changing, mutating, and morphing into something else. Perhaps most of all, this spiritual search is interesting because it gives implicit permission to cross boundaries because they hold out the promise of finding what is real on the other side. It validates what, in a Christian context, is called lawlessness.

The presumption of this search is that the sacred can be directly accessed from within, accessed by the self. Harold Bloom, seeing all of this happening, claimed in his book *The American Religion* that this is resurgent gnosticism and that gnosticism now is the American religion. This is a hard case to prove.

It is undoubtedly true, though, that across the ages a spirituality has appeared in one form or another that has made the same assumptions as are being made today. Gnosticism was a particular form of this, against which both the apostles and the early church battled. This postmodern search is another form of it. What they all have in common, despite other differences, is that they are self-focused. They oppose "faith" to "knowledge." They live by intuitive insight and dismiss doctrinal teaching. Their authority is internal rather than external, subjective rather than objective. They are spiritual but not religious. All these forms of spirituality are about exploring the psyche to find, deep within the self, spiritual realities larger than the self, spiritual secrets that unlock meaning in life. This kind of spirituality is a perfect reflection of the shift from the moral world we once inhabited to the one we now live in that is psychological and therapeutic. Christianity requires a moral world, the one God sustains. This new spirituality has abandoned every vestige of the moral world and is happily ensconced in a psychological world.

We today are living in the world our Enlightenment forebears said would be moving forward toward a brighter and better future. We are the future toward which they looked!

But one thing does seem clear: while the world has been "progressing" in some ways, it has become far more dangerous in others because technology magnifies the possibilities for human depravity. Life has also become far more stressful and difficult. The Enlightenment looked at material progress and imagined that somehow the human spirit, in due course, would follow along. Postmoderns know that the human spirit is fragile and empty, and is not following along. They are not looking to the triumphs of the modernized world to produce its solace within them. They are looking elsewhere.

This sense of dis-ease, of the uneasiness of the human spirit, has now been hitched up to a search for what is ultimate, what is sacred, what is real beyond our world of commerce and high-rises. This is being pursued through the self.

We are sensing within ourselves that we are more than what we buy, more than what we experience, more than what we see. We are more than our sexual experiences, more than our ethnicity, more than our generation, more, more, more. . . . Yes, but what is this "more"? We know that to find it we must transcend this flat plane of buying and selling, connecting and disconnecting, moving and changing, posing and posturing, seeing and being seen, using and being used. Yes, but what is it we really seek? And how do we find it? These are our questions today.

Secular but Spiritual

The emergence of this new, but ancient, spirituality has been one of the really startling developments of the last few decades. Very few saw it coming.

In the 1970s secular humanism seemed poised for triumph. Certainly its advocates thought it was. A flourishing literature emerged promoting the cause even as the religious sounded warnings from the other side. It may well be that the secular humanists became the victims of their own ideology with its centerpiece idea of progress. It must have seemed a foregone conclusion to them that it was only a matter of time before their views would triumph. The map would be wiped clean of all religions and all spiritualities. The world would soon become wholly "rational" and all "superstition" would disappear.

That was not to be. Even while the United States was modernizing, a considerable amount of Christian believing was also going on in the 1970s, 1980s, and 1990s. America, at one and the same time, is both highly modernized and full of believing.

This fact prodded theorists to ask whether their understanding of how secularization works had not been a little too wooden. They had assumed that the processes of modernization would push all things religious to the periphery of life, marginalizing them, and make God irrelevant to everything that is important. However, something a little different from this has been happening in America.

So it was that in the 1970s, a more subtle understanding of secularization began to emerge. The way it works, it came to be seen, is not necessarily by eliminating all religions and all spiritualities but rather by forcing a sharp divide between what is public and what is private, as we saw in an earlier chapter. It seizes the public sphere for itself but allows people to believe and think what they want in their private lives.

In fact, it puts great pressure on all religious belief to become completely private and keep itself out of the public view.

The American ethos has always protected private rights to belief and defended the freedom to express those beliefs in public. The separation secularization was forcing between public and private, therefore, did fit in partially with the American ethos. America defends the individual right to believe whatever seems believable.

However, this ethos has also created some awkward moments. Private beliefs of a religious kind have been asking for the same protections of expression in the public domain as all other beliefs enjoy. This expression of private belief in the public square has now run headlong into the more ardent advocates of secularism. They are insisting that religion is only for homes and hearts, that religious belief of all kinds does not belong in the public square.

These fights, though, are on the surface. They obscure what is beneath the surface. Here an overwhelming percentage of people now say they are spiritual. Secularization does not mean that all religion and spirituality must wither away. It simply means that all religion and spirituality need to be kept private. By a strange turn of events, secularization itself has opened up the way for the emergence of our new, surging, private spiritualities as well as a flourishing industry to service them. We are now both secular and spiritual.

How Spiritualities Work

These new spiritualities, coming as they do in all forms and shapes, are making several assumptions about which we need to be clear. These are the mechanisms of this spirituality from "below." They are, first, that we have natural access to the sacred; second, that sin has not disrupted this access; and third, that spirituality is always a private matter, discerned intuitively and internally, not a matter objectively anchored in history. That is why it is so content to live with this public/private separation.

NATURE

The thought that we have natural access to the divine is not new, and we in fact already considered it when thinking about the self movement. However, we need to revisit this briefly to set the contemporary context for thinking about the person and work of Christ.

The assumption that we all have a natural access to the sacred is as old as the oldest forms of paganism. In paganism the boundaries between the natural and the supernatural, as well as between the living and the dead, became blurred. The gods came down and cavorted with women sometimes, but humans were constantly traversing the terrain of the gods and goddesses themselves and had to sense from within themselves how they were related to these divine presences.

Pagans were deathly afraid of the gods and goddesses. And with good reason. These divinities were unpredictable, dangerous, capricious, and sometimes vengeful, and they often made war on each other at human expense. By contrast, we are unafraid of the sacred today. More than that, we feel that the sacred will be pleased to have us, will spread out the welcome mat, so to speak, and will be grateful for our attention.

The second new element is our consumer mentality. As consumers we expect to get what we want immediately, without waiting, on our own terms, and with the right of return. That is the mind-set that now invades this new spiritual quest, as it does also many of our churches. This is quite different from the uncertain, quaking, or fanatical demeanor of ancient pagans.

Today we come confidently seeking, assuming an instant welcome, an immediate access when we have time for this in the midst of our busy lives. We are in the market for some spiritual dimension to complete our selves, some solace to fill what has been lost somewhere along the road to modernity. We expect access to the sacred without cost, without thought, without pain, without waiting. We have learned this in the malls. After all, this is our right. It is also our right to walk away from our experience of the divine if we are not satisfied. And many of us do. To see this at work we need not look for strange cults or covens. It is there among our most ordinary neighbors. It is going on at the next desk over on the office floor, in break rooms, in meditation rooms, and on the way home in the car.

And it is going on in the garden-variety evangelical church of a seeker-sensitive or emergent kind. There you can see this very same consumer spirituality at work, completely unafraid, buying, matching product to need, at work in all these ways. Instant access! An experience to be sized up. Help when we want it, but on our terms.

Here is this earthy spirituality trying to move up to God. Here is the projection of the human spirit into eternity, trying to immortalize itself. And here the sacred is loved for what the spiritual seeker gets in return. What people want is their needs satisfied. Satisfaction is of a therapeutic kind, so it varies from person to person. Some feel abandoned and need comfort. Some feel lost and need to find direction. Some feel empty and need to feel filled. Some are unsatisfied, even with the surfeit of our affluence, and need to taste something from another world.

But what always happens in every form of spirituality from below is that the seeker ends up controlling what is sought. We the seekers come to determine when we will seek, what we will seek, and when we will declare ourselves satisfied. Soon we fall into the habit of thinking, since we receive no rebukes, that the sacred is there simply for our satisfaction and for our use. We use the sacred when we want, just as we do any of the other consumer goods we buy.

The Christian doctrines of creation and sin set this right. What is created is finite and dependent. The one who created it all is sovereign, self-sufficient, and independent. He is the one who makes himself known. It is not we who find him, and we especially do not find him in ourselves. This is the old habit that has surfaced throughout history. It is a pagan habit based on pantheistic assumptions, that the sacred can be found by searching the self, the psyche.

Here are the spiritual life-and-death distinctions. Across the ages the church has framed them by establishing some basic categories: natural and supernatural revelation (this is Protestant language) and nature and grace (which is more typically Catholic). The point about both distinctions is that, against the assumptions of this ancient and now contemporary spirituality, there is no *natural* access to God in a saving way. Protestants and Catholics have other differences, and differences in exactly how they articulate these distinctions, but on the main point they are in agreement.

189

Natural revelation — what is disclosed about the existence of God (Ps. 19:1-6; Acts 14:17) and his moral nature (Rom. 2:14-15) — is a disclosure that is general. It is made to all. It is a revelation that all people not only receive but that renders them "without excuse" (Rom. 1:20). It is made, then, to us as *humans*. But it is not a saving revelation.

The revelation that leads to salvation is different. It is supernaturally given, given in the fabric of space and time in God's redemptive acts in Israel's history (e.g., Pss. 78; 80; 114; Acts 7:1-53). We have the inspired account of these acts and their meaning given to us in Scripture. We know that these acts were summed up and consummated in the life, death, and resurrection of Christ. All of this constitutes a revelation made to *sinners*.

The point I am making is quite offensive to us today. It is that God hides himself from us, that he cannot be had on our terms, and that he cannot be accessed from "below" through natural revelation. In the malls, and in much of life, we encounter nothing like this. We expect access. We expect to be able to get what we want, when we want it, and on our terms. Here this is not the case. Here we have to be admitted to God's presence, on his terms, in his way . . . or not at all. We cannot simply walk into his presence. Here nature does not itself yield grace. God's grace comes from the outside, not the inside, from above and not from within. It is not natural to fallen human life. We enter the presence of God as those who have been estranged, not as those who have been in continuity with the sacred simply because we are human. We are *brought* into a saving relationship through Christ; we do not put this together from within ourselves.

To speak of these contrasting approaches to spirituality, the one reaching down and the other feebly trying to reach up (or in), is simply to state that there is a boundary between God and human beings. This boundary is not self-evident at all. If it were, there would be no shadow culture of spirituality in America today. In fact, without God's revelation we do not know that God is hidden from us and that we are blind, as Karl Barth has rightly observed.

This new spirituality, in sum, assumes that all natural revelation is supernatural and that all nature is graced. What it assumes is what Scripture resolutely, insistently, and in every instance denies.

SIN

Why are we at such odds with the way Scripture sees things? The answer, of course, is that we are sinners and, apparently, are unaware of this fact. Americans, as we have seen, do not believe in original sin.

Sin, we need to understand, has reality-defining capacities. Defining reality, though, is a *divine* prerogative, not one that has been passed off to us. The first temptation was a temptation to be "like God, knowing good and evil" (Gen. 3:5). Presumably, Adam and Eve were lured by the thought that, like God, they could be in close and intimate contact with evil and remain unpolluted by it. That was a lie. The experimentation with evil, the defiance of what God had said, led to their internal corruption and then to their banishment. Angels with flaming swords barred their reentry.

We have no such difficulty. The angels have gone. And so has that older, moral universe whose fabric reflected the character of God. We have abandoned that universe and are now in the business of redefining what is real and what is ultimate. In this sense sin is both self-deifying, since only God can define reality, and blinding, because we no longer see things as they actually are nor understand what we are doing. To the self-defined who inhabit a world with no absolutes, sin has disappeared. There is therefore no earthly reason, if I may put it this way, why I should not gain access to the sacred on my own terms, in my own time, in my own way, for my own benefit.

SPEAKING

The differences between the two types of spirituality come into focus further when we talk about speaking. In the earthly kind of spirituality, *we* speak because there is no one who speaks to us. We receive no address. We have no Word from beyond ourselves. Unlike the earlier paganisms, there is no one who hears us. It is an impersonal, empty universe that we inhabit.

In the biblical spirituality, there is address. We are summoned by the Word of God. We stand before the God of that Word. *He* speaks. If this introduces the solemn note of accountability, it also introduces the grounds of hope. We have not been abandoned as orphans on the streets of a vast, inhospitable, and dangerous city. We are not adrift upon an infinite ocean. We are in fact spoken to, confronted, called to account not by ourselves but by God, from his Word. He draws near through his Word, whose speech is his own. Through the hearing of his law and the believing of his promise he lifts the fallen, instructs the bewildered, fills the hungry, and dispenses the sweet fragrance of his grace through Christ.

That is where we need to go next, to this other kind of spirituality that is so very different from that which is from "below."

From Above

It was Luther who noted, rather strikingly, that the basis of our fellowship with God is not holiness but sin. This spirituality from "above" comes to us from a completely different universe than that inhabited by the spiritualities from "below." It starts with the premise of the utter, incomparable holiness of God; we, in our spiritualities, start with our own self-perceptions and our own acceptability to the sacred.

These are entirely different starting points with two visions of life that are starkly, relentlessly, and irreconcilably different. It takes a major effort to wrench ourselves free from the world we inhabit so comfortably, and so commonly, to enter the world God inhabits. It is hard to do this. However, let us try!

One way to do this is to think about the two contexts in which "above" is used in relation to Christ. He who was "above" was sent on a mission, was incarnate, and in his death confronted sin, death, and the devil at the cross, conquered them, was raised from the dead, and now reigns from "above." He journeyed from a place where he was "above," through the valley of human life, humiliation, and conflict, and back to the same place from which he departed and where he is now "above," crowned with glory and honor.

I want to think about what has changed between when Christ was "above" but had not been incarnate and now, after his ascension, when he is once again "above." This is the journey in which the love, grace, and wrath of God are all fully defined and define for us what spirituality is actually about. Let us work out the beginning and end points, the descent and ascent of Christ, as Scripture lays these out for us.

Above but Incarnate

CHRIST'S DESCENT

The New Testament writers all have their own style, their own ways of arguing, their own perspectives. That does not mean for a second, though, that we have multiple theologies in competition with one another. That is what postmoderns yearn to think is the case because of their penchant for relativism. They embrace multiple perspectives on everything. No one perspective is definitive.

But God has not allowed for that in the Scriptures. Such a disappointment! What we have, instead, is complementary angles. Those who have a mind to do so are able to piece together, into a single, coherent whole, these different angles on Christ.

The author who makes the sharpest use of the above/below contrast is John, correlating it with his glory/flesh distinction. Jesus said he was from "above" (John 3:31; cf. 6:33), where he had preexisted (8:42, 58; 17:8). That is, he existed before there was a creation. He existed apart from this world. In his incarnation, what was eternal came into time. He who had shared in all the glory of the Godhead became enfleshed. He left God's presence (6:62; 8:38; 10:36) and descended (6:38). Forty-two times in the Gospel we read that he was "sent" from this realm of glory by God and came into this world of sin (e.g., 8:42; 10:36; 13:3; 16:27-28; 17:8).

Thus it was that the Son, who came to reveal the Father, was the same Son as the one from whom the creation itself had arisen (1:3). It is true that his human flesh veiled the brightness of his divine glory, but it would be a grave mistake to imagine that the Son enfleshed was other than what the fully divine Son had been. To see the Son is to see the Father (14:9), for the Father is in the Son and the Son is in the Father (10:38; 14:10) and they are one (10:30). Because of who he was, because his godness was undiminished, he naturally assumed the divine functions of judging, giving eternal life, giving commandments, and answering prayer (5:22, 24, 40; 14:14; 15:17).

All of this is John's way of setting out the essential truth about the identity of Christ. But he is not alone in this. Paul, in Philippians 2:5-11, comes close to reiterating John's above/below language.

Despite some inventive new exegesis, it is probably still best to see Paul's language of "form" — "though he was in the form of God" (Phil. 2:6) — as meaning the essential characteristics of a thing, its very essence. In this passage Paul asserts that he who was of the very essence and nature of God took on the very nature and essence of a servant. This transition required that he "empty" himself.

Of what did he empty himself, the church has asked across the ages? His divine attributes? It is probably best to answer this question not with what precedes this statement — "the form of God" — but with what follows it. Christ assumed "the form of a servant." To be true to that role, he limited and qualified the ways in which his godness could show. That, I believe, is the answer to this question. Far from reducing or minimizing the Son's deity, Paul brings us to a deeper understanding of it. Christ was not only God in human flesh, but what we see is the God of self-effacing, self-giving, self-sacrificing love. Here is agape love incarnate. Christ in his person thus gives us the unique exegesis of the character of God within the limits of a full and authentic humanity. And he does so in such a way that to see him is to see the Father. Once and for all Christ by whom all reality was made, and in whom all things subsist, stripped away the insignia of his majesty and allowed his glory to be muted by our flesh. In him the triumphant messianic age arrived. In him the "age to come" dawned. Only God could establish this age, and only in Christ was it established. In him we are face-to-face with God, and before him we are in the presence of eternity.

AN AGE DAWNS

The Bible gives us several different angles on this. It speaks, for example, of the inbreaking into this world of another "age." This strikes modern ears as strange, for we think of ages in terms of what we know. When we think about our present time, we divide it by decades, speaking of the Roaring Twenties, or the Rebellious Sixties, or the Greedy Eighties. Or we divide it generationally, into the postwar builders, the boomers, the Gen Xers, and the millennials. But however we do it, we are thinking about the ordinary course of life, the life we see, experience, and know, its events, its clock time, its conflicts, its evening news, its aspirations, its products and opportunities.

The Bible speaks a different language about this. It speaks of another kind of reality, a supernatural reality, one not limited by the constraints of human life, one that goes on forever, and one that is actually penetrating human life as we know it. It is called the "last days," and it comes from "above."

Paul tells us that God sent his Son "when the fullness of time had come" (Gal. 4:4) and that he made known his plan in Christ in "the fullness of time" (Eph. 1:10). We would be quite mistaken to suppose that all he meant was that the incarnation had happened at a propitious moment. In Ephesians, his thought is that the redemptive-historical work that God had been doing reached its end in Christ. This coincides with the fact, as he puts it in Galatians, that this present age ended. He clearly does not mean that clocks suddenly stopped, but that with Christ the old order died.

This present age is dead? That is not our perspective! We are fully caught up with life's buzz. It all seems very much alive to us!

We are encountering here a distinction that goes to the heart of the Christian message. It is the distinction between what comes from above and what comes from below. What comes from below, including all our new spiritualities, is dead. But not only our spiritualities come from "below." There is not a self-help program on the market today that is not, in some way, utilizing the knowledge, resources, techniques, products, and tools of this present "age" to transform lives. But what they are using comes out of an age that is spiritually dead and can only continue to impart death. Our world is filled with offers of help and of hope, of meaning and of fulfillment, and even of surrogate regeneration, but they all come from a world that is spiritually dead and therefore ultimately worthless. That is an extraordinary, a breathtakingly radical, position to take. The New Testament takes it unapologetically.

This new age began its final act of invasion with the birth of Christ. There was, under the Holy Spirit's leading, an acute sense at that time that the old period was coming to a close and the "last days" were beginning, the days inaugurated from "above." In Hebrews the incarnation of the Son inaugurates the "last days" (Heb. 1:2-5). In the consummation of the ages, the Son put away sin (Heb. 9:26). As Paul put it, upon us "the end of the ages has come" (1 Cor. 10:11). And the deception, false teaching, and rebellion characteristic of the last days or the "end days" were already present in his time (1 Tim. 4:1; 2 Tim. 3:1).

This discussion had been heard in the many things Jesus said about the coming of the kingdom. The kingdom of God, in the Gospels, is never a realm. It is a rule. And it is the rule of *God*. The primary idea in this language is that God himself has begun to rule. It is present, but this reign still has to be concluded and consummated at some point in the future.

Let us not miss an important point here. It is that this reign, this rule, is something *God* is doing. The reason, clearly, is that this is not something that emerges from "below," which we ourselves can get going. It must come from "above." We cannot bring it about; only God can.

We can search for the kingdom of God, pray for it, and look for it, for example, but only God can bring it about (Luke 12:31; 23:51; Matt. 6:10, 33). The kingdom is God's to give and to take away. It is ours only to enter and accept (Matt. 21:43; Luke 12:32). We can inherit it, possess it, or refuse to enter it, but it is not ours to build and we can never destroy it (Matt. 25:34; Luke 10:11). We can work for the kingdom, but we can never act upon it. We can preach it, but it is God's to establish (Matt. 10:7; Luke 10:9; 12:32).

God's inbreaking, saving, vanquishing rule is his from first to last. It has no human analogues, no duplicates, no parallels, and no surrogates. It allows of no human synergism. The inbreaking of the "age to come" into our world is accomplished by God *alone*. This is all about the spirituality that is from "above" and not at all about that which is from "below." It is about God reaching down in grace and doing for sinners what they cannot do for themselves. For if this is *God's* kingdom, his rule, the sphere of his sovereignty, then it is not for us to take or to establish. We receive, we do not take; we enter, but we do not seize. We come as subjects in his kingdom, not as sovereigns in our own.

In John's Gospel the intrusion of the "age to come," this inbreaking of God's sovereign, saving, and judging rule through Jesus, is expressed in the language of "eternal life." Jesus is this "life" (11:25; 14:6) that was eternally with the Father but has now been historically manifested (1 John 1:1-3). Jesus' words are the very words of God (John 3:34; 8:14; 14:10), and so they bring "life" (5:24; 6:68; 8:51). Eternal life is something that has already been given to believers (10:28; 17:2-3). It does not await the final unfolding of events at the end of time. This eternal life is a present reality, received by believing in Jesus (3:36; 6:47, 54). And judgment, even though a future reality, nevertheless for believers was brought into time. For the believer the judgment has already passed (3:18), and already he or she has been resurrected (5:24; cf. 11:23-26), even though a bodily resurrection will occur later. The one is an anticipation, a down payment, of the other.

In Paul the present age is characterized by sinful rebellion against God, and that is why it is dead. The age to come is that in which Christ reigns, and this is an age of life. However, this reign has already begun redemptively in the regenerate, those for whom Christ is their head. We hear this distinction between the ages quite clearly in Paul's prayer that Christ might be seen in his exaltation "far above all rule and authority and power and dominion, and above every name that is named, not only in this age but also in the one to come" (Eph. 1:21; cf. 1 Cor. 1:20; 2:6-8; 3:18; 2 Cor. 4:4; Gal. 1:4; Eph. 2:2; 1 Tim. 6:17; Titus 2:12). This present age belongs to Satan, "the god of this world" (2 Cor. 4:4), but for the believer this age or world has passed and its so-called wisdom has been exposed by Christ (1 Cor. 1:20). May we say that what has been exposed includes how we are today thinking, in this postmodern world, about how to be spiritual?

For Paul, to believe on Christ is the same as entering the kingdom in the Synoptic Gospels. It is to become a part of the age to come. And whether in the starlit firmament of this vast universe now, or within human consciousness, or in the world to come, anticipations of which we already have, Jesus has "supremacy." So Paul declares in Colossians 1:15-20.

Above and Reigning

The incarnation was for the atonement. The atonement was about Christ's conquest over sin, death, and the devil so that the whole of life might be cleansed and restored, that Christ's reign might be established, uncontested, and unobstructed. We are not there yet but are moving toward this great moment. He came from "above" in order that he might rule from "above" redemptively as well as sovereignly. It is the second half of this movement that we now need to trace.

There could be no such rule, no such conquest, unless Christ first bore our sin, in our place, and in that act bore the penalty of our sin and overcame the powers of evil behind it. From the time of the Reformation, justification by grace alone and received through faith alone has been considered the central, defining motif in this New Testament gospel. It was upon this doctrine, Luther declared, that the church either stands or falls.

IN CHRIST ALONE

The doctrine of justification is interwoven in the New Testament with other motifs that together express the gospel. Paul, for example, associates reconciliation with justification when he says that "in Christ God was reconciling the world to himself, not counting their trespasses against them" (2 Cor. 5:19). He associates redemption with justification when he says we "are justified by his grace as a gift, through the redemption that is in Christ Jesus" (Rom. 3:24). Propitiation belongs alongside justification (Rom. 3:24-25). And justification is also the way in which the forces of evil have been routed. God not only "cancel[ed] the record of debt that stood against us with its legal demands" but also, in so doing, "disarmed the rulers and authorities and put them to open shame, by triumphing over them in him" (Col. 2:14-15). It is important to see that for Paul these doctrines are not loose threads unrelated to one another. They are woven into a single fabric of understanding.

New Testament passages about Christ's death can be put into two groups, those that are general and those that are explanatory. In the first category we have statements averring that it was "for many" that Christ gave his life (Mark 10:45), it was "for the sheep" (John 10:15), "for the ungodly" (Rom. 5:6-8), "for us" (1 Thess. 5:10), "for the unrighteous" (1 Pet. 3:18), and it was "for his friends" (John 15:13-14) that he came to die.

But these general statements are interpreted by more specific ones. Why, then, did he die on behalf of others? The answer is that he gave himself "for our sins" (Gal. 1:4; 1 Cor. 15:3), he "bore our sins" (1 Pet. 2:24), and because of his death we have "the forgiveness of our trespasses" (Eph. 1:7). He was "delivered up for our trespasses" (Rom. 4:25), he is the propitiation "for our sins" (1 John 2:2; 4:10), and we are now "justified by his blood" (Rom. 5:9). The logic is simple but inescapable. God forgives us because Christ died for us. God forgives us our sins because Christ bore their penalty in our place. His death in our place must, then, be counted as a death that was really ours, otherwise God in his holiness would not be satisfied.

These simple affirmations about Christ's penal substitution, which are at the heart of the doctrine of justification, are easy to ridicule because they are not tidy at a rational level. This transference of guilt from one person to another, which justification requires and legal systems typically do not allow, is only one of the issues in play in this doctrine. Alongside it is the fact that God's character includes aspects that, at a rational level, seem to be incompatible. He is, for example, simultaneously holy and loving, just and merciful, the God of salvation and the God of judgment. Also left unexplained by the apostles is what exactly the relation is between the punishment Christ bore in place of sinners and the suffering he endured. Was his suffering itself the punishment, or was it the indication of the punishment? If the suffering was the punishment, then the door is open, as Horace Bushnell saw, to thinking that any kind of suffering can dissolve the consequences of sin, that in every human tear there is the hint of a Calvary. If not, then what exactly was transpiring in the moments when Christ experienced such deathly God-forsakenness on the cross?

This raggedness has been exploited by those hostile to penal substitution. How can God be simultaneously loving and angry with the same person? How can he declare a sinner righteous when he knows perfectly well that he is not? How can God clear the guilty knowing how guilty they are? No human judge is permitted to let the guilty off scot-free. How can one person bear someone else's penalty when under every system of law people remain responsible for themselves? If the penalty for sin is eternal separation from God, how could Christ have been resurrected after only three days?

Paul, of course, was not unaware of the dilemma at the heart of justification. The dilemma is how God can remain just while justifying sinners (Rom. 3:26), but his doctrine does not require the kind of literal parallels to the human courtroom that defenders have sometimes looked for and attackers have often exploited. This language operates more like a metaphor in which there are some parallels but also some dissimilarities.

To say that a senator fought like a lion for the passage of some legislation, or was a lion in the fight for that legislation, suggests only parallels. Lions and senators are different in many ways, but in some particular ways they can act similarly.

We should not imagine, therefore, a literal courtroom with a literal prosecutor, judge, verdict, and sentence. The way human courts work has some parallels in the Pauline doctrine of justification, but they are not literal and exact. The parallels do hold at the point that this is a moral universe in which there is accountability. This accountability requires God's judgment since he is morally bound to uphold what is right. Rejecting the authority of God and his law therefore has unavoidable consequences. Punishment is inescapable. And once this punishment has been rendered, the law has been satisfied.

It is impossible to understand Paul's doctrine of penal substitution without placing it in the center of the matrix of God's character. God is simultaneously the God of love and of wrath — the one side cannot be surrendered to the other — and in his wrath he judges justly and in his love he himself bears the penalty of his judgment. Paul picks up this theme early on in Romans where he introduces the reader to the "righteousness of God" (Rom. 1:17; 3:21-26). This much-debated phrase, which opened up the gospel for Luther, speaks of this righteousness as God's saving intervention made known in "the gospel" and "apart from law." It is therefore what constitutes a person's standing before God. It reveals God as being right in condemning sinners and in fulfilling his promises to provide salvation. The primary reference is not to his righteous character, although his righteous character is revealed in his actions of both judging and saving (cf. Judg. 5:11; 1 Sam. 12:7; Ps. 103:6; Dan. 9:16). These acts bring Israel salvation and her enemies judgment (Isa. 45:8, 23-24; 51:6, 8; Pss. 71:19; 96:13; 98:9).

When Paul adapts this language, he does so in the interests of declaring that outside of Christ God is really angry with sinners, alienated from them by their sin, irreconcilably opposed to them in their sin. Inside of Christ, the love of God is seen and known in all the richness of its splendor and believers are covered in that righteousness in which alone they can stand before him. God is the God of wrath and love, judgment and mercy, and each of these is simply another facet of his holiness.

However, I believe that it would be more felicitous to say that Christ took upon himself the penalty of our sin than to say that he was punished for sin. His work on the cross was one in which Father and Son were united in the common task of saving lost sinners, and what Christ bore he bore without any sense of personal desert (2 Cor. 5:21). He willingly bowed under the weight of a judgment whose justness he accepted. From eternity he had purposed to accept this judgment in our place. And thus it is that at the cross, God's triumphant and changeless grace is exhibited in space and time, his holiness is revealed through the necessity of the cross, and in that revelation is also seen the sinfulness of sin. This revelation, as well as that of God's holiness, shows us the length, breadth, and height of his love. Christ did not simply establish in his atonement the possibility or the hope of redemption from the righteous wrath of God. He accomplished that redemption.

Thus it is that God takes action in Christ against sin, death, and the devil. The doctrine of justification is not about the workings of impersonal law in the universe, or about manipulating its outcomes, but it is about God. The moral law is simply the reflection of the character of God, and when God acts to address the outcomes of the broken moral law, he addresses these *himself,* himself taking the burden of his own wrath, himself absorbing in the person of Christ the judgment his righteous character cannot but demand, himself providing what no sinner can give, himself absorbing the punishment no sinner can bear and live.

The mechanism of this in Paul is the imputation of sin to Christ and of his righteousness to the believer. Thus it is that Paul argued that Abraham was not accepted by God on the grounds of what he had done, for then that acceptance would have been earned and expected. The situation was quite the reverse. His acceptance was not earned but "credited" to him (Gen. 15:6; Rom. 4:3). This crediting or counting does have the feel of the accountant's ledger. It is in this sense that Paul told Philemon that if his runaway slave "has wronged you at all, or owes you anything, *charge that to my account*" (Philem. 18, italics mine; cf. Rom. 5:13). It is the penalty of sin that is charged to Christ's account, and so God "[reckons] righteousness apart from works" (Rom. 4:6; cf. Phil. 3:8-9) to those who receive it by faith. The righteousness we cannot provide for ourselves is provided by God through Christ on the basis of which we are declared to be free of the law's penalty and free to stand in his presence without condemnation.

This, however, is not a matter of cold, impersonal bookkeeping. It is a matter of great, earthshaking, eschatological reality penetrating the routine circumstances of everyday life. The consequences reach far beyond our own individual experience. They reach into the wounded cosmos, and into the dark reaches of the universe where evil continues to live out its doomed existence. The reach of evil, in its most vital aspect, is now severed. Its domain, this age, is under sentence of death and has no future. The future, the age to come, is already known and is even now reaching into the present. In Christ eternity has been brought into time. In time, hope, which is the result of this spirituality from "above," reaches out and back into eternity.

The most widely reproduced image of Luther is Lucas Cranach's portrait. The painting itself hangs in the Uffizi Gallery in Florence. This gallery housed many of the treasures gathered by the Medici family. Today, they are arranged chronologically so that one begins with Roman sculptures and moves on to extraordinary medieval art from the life of the church, some of which used actual gold, and then on to the high Renaissance. This gives the viewer valuable perspective. In comparison to so much of the art one passes, Cranach's portrait stands almost alone in its stark simplicity. It is unadorned, unassuming, painted in muted tones, and it is straightforward.

Luther, of course, was a peasant and not a prelate. Nevertheless, in the simplicity and directness of that painting, Cranach also caught something that is at the heart of the gospel Luther struggled to recover. It is a gospel that stands over against all human efforts to substitute devotion, self-experience, or the church for its truths. Those truths have depths and complexities to them, but their essence can be communicated in simple, unadorned, straightforward, and direct ways.

DOES THIS PREACH?

So much has been made of the fact that in a video generation such as ours, images dominate the way people process reality rather than words. This, in fact, is part of the postmodern attack on modernity, that the centrality of words in our processes of knowing needs to be demolished and the deck thus cleared of the rationalism that dominated the period of modernity.

However, the use of reason and with it, language, was not itself the distinguishing mark of the Enlightenment. After all, we encounter the use of reason in remarkably developed and sophisticated ways in the early fathers, in Augustine, in medieval scholastics like Duns Scotus and Thomas Aquinas, and even in the Protestant Reformers, all long before it was taken captive by the narrow, humanistic agenda of the Enlightenment. Whatever merit there is in stressing that postmoderns place great premium on images, on imagination, on relationships, on being part of a community, none of these things can substitute for the fact that the church has to *proclaim* the truth about Christ, that it cannot do so without using words, that words are the tools for expressing our thoughts, and that our thoughts must correspond to the reality of what God has done in Christ.

The central and simple message of the New Testament is that the promised age to come has dawned, the promised victory over what has emptied life of meaning and filled it with confusion and dismay has been won. Postmoderns who have, in one way or another, pointed to the emptiness of life, the absence of meaning and of enduring, stable value structures, are astonishingly close to the truth, far closer in fact than many in the Enlightenment period who lived off fraudulent meaning. Were it not for the resurrection, Paul suggests, abandoning ourselves to a life of empty party-making and a fatalistic sense of doom would be quite logical. There is no hope in "this age." It lies under the judgment of God. It is all, despite its brilliance, now dying. It has no future. It can offer many pleasurable experiences, many momentary distractions, but it is doomed. It has no long-term future and can offer no meaning besides what it manufactures for the moment, which is as fleeting as the morning mist.

Meaning comes from God alone. In the person of Christ, the age to come, which alone will endure for all eternity, has arrived. It arrived in his person and was made redemptively present through his work on the cross. In that work, not only is the eternal present in time, but so is the judgment of the end of time now exhausted within time. For the people of God the "end time" judgment has already happened. Not only so, but the resurrection the Old Testament saw as coming when time had run its course is now the way in which the New Testament speaks of the "new creation." This present age is in the sunset of dissolution; the age to come is the dawn whose light bathes life, banishes its shadows, and illumines its meaning because this age is moving the people of God to that time when everything has become subject to Christ and he has rendered it all up to the Father (1 Cor. 15:20-28).

Does this preach? I believe it does. It connects with the deep things of God on the one end and our own shallow emptiness on the other. Is that not what Christianity has always been about?

CHRIST'S RULE NOW

And so it is that Christ has ascended and begun his rule. Christ has been elevated, Paul tells us, "far above all rule and authority and power and dominion, and above every name that is named, not only in this age but also in the one to come" (Eph. 1:21). Paul uses a rich vocabulary in describing the sweep of this conquest. Sometimes angels are the conquered, and sometimes powers, or rulers, or depth, or authorities, or creatures, or spiritual forces, or height, or depth, or things to come, or death is conquered (Rom. 8:38-39; 1 Cor. 2:6). Christ is at God's right hand now "with angels, authorities, and powers having been subjected to him," Peter adds (1 Pet. 3:22).

What is new in this picture is the understanding about how Christ is working out his sovereign rule now. What is new is that we see more clearly the eschatological dimension in it. While "all things" have been delivered to him by the Father (Matt. 11:27; John 3:35), and "all things" have been put under his feet (Eph. 1:22), and such is his power that he is able "to subject all things to himself" (Phil. 3:21) so that we can say unequivocally that Christ "is Lord of all" (Acts 10:36), yet this is a contested reign. Here again we find the "already" but "not yet."

Christ's rule is contested in the sense that while evil is even now under his sovereign rule, and even though its doom has been declared, and even though its back has already been broken at the cross, it has not yet been taken to the scaffold. The church, therefore, has to be wary as long as it is in this world. It cannot become triumphalistic. It must seek the protection of God's armor (Eph. 6:10-18), grace, and power. We have not yet come to the final moment of conquest when Christ "delivers the kingdom to God the Father after destroying every rule and every authority and power" (1 Cor. 15:24). Only then will all of created reality that has been fractured and broken by the intrusions of satanic disorder be eternally cleansed.

The authority over "all things" that Christ had at the beginning when he acted in creation (Col. 1:15-16) has been reasserted over this fallen world (Eph. 1:9-10). Because of this, he who "descended is the one who also ascended far above all the heavens, that he might fill all things" (Eph. 4:10).

And yet this sovereign reign is, in important ways, concealed, just as Christ's preexistent glory was during his earthly days. Of the fact of this rule there should be no doubt, but exactly how Christ is exercising it is most often lost on us. Undoubtedly we have clear evidence of it in sinners who turn from their self-absorption, their privately created reality, to trust in him alone, to see their sin as having been made his at the cross and his righteousness theirs, received by faith alone. Anytime that happens, Christ's rule has taken root!

But beyond this we are often in the dark. None of the visible trappings of regal power are being displayed, as they are by earthly rulers, kings, presidents, and prime ministers. His is a reign that we apprehend by faith and not by sight. We see the tangible results of the hidden work of the Holy Spirit. We know it is his work to apply what Christ secured on Calvary. We see the results but have no explanation for how he has worked. The Holy Spirit is like a wind that "blows where it wishes, and you hear its sound, but you do not know where it comes from or where it goes" (John 3:8). Nor are we told how he works in world affairs, in the events and course of history. These matters belong to the mysteries of God's providence, and unless we are sent a prophet to interpret this work, we are wise to conclude that we have not been made privy to what God has been doing.

Christ's sovereign rule is hidden in this interim period between the "already" and the "not yet" until that time when "every knee should bow, in heaven and on earth and under the earth, and every tongue confess that Jesus Christ is Lord, to the glory of God the Father" (Phil. 2:10-11). The mystery of iniquity is at work in the world during this interim time, and it is not always clear how its malignant work is being checked, overridden, or woven into the glorious purposes of God. We need to remember, though, that while Judas betrayed Christ, and woe to him for doing so, it was by God's plan that Christ was thus betrayed. Evil by its very nature opposes the purposes of God, but God, in his sovereignty, can make even this evil serve his purposes.

How modest we need to be in using a word like "theodicy"! For the judgment that has befallen us, we who live east of Eden, is that we have been exiled. Our reconciliation has overcome our broken relationship with the Father, but it has not conferred on us vast powers of understanding into his governance of the world! From us as sinners God has hidden himself, and his ways are ultimately known only by himself. God alone knows himself in the depths of his being. What we know is only what he has chosen to make known to us, and he has not chosen to make known much of his dealing with evil in the world or exactly how his purposes are ripening in the church that now seems so battered.

Christian hope is not about wishing things will get better. It is not about hoping that emptiness will go away, meaning return, and life will be stripped of its uncertainties, aches, and anxieties. Nor does it have anything to do with techniques for improving fallen human life, be those therapeutic, spiritual, or even religious. Hope has to do with the knowledge of "the age to come." This redemption is already penetrating "this age." The sin, death, and meaninglessness of the one age are being transformed by the righteousness, life, and meaning of the other. What has emptied out life, what has scarred and blackened it, is being displaced by what is rejuvenating and transforming it. More than that, hope is hope because it knows it has become part of a realm, a kingdom, that endures. It knows that evil is doomed, that it will be banished. This kind of hope has left behind it the ship of "this age," which is sinking. And if this other realm, this place where Christ is even now ruling, did not exist, Christians would be "of all people most to be pitied" (1 Cor. 15:19). Their hope would be groundless and they would have lived out an illusion (cf. Ps. 73:4-14).

Vast, mysterious, and mostly unknown as the universe is, we are neither aliens nor strangers in it. It is our alienation from God that makes us see the world as if we were aliens. It is our estrangement from him that leaves us with this haunting sense that we are alone, strangers in a cold and indifferent universe. So it is that life comes to seem like only a "chance collocation of atoms" destined to disappear beneath the rubble of a universe in ruins, as Bertrand Russell put it. It can all seem so meaningless, so ephemeral, so pointless. And it is meaningless, a vanity of vanities, until we see that fallen life yields up no meaning higher or deeper than its own fallenness. And that is only as high as the spirituality from below can ever ascend.

The only future there actually is, is the one established by God in Christ, the one wrought in time at the cross that alone reached into eternity. But we must receive entry into this future. We cannot seize it. It is not there to be had on our own terms. This is not our self-constructed future. It is *God's*. It comes from above, not from below.

This is why those churches that have banished pulpits or are "getting beyond" the truth question are going beyond Christianity itself. The proclamation of the New Testament is about *truth*, about the truth that Christ who was with the Father from all eternity entered our own time. As such he lived within it, his life, like ours, marked by days and weeks and years. He lived in virtue of his unity with the Father, living for him, living as the representative of his own people before the Father, his very words becoming the means of divine judgment and of divine grace. But in the cross and resurrection the entire spiritual order was upended, his victory reached into and across the universe, and saving grace is now personalized in him. The world with all its pleasures, power, and comforts is fading away. The pall of divine judgment hangs over it. A new order has arisen in Christ. Only in this new order can be found meaning, hope, and acceptance with God. It was truth, not private spirituality, that apostolic Christianity was about. It was Christ, not the self, who offered access into the sacred. It was Christ, with all his painful demands of obedience, not comfortable country clubs, that early Christianity was about. What God had done in space and time when the world was stood on its head was Christianity's preoccupation, not the multiplication of programs, strobe lights, and slick drama. Images we may want, entertainment we may desire, but it is the proclamation of Christ crucified and risen that is the church's truth to tell.

CHAPTER VII

Church

"Yet even now," declares the LORD, "return to me with all your
heart, with fasting, with weeping, and with mourning; and
rend your hearts and not your garments." Return to the LORD
your God, for he is gracious and merciful, slow to anger, and
abounding in steadfast love; and he relents over disaster.

JOEL 2:12-13

What someone thinks about the church tells us exactly what
that person is thinking about Christianity. There is, of
course, much more to Christianity than simply our experience in the church. Christian faith is about much, much more than
what happens on the weekend.

Nevertheless, what happens in churches speaks volumes about
the kind of Christian understanding that is at work. It tells us how people are thinking about God, how they are relating themselves to the
truth of his Word, how they see the world, how they think about human
corruption — or if they think about it at all — how they think about the
gospel, how they think about the poor and dispossessed, their own
generation, affluence, and many other things besides.

It was when the historic Protestant perspective on these matters
began to slip away in the 1970s in America that the impulse to "do

church" differently started to surge. It surged first among the seeker-sensitives, and now it is surging among the emergents. That the slow disintegration of core Protestant beliefs was followed by these new experiments in church-doing was not accidental. The one followed the other as predictably as night following day.

These issues go to the heart of evangelical faith. Indeed, they go to the heart of the question whether evangelical faith is going to survive in the West. I began, when I first raised this question, by suggesting that evangelicalism had two flaws that have been there from the beginning in its post–World War II phase.

The first flaw is that evangelicalism has an inclination to allow its biblical core to shrink. In parts of the evangelical world today, it has shrunk so much that virtually nothing remains. This was so initially because evangelicalism has been a populist movement that owes much of its temper to democratic impulses. When it also became a marketing phenomenon, further emptying-out happened.

Second, and alongside this, evangelicalism's inherently *para* nature asserted itself so that it increasingly became parachurch to the point where the local church, in biblical terms, became increasingly irrelevant. Once these things began to happen, I believe, evangelicalism was on its way to decline.

I now need to explore these inherent weaknesses a little further. After that I will frame what has happened in the light of historic Protestant thinking. I will then return to what is also a part of historic Protestant reflection, and that is to consider how we should judge the church's authenticity. Finally, I am going to return, one more time, to the issue that is central to all these changes.

Trouble in the House

Middling Standards

The postwar resurgence of evangelical believing in the West gained a great deal of strength from the fact that its many churches and organizations could work together around commonly held beliefs. Centrally, these were the authority of Scripture and the necessity of the cross. The core was narrow, in the sense that diversity of belief around it was allowed, but it was deep. With the passing of the years, however, the core began to disintegrate and, certainly, has been losing its depth. It has now become very shallow. Why is this?

There are no doubt many reasons, but I can focus only on one or two here. What I have been describing is a tendency to which all mass movements are prone. American evangelicalism is a mass movement, and being in America, it has reflected the deep democratic impulses at the heart of American life.

Alexis de Tocqueville noticed this when he visited America in the nineteenth century. What he described then is still with us today. The tendency is toward the average in American society, he observed, the "middling standard." That was the tendency because it was the standard most could attain.

It is remarkable to think about the many ways today in which this democratic impulse toward the "middling standard" is realized throughout society and not simply in that part of it that is self-consciously evangelical. This tendency is evident wherever democratic capitalism has taken root.

Never have the poor and the rich in Western societies, for example, lived more like one another than they do today. They dress alike, eat the same packaged foods, go to the same entertainments, watch the same television programs, drive on the same highways, and do so in cars that increasingly look alike. We who live in suburbs live in houses that look quite alike, we buy clothes that are similar in style and quality, and have expectations about life and affluence that are very similar. We are all part of the same democratic systems and believe in the same kinds of equality. Modernized societies, in fact, tend to produce the same mass expectations. They are carbon-copy expectations generated by the same context, the same experiences, the same marketing, and the same sights. They tend to settle on the same simple, common denominators when people are thinking about life. The result is that we are prone to thinking alike.

Modernized societies, therefore, tend to create the same kind of experience. It is one that has neither height nor depth. It is a kind of homogenized experience in which the average is exalted. This is both the blessing and the curse of modernized societies. It is a blessing because they include so many in their abundance who were once excluded from having wealth, opportunity, and choice. It is a curse because the life of our highly commercialized cultures tends toward a homogenized, flat, and common sameness in the way we think and what we want.

This is certainly evident in the evangelical church. A strong undertow, a current beneath the surface, pulls it toward ways of thinking and living that are minimalistic, gray, and average, the lowest common denominator, something very much on a par with what is served up daily on commercial television.

In the church the same two sides to this are evident. The good side is that evangelicals have taken to heart the biblical imperative to take the gospel to the whole world. Christianity is not just for the privileged, the wealthy, the well educated, those higher in the social hierarchy, or those in the West. The gospel is for all. This evangelistic impulse has been responsible for innumerable gospel meetings, crusades, organizations, church plants, and missionary endeavors.

The bad side is that this outreach has coalesced with the deep egalitarian currents that have flowed through the American psyche, at least since the Revolution. These have tended to produce an understanding of Christianity that is accessible to all but tends to lose its depth and profundity in the process.

Since the war, evangelicals have focused on the thought that the gospel was so simple even the simplest could understand it, and therefore evangelical churches must keep low thresholds so that all can find their way in.

Of course, this principle has not always been practiced as well as it should have been. Exclusions along racial lines did happen. Nor has this bad habit been fully conquered. To these earlier racial exclusions are now being added generational exclusions. One seeker-sensitive church in the Midwest advertises itself as being "not your grandmother's church." If some churches are going to turn their backs on older generations, why should they not also turn their backs on those who are not middle-classed and well-heeled? And they have. This principle is sometimes honored as much in its breach as in its practice.

In gearing church life around this principle, evangelicals have taken up the gospel's *simplicity* and, because they affirmed that, have felt that they could walk away from its *profundity*. In its biblical setting,

212

though, the gospel does not give us a choice between its simplicity and its profundity. It is both. It is both so simple that everyone can understand it and so profound that none can fully plumb its depths. It is this matchless combination of simplicity and profundity that has to be preserved if Christian faith in its biblical fullness is to be preserved. Those evangelicals who took its simplicity and abandoned its profundity are now finding that Christian faith itself is beginning to crumble in their hands.

Be Appealing!

This tendency to focus entirely on Christianity's simplicity, which is so natural to a modernized and democratic society, has now been deepened as the marketing impulse has taken hold of the churches. When this disposition toward the average married the marketing impulse — which it has throughout the American evangelical world — the average was first exalted and then emptied of substance by being simplified in what have turned out to be extreme ways. That is what marketing does. It flattens, simplifies, and converts everything into what is appealing. That is what it has done in the evangelical church. The gospel, understood as a product, loses its depth and cost. This happens so that its appeal and salability can be elevated, but along the way Christianity becomes flat, empty, and banal.

The result is a set of damaging triumphs: the triumph of appeal over depth, of technique over truth, and of consumption over cost. At the bottom of it all is the triumph of the seller over the product. The remnants of the gospel that can still be found, in the mercy of God, do bring people to Christ, but the churches that spring from these denuded and trivialized gospel messages tend to carry into their life the very same qualities with which they began. They seem to rise no higher than the emptied-out, shallow gospel messages they started with in this massive outreach of being sensitive to supposed seekers.

The local church should be a corrective to this. Why has it not been? Even if Christian faith starts out on shaky ground, why is it not becoming solidified? The answer is that the invisible and visible churches are now increasingly disengaged, so the corrective is no longer there. This is the other flaw that we see lying latent in evangelicalism in these postwar years.

Losing the Church

The original intent of making the distinction between the church visible and the church invisible was not to make what is visible unimportant. It was simply to recognize that there are likely to be tares among the wheat (Matt. 13:24-43), that in a local church, side by side, may be seated as supposed fellow Christians the regenerate and the unregenerate. Outward patterns of churchgoing, and of Christian profession, may not be telling the full story. Not all who are in the visible, local church are in the invisible and universal church. Because someone attends a church does not necessarily mean that person is in Christ. That was the intent of this distinction.

The result today, however, has often been an unhappy one. Evangelism has often become an enterprise separate from the life of the church. Indeed, among the marketers the separation is deliberate and visual. The services have been entirely emancipated from anything and everything "churchy." No pews, no crosses, no collections, no hymns, no pulpit, no sermon — nothing that will in any way lead an unbeliever into thinking that he or she has entered a church.

We need to be as generous as possible and say that this is the realization of evangelistic passion. It is nevertheless a grievous flaw. Its consequences are now stark, plain, unavoidable, and devastating. The gospel so preached has been separated from discipleship. The reason is quite simple. Marketers are looking for buyers. If disciples somehow also emerge, one has to say that it is an anomaly. It is buyers that are wanted. In droves. Instead of evangelism being the doorway to the life of discipleship, now the gospel enterprise stands alone and the church is left outside the door, rejected and despised. The invisible church becomes everything, and the visible church, in its local configuration, loses its significance and its place in Christian life.

Nowhere perhaps is this more evident today than in the "electronic church." There are literally millions of Americans who not only watch television preachers but for whom these preachers are their only engagement with the "church." Week by week they are "going" to church but are alone. Their "church" asks for no involvement except the financial one, provides no opportunity for service, assumes no responsibility for discipline, offers no sacraments, offers no pastoral care, and rarely provides any sustained teaching. This yields only a deeply privatized understanding of Christian faith. It is a situation rife with bad possibilities. Venal preachers have golden opportunities to exercise their venality, and many have. This is an embarrassing travesty of the New Testament teaching on the church.

The counterpart to this on the mission field is what Herbert Hoefner argued in his 1991 book *Churchless Christianity*. His argument seemed to lie dormant initially, but a decade or so later it came back to life like some dreadful specter that materializes out of nowhere. His argument seems now to be gaining momentum.

The book was an analysis of Christians living in India who remained within their Hindu communities, went to Hindu worship (but focused on Jesus), never made a public profession of faith, and never joined a local church. This paradigm was offered as a "magic bullet" to missionaries working in hostile religious contexts. Why should converts declare their faith by joining a church and thereby put themselves in jeopardy? Why can they not remain in their own religious settings as secret believers?

When Christianity becomes churchless, it is able to fly under the radar of hostile opposing religions and ideologies because it has become invisible. This offers the enormous boon of providing a way for people to be Christian and to avoid all the persecution that would otherwise come their way. They simply are unknown in their believing.

It is an ingenious proposal, but sadly it suffers from a defect: it violates the biblical norm. God's people should not neglect "to meet together, as is the habit of some, but encouraging one another" (Heb. 10:25). Indeed, it is striking to note that in many cases in the New Testament, God's blessing came, not simply in private moments, but when people were gathered together (e.g., Acts 2:1; 4:31; 10:44). They obviously met at their peril, but meet they did. And it was in their company that outsiders saw the reality of God's redemption at work.

Furthermore, if the local church is as dispensable and irrelevant as Hoefner suggests, why does Paul spend so much time talking about it and the qualities of its leaders, and setting up its structure and how it is to function? Let us be clear. Churchless Christianity has nothing to do with biblical Christianity and everything to do with pragmatic, methodological, and reductionistic thinking. It is very remote from the biblical teaching.

In this case from India, the argument is that the local church is needless. In America the argument is that the local church is a failure. The failure of the market-driven, seeker-sensitive churches to produce serious Christian life is what has produced Barna's despair about the local church.

However, does not the failure really lie in the marketing methodology? Certainly the gathering weakness in the born-again churches, where only 9 percent have even a minimal Christian worldview, and where lifestyle differences between the born again and secularists can no longer be discerned, does raise troubling questions. Why has Christ become so indistinguishable from culture? Why are supposed Christians not different from the world?

The American "can-do" spirit is inclined to see in this situation a challenge, one that can be overcome only by a frontal assault. The local church must be reorganized! It must be made more appealing! It must have Starbucks! It must lure people in to spend more time there! It must offer amenities, a food court, theater tickets, a travel office, and who knows what else? Preaching must go! The best videos must be run! Let's make it more like a country club!

It is, in other words, being considered like a business whose bottom line has become a bit shaky. What to do? Reorganize, thin the workforce, get new leadership, seek new markets, hire a new advertising agency, put a fresh face on it, and change the product!

That may work in the business world, but it is catastrophic when applied in the church world. The reason is that God is not subject to our manipulation, our systems, our organization, or our marketing. We cannot force the hand of God by reorganizing, hiring a new ad agency, honing our marketing skills, mimicking Disneyland, importing Las Vegas–type entertainers, building ever more splendiferous auditoria in which our celebrity-type preachers can perform. No, we need to think about this in an entirely different way. But which way?

My Critics

Some of my critics have said that my books have all been about this kind of diagnosis but that I have offered little prescription. It is all too negative, they say. There is not enough that is positive.

In a way my critics have a point. It is true that I have not offered practical solutions. I have not suggested a solution to the worship wars. Nor have I proposed a Sunday school curriculum, or ways to combat the self movement's effects in the churches. Nor have I offered solutions to the many other issues raised for the church by our highly modernized culture with its deeply postmodern ethos.

Why not? In part the answer is, I confess, that I have underestimated how remote a robust, biblical faith of a Protestant kind has actually become to many people today. I thought they would know what they had departed from and needed to return to. Memories, though, are obviously fading, or maybe the experience of this kind of belief, and its practice in the church, was never there in the first place. I miscalculated on this point. Knowing how postmodern culture impacts biblical faith, how it can unravel that faith or rearrange its priorities, or how it masks some things and magnifies others, or seduces biblical faith, or perverts it, is not the same thing, I acknowledge, as saying what we should do about it.

If there is an analogy here, perhaps it is in young people who bear the marks of the broken homes from which they come. At some point some of them come to faith. It is then that they begin to realize that the chaos that once passed for normal in their world, what they saw in their suburb or neighborhood, what they heard every day in school, was unacceptable to God. The problem, though, is that these young people have known nothing but broken homes, absentee fathers, live-in boyfriends or girlfriends, stepfathers and stepmothers, the drug culture, and all the complications of life in great disarray before the changed moral climate of the postmodern world. What, then, should a home look like? What does it mean to be in a Christian marriage, to be a Christian father or mother? There is little in their experience from which they can draw. That, I think, is the situation we face in the evangelical church today. We are increasingly remote from the practice of historic Christian believing. Many of us have little experience of a deep, robust, biblical kind of faith on which to draw in thinking about what the alternative to what we have today looks like.

Of course, it would be very desirable to have this kind of picture in mind, even if we have never been in such a church ourselves. Nevertheless, I remain convinced that recovering such a church is not a matter of technique, searching for some lost formula, rereading a forgotten confession, introducing an ancient litany in worship, or finding some business strategy. No twelve-step program will lead the church to its recovery. I continue to think such strategies for recovery may bring the church even lower if all they do is deepen our present love affair, as pragmatists, with technique. No, we need to think a little more deeply than this.

The Church's Two Sides

Let us begin by revisiting the distinction between the church visible and the church invisible. This was a distinction the Reformers saw in Scripture, so I want to think a little about the grounds for it. I then want to add a line of thought that is today more Lutheran than Reformed. It is the distinction between the church hidden and the church manifest.

Visible and Invisible

In discussing the first distinction, between the church visible and the church invisible, we will be asking whether more recent evangelicalism has understood this distinction correctly. For the second, between the church hidden and the church manifest, we will touch on the other evangelical weakness, its loss of profundity.

We begin with the first distinction. The word "church" is always used in the New Testament of people, never of buildings or bureaucratic structures. The church is made up of those believers who are gathered at a specific place for worship (e.g., 1 Cor. 11:18; 14:19, 28, 35) or those who normally gather for worship at a specific place but are scattered at the time of writing (e.g., Rom. 16:4; 1 Cor. 16:1; Gal. 1:2). This is the church visible, the church that can be seen locally as it worships and witnesses.

The word "church" is also used more generally of everyone, in all ages and places, in heaven or on earth, who belongs to Christ. The writer to the Hebrews spoke of coming to "the assembly [and church] of the firstborn who are enrolled in heaven" and to "the spirits of the righteous made perfect" (Heb. 12:23). Certainly Paul, in addition to thinking of the church as the local gathering of believers, also thought it encompassed all those, in all ages, who made up Christ's body (Eph. 1:22-23). It is through the whole church, in all ages, that God's wisdom is manifested (Eph. 3:10), and he is to be glorified in the whole church (3:21; cf. 5:23-25, 27, 32) now.

This twin usage of "church" early on, beginning with Augustine, led to the distinction between the church local and the church universal, with its parallel distinction between the church visible and the church invisible. This distinction is making a very important point, but it is also subject to serious abuse, abuse that is everywhere present today.

The important point, as I noted, is that those who belong to a church do not necessarily belong to Christ. At the time of the Reformation, this case was made against the Roman Catholics, who insisted that the only way one could belong to Christ was by belonging to the Catholic Church, submitting to its teaching, and receiving the grace available through its sacraments. To be in the church was to be in Christ. Furthermore, it was not possible to be in Christ except by being in the church, with a few very carefully guarded exceptions. Outside the church there is no salvation.

The Reformers countered that we come to be in Christ by *faith*. We are joined to Christ by faith alone, faith in his finished work on the cross whereby he took our sin, bore God's judgment in our place, and now clothes us in his righteousness. From first to last, God's acceptance of us is by his grace, and so, too, is our capacity to believe in what Christ has done for us. It is true that Luther muddied these waters by his doctrine of baptismal regeneration, but in deference to his otherwise magnificent achievements, let us chalk this up to some uncompleted thought on his part, for his understanding of justification was always thoroughly biblical and profound.

This is the line of thought that has come down into the evangelical world. The good side of it has been the insistence that we come into a saving knowledge of Christ only though believing the gospel. Church membership itself avails nothing. Nor do the sacraments. Nor does moral effort. Nor does self-realization. Nor does psychology. Nor do any twelve-step programs. Nor does any spirituality. Nor does anything else we think we might do to make ourselves more acceptable to God. The great strength of the evangelical world has been that it has run with this message. It has taken this gospel to the airwaves, onto television, into home Bible studies, and into evangelistic programs. Organizations for evangelism have been formed, tracts have been distributed, books have been written, sermons have been preached, crusades have been held, and converts have been made.

However, in practice this distinction has become quite injurious to Christian faith because it has been taken to mean that all we need be serious about is the gospel. The church has become an irrelevance or, at best, a luxury. It has become more of an optional extra, less of a necessity. And in fact, as evangelicalism has lost its seriousness, even as the gospel has lost its profundity, the local church has lost its capacity to serve as a corrective to this.

What Is Hidden

It is here, against these tendencies, that I find the distinction made by some Lutheran thinkers to be helpful. They have spoken of the difference between the church hidden and the church manifest. This puts a twist on the distinction between the church visible and the church invisible. It says there is a reality to the church's life that now is invisible but, in time, will become fully visible. They are thinking less of believers who have died and belong to the church universal and more of those who live now but in whose lives God's reign, the "age to come," has not been fully concluded. This reign is established only by God and only on God's terms. We march as those who know the City to which we move, but we march as those in whom God's reign is, at this time, incomplete. This is what is "hidden." We know it too little and the world sees it too little. Right now it is grasped only by faith, not by sight, and it cannot be forced by organization or technique.

There is a profound insight here. And it grows out of very familiar biblical teaching. We mentioned this teaching earlier in the book.

Christian life has about it a quality of the "already/not yet." We have been redeemed in full, inasmuch as nothing can be added to or taken away from what Christ did on the cross, but at the same time we are not yet fully redeemed. We know ourselves to be sinful even though we have been redeemed. We are, at one and the same time, justified and yet sinners. We are in Christ even though we are still bonded to our world by sight, sound, and appetite. We are utterly secure in him, but we are also prone to wander, prone to substitute our plans for God's, our ways for his, our thoughts for his. Not only so, but we also know ourselves to easily and naturally presume that God's will awaits our choices, that his plans are subject to ours, that we control what he does, that we control the church and he is dependent on us, that we are its leaders and he is just waiting for us to lead and devise ways to make us successful. Without us, it almost seems, his rule is rendered powerless.

The reality, however, is that God's kingdom is not a human business open to our control and manipulation. God hides himself from the eyes and the powers of "this age." There is a seeming wildness about him. He is uncontrollable. He is not obliged to our schemes, our leaders, our programs, or our marketing. To know him through Christ we must die, and in our death we give up not only any claim upon his mercy but also any belief that our plans, programs, and schemes can be ways of manipulating his grace. The gospel is a message of death before it is a message of life. It is a message we live in a world that is on death row. This world will remain there until faith in Christ's justifying work swings open the prison door. And when we walk through that door, trusting not in ourselves but in Christ alone, we enter another universe.

This new universe is not the same world we have just left. The one we now enter is one of eternal life, not death, of God's glory, not of sin. It operates by different rules because it is under different management. In our fallen world, we who are sinners have seized sovereignty and set up shop on our own terms — that we have the right to think what we want, live as we will, behave as our appetites dictate, and run our enterprises the way we want. We do our business in our own way. There is a logic to fallen life. Once we assume our own sovereignty in one area, we go on to seize it in every area.

These habits enter the churches. Is it not natural to think that what makes us successful in the fallen world of the marketplace will also make us successful in the church? If we can profit in the commercial world, we can surely "profit" in the church by the same techniques.

When we are reconciled to God through Christ, we should surrender all of this seized sovereignty. If we accept the gospel offer of forgiveness, it is that we might accept God's reign over and in us. That is what it means to repent and to believe. We repent of every exercise of our own sovereignty. We take hold of the promises of God in its place. It is then that we become these strangely amphibious creatures, tied into a world that is dying because of our fallenness and yet already part of a world that is not yet finally realized but is eternal. We have been redeemed in full, but we are not yet fully redeemed.

Forget Rethinking the Church

The result of all of this is that we do not need to be rethinking the visible church. Today, prodigious amounts of energy are being poured into this effort. Everything about the church must be rethought! We must rethink how it becomes successful! We must rethink it all because this is what businesses have to do! Their products are all the time dying as new niches and needs arise. So it is in the church! Rethink or die!

In my view, so much of this rethinking confuses rethinking the nature of the church with rethinking its performance. For the multitude of pragmatists who are leading churches in America today, these are one and the same thing. The church is nothing but its performance. There is nothing to be said about the church that cannot be reduced to how it is doing, and that is a matter for constant inventories, poll taking, daily calculations, and strategizing.

I beg to differ. These are two entirely different matters. We intrude into what is not our business when, in our earnest pursuit of success in the church, which we think we can manufacture, we confuse its performance with its nature. Let me explain.

The church is not our creation. It is not our business. We are not called upon to manage it. It is not there for us to advance our careers in it. It is not there for our own success. It is not a business. The church, in fact, was never our idea in the first place. No, it is not the church we need to rethink.

Rather, it is our thoughts about the church that need to be re-thought. It is the church's faithfulness that needs to be reexamined. It is its faithfulness to who it is in Christ, its faithfulness in living out its life in the world, that should be occupying us. The church, after all, is not under our management but under God's sovereign care, and what he sees as health is very often rather different from what we imagine its health to be.

The church, let us remember, is called the "church of God" (Gal. 1:13; 1 Cor. 15:9). Churches are "the churches of Christ" (Rom. 16:16) because they are his, bought by his precious blood. Christ not only constituted the church (Matt. 16:18), but God has given us the blueprint for its life in Scripture. What we need to do, then, first and foremost, is to think God's thoughts after him, think about the church in a way that replicates his thoughts about it. We need to ask ourselves how well, or how badly, we are realizing our life in Christ in the church, how far and how well churches stand as the outposts of the kingdom of God in our particular culture.

Distance and Impact

It follows from this that while the churches are identified with their own cultures, because they are filled with people from those cultures, they also should experience a jarring and internal distance from those cultures. Those in a church are unlike other people in their culture because they are hearing, in their church, a Word from outside this world. They are worshiping a God who, in his greatness and holiness, is completely unlike anything in fallen life. Those in the church are in this world, but the world should not be in those who are in church! They are not there to live on its terms, with its ways of doing business.

It is true that churches are also organizations. But it is not their organizational side that defines them. Organizations are everywhere in the Western world, and there is nothing unique about an organization. The church is utterly unlike any other organization in the world. In the church are those who belong to another world. At least that is sup-

THE COURAGE TO BE PROTESTANT

posed to be the case. Why is this? Because when it gathers, it is hearing a summons to stand before the God of all eternity, to worship in awe before him, to acknowledge his greatness, to humble itself, to learn to live in this world on *his* terms, and to do its business as *his*. It is in all these ways otherworldly.

Churches that want to influence their culture are so often tempted to think that to be effective they must hide their otherworldliness and become slickly this-worldly. They think they must identify with their culture as if they knew nothing but that culture. They imagine that their chief tool, if not their only tool, of influence is friendship with their world.

Churches that actually do influence the culture — here is the paradox — distance themselves from it in their internal life. They do not offer what can already be had on secular terms in the culture. They are an alternative to it. They stand outside of its life. They stand over against it in their preoccupations, because their preoccupations are with the God of their salvation who in his holiness and grace is completely unlike anything we find in life. In life we find preoccupations that are thoroughly this-worldly. The preoccupations we should find in the church arise from the knowledge of God in Christ and from his written Word. Because of this, they are necessarily "otherworldly."

This is what gives the church its character and message. This is what gives it a place to stand in the world, one not derived from the world. This is what sustains the church in its minority status. Indeed, in many countries today it is also a persecuted minority. The temptation the church always experiences is to be like the world. It is the temptation to enjoy the comfort of a majority, to be at home, to be at peace, to have no enemies. Is it not true that we all yearn for such an experience?

However, if the church is to be truly successful, it must be unlike anything else we find in life. As a result, it will undoubtedly make enemies. It will have enemies, even if they are merely voices in the culture whose intent is to secure ways of life that are antithetical to Christian faith. If the church ever becomes just like anything else we can find in life — as many born-again churches have become — then we can have it without God's truth or grace and without cost. Indeed, we can have it on our own terms.

The church, however, cannot be had on our terms, and to try to do so is to destroy both the church and its capacity to influence its world. To be successful it must reveal in what it says and does that it is not of this world precisely because it is the "church of God," born of his grace, and called to live out its life in accordance with his truth. And that is very different.

Where do we find the evidence of this? What does a church look like that has this character? How can we see that it knows that it is the enterprise of God and not a product of merely human engineering or interest?

The answer given at the time of the Reformation is that we can see this in the churches where the Word of God is preached, the sacraments are rightly administered, and discipline is applied. But these signs, or "marks," are not infallible. One can find churches that exhibit all three that are nevertheless moribund and lifeless and may have little impact upon their culture. These marks are not foolproof. However, they are helpful in pointing to the otherworldliness of the church that, in today's climate in the West, is fast being erased.

These three marks of the true church also do not make up a complete list. The church's invisible nature in Christ is manifest in many other ways. It is difficult to imagine, for example, how a church that is being true to itself as God's creation in Christ will not be one where all the fruit of the Spirit will be in evidence, flawed though we all are. There we will also see the desire to make the good news of that salvation known. We will see in practice God's compassion for the needy, the unjustly treated, and the displaced.

Nevertheless, these three marks do get at things that are indispensable in the life of the church. Therefore, I will use them as illustrations of the larger whole.

Marks of Authenticity

Word of God

SUFFICIENT

What the Reformation recovered can be seen in the earliest churches. It is the understanding that whatever is given to us by the inspiration of the Holy Spirit, whatever constitutes Holy Writ, is binding and authoritative. As such, it is the touchstone by which we measure ourselves and test every claim. It is the guide by which we learn to live before God in a way that is pleasing to him. Scripture *alone* is our authority.

The Reformers had to defend this position against the Roman Catholic Church, which was claiming for its own teaching a comparable authority. It saw Scripture and tradition as the two fountains from which the church received revelation. Its teaching authority, the magisterium, resolved how Scripture and tradition were to be made compatible with each other.

The effect of this, Luther said, was to place a "gag" over the mouth of Scripture. What he meant was that Scripture was free to deliver its truth only to the extent to which the church's teaching authority was in agreement with it. Where it was not, Scripture had to remain silent. This left the impression that the Catholic Church was under the authority of Scripture, but in fact, that authority had migrated to its teaching authority, the magisterium. The church, therefore, could no longer be reformed by the Word of God since it stood outside the reach of that authority in many aspects of its life. That was the force of this Reformation slogan. There were not multiple authorities but one, the written Word of God.

Many today marvel at this attempt by the Catholic Church to mute the full authority of God's Word by its own authority, but they then fail to see that something rather similar is happening in the Western evangelical church. It is not that evangelicals today, or Catholics then, actively oppose the authority of Scripture. Catholics did not oppose biblical inspiration, nor do evangelicals today. Rather, then as now, the church's *practice* belies its profession of belief in the Bible's authority.

Scripture cannot function authoritatively if the church is not will-

226

ing to put itself under its authority and learn from it as God's sole, authoritative guide for its belief and practice. The Catholic Church then could not claim that it believed in Scripture's authority while it was also negating that authority by its own teaching. And we today cannot claim we believe in the Bible's authority if we set it aside to build the church in our own way.

For evangelicals, this has taken the form of using polling, marketing, and business know-how to adapt Christian faith to generational niches. It has also involved recasting Christian faith in therapeutic terms for those who have left a moral world and now inhabit a psychological world. It has also taken the form among emergents of making the authority of Scripture uncertain and elastic in order to blend in more fully with postmodern ways of thinking. These are the ways in which evangelicals imagine that they are becoming "relevant." The only reason evangelicals in great numbers are walking these paths is that they have lost their belief in the sufficiency of Scripture. They have lost their understanding that the truth of God, in the hands of God, is sufficient for the life of the church in this world.

Relevance is not about incorporating something else as definitive in the life of the church, be it the hottest marketing trend, the latest demographic, the newest study on depression, what a younger generation thinks, Starbucks, or contemporary music. None of these is definitive. None should be allowed a defining role in how the church is strengthened and nourished. Studies on contemporary life, whether of a demographic or psychological kind, are helpful in understanding the way life is in a (post)modern world, but these studies do not themselves give the church its agenda. At least they should not. The agenda comes from the Word of God. In the rhythms of marketing, and the pandering to generational tastes, this agenda is often being lost. The agenda, in fact, is coming from the culture, from its consumers, from the world. In these churches it is *sola cultura,* not *sola Scriptura.* Unless evangelicals recover their confidence in the sufficiency of Scripture, their claim that Scripture alone is authoritative will remain empty. It will remain a charade.

The apostles' understanding about the sole authority of Scripture, and hence its complete sufficiency, explains why Christianity took the form it did. The apostles taught this truth in the form of *doctrine.*

DOCTRINE

It's not like they had no alternatives. There were many other options, from Greek "wisdom" to the "mysteries" of gnosticism. On none of these ways of knowing was the foundation of the church laid. It was laid upon the teaching of "the apostles and prophets" (Eph. 2:20). If these were not the prophets of the Old Testament, we can only assume that the revelation they delivered was either circumstantial and therefore not normative for the church in later periods, or was simply repetitions of what the apostles had already said. It is upon the apostles' writings that the church now rests. Under the inspiration of the Holy Spirit, they gave the church the definitive statement of what Christian faith is. And this revelation was *taught* to the churches because it came in the form of *doctrine*.

The New Testament, it is true, contains historical narrative, parables, and practical discourses. It would be foolish, though, to say that this militates in any way against the fact that Christianity as the apostles delivered it was doctrinal in form.

Jesus was a teacher. The crowds marveled at "his teaching" (Matt. 7:28; Mark 1:22). This teaching, read within and against the framework of the Old Testament, is what the apostles expanded and applied to the churches under the inspiration of the Holy Spirit. They gave us the doctrine by which the people of God are defined and by which they should live. To be a believer is to believe this teaching. And that is the point made by an impressive array of passages.

Sometimes, as we have seen and as John Stott has also noted, this apostolic doctrine is called the "teaching" (Rom. 16:17), "the faith" (Titus 1:13; 1 Tim. 3:9; Jude 3), "the truth" (1 Tim. 2:4; 3:15; 4:3), and "the deposit" (1 Tim. 6:20; 2 Tim. 1:14). It is called "the pattern of the sound words" (2 Tim. 1:13), "the traditions" (2 Thess. 2:15), "the apostles' teaching" (Acts 2:42; cf. 2 Tim. 2:2). Elsewhere it is "what we have heard" (Heb. 2:1) or what was heard "from the beginning" (1 John 2:24).

It is about this body of teaching that the apostles wrote to the early Christians. This doctrine was given by God for the instruction, moral guidance, and nurture of God's people. The apostles therefore say they are writing to "remind" the churches of this doctrine, that they are to "recall" it, to "stand firm" in it, to "follow" it, or, in Hebrews, not to "drift" from it. This, the apostles say, is what they "delivered" to the church. This is what has been "entrusted" to the church.

Christians, therefore, are those who "know" this doctrine. They "believe" it, "have" it, "hold it fast," "guard" it, and "contend earnestly" for it. That is the central and defining place it should have in the life of the church. This apostolic teaching is what should describe what all Christians believe. It should explain how they think and who they are in their very souls. It should be their identifying mark. They are the ones who "have" the apostolic teaching. They guard it, treasure it, teach it, defend it, and are nourished in their lives by its truths.

Today, however, the evangelical church has drifted far from this norm. The doctrines of the New Testament are terra incognita to many in its churches. That is what Barna has been told by the born again, and there is plenty of evidence to suppose that what he has been told is true. There is abysmal ignorance of biblical truth in evangelical churches today.

The reason, quite simply, is that these doctrines are no longer important to many born-againers in their understanding of Christian faith, or in how the gospel is framed, or in how Christian life is taught, or in how it is lived, or in what its preoccupations are. Evangelical Christianity today is no longer doctrinal in nature. Let us be clear about what is at stake in this drift. It is not just that we no longer think in doctrinal terms. More basic, and more important, we no longer think in *truth* terms. Christianity is about many things now, but truth increasingly is not one of them. That also explains why preaching of a biblical kind is such an uncommon occurrence in the life of the church.

PREACHING

Preaching, in fact, has always held a central place in the life of historic Protestant churches. This is the way they have practiced their belief in the sole authority and consequent sufficiency of Scripture. This Word of God has been preached and preached so that those who hear will come to a knowledge of its truths. Those truths have a doctrinal shape. Christianity is not simply about experience, not at all about experience which is exclusively private, not at all a spiritual version of what is therapeutic, and it is not a product on sale at the church's counter. These serious distortions are influencing pulpits and account for the cata-strophic weaknesses in both belief and behavior everywhere evident in Western evangelical churches today. As this happens, one of the "marks" of the true church makes its way out the back door.

Yet we must go further. Scripture is not only authoritative. It is the Word of *God*. It is the way God, in all his magnificent glory, as it were, hides himself in very human words in order that we might be able to stand in his presence, listen to him, and learn. It speaks to his humility that his greatness should be so cloaked that we can bear it. It speaks to our pride that we have turned away from hearing him, abandoning se-rious preaching in our churches.

Preaching is not a conversation, a chat about some interesting ideas. It is not the moment in which postmoderns hear their own pri-vate message in the biblical words, one unique to each one who hears, and then go their own way. No! This is *God* speaking! He speaks through the stammering lips of the preacher where that preacher's mind is on the text of Scripture and his heart is in the presence of God. God, as Luther put it, lives in the preacher's mouth.

This is the kind of preaching that issues a summons, which nour-ishes the soul, which draws the congregation into the very presence of God so that no matter what aspect of his character, his truth, his work-ing in this world is in focus, we leave with awe, gratitude, encourage-ment, and sometimes a rebuke. We have been in the very presence of God! That is what great preaching always does.

About preaching, I think I discern two rather clear and rather dif-ferent viewpoints. On one side are those who have become convinced that it is the biblical text that must be preached. Perhaps they come to this opinion through reading older sermons, or by understanding the emptiness of topical preaching, or as a reaction to the older liberalism. But they hold a conviction that the Word of God, in the hand of God, is sufficient for the people of God. The form this conviction most often takes is the expository sermon, in which the text or passage provides both the structure and content of the sermon.

On the other side are those who have become acutely aware of how postmoderns think. These are the preachers who want to meet their audiences on their own turf in a way they think addresses their world and needs. Sermons here, most commonly, begin not with a text but with something in the postmodern experience. Perhaps a movie, a sitcom, an excursion into the mall that yielded an amusing anecdote. If the intent is to be biblical at all in these sermons, the preacher will then try to find his or her way back from the opening story to some aspect of biblical truth.

In my view, both approaches contain a valid insight. In the one, the insight is the sufficiency of God's Word for his redemptive work and for our life in this world. The conclusion drawn from this is that preaching is no more than simply doing exegesis on a passage from the pulpit. It is God who must apply that truth, it is assumed, and he will do so because Scripture is all we need for a life of godliness in this world. The preacher's task is finished when the text has been explained. Personal applications are sometimes added, but little effort is typically made to place that text's truth in the context of the world that people inhabit and have to understand, and that must be coped with every other day of the week.

The insight in the alternative approach is that our experience in the (post)modern world is complex, baffling, difficult, perplexing, highly stressful, and confusing. Every day we face situations that are difficult or taxing. Our marriages are not holding together very well, our souls are often rent in two, our children sometimes break our hearts, and more often than most other people know, we just don't know what to do. It is good to hear words of comfort on Sunday (or Saturday evening), but what we really need is a way to understand our lives. It is this yearning that has unfortunately driven so many preachers into a psychological world, and they emerge replete with all the latest therapeutic talk. All too often, as a result, they serve up nothing but pablum to their hearers. Or worse. Sometimes they serve up entertainment in the sermons, performing before an audience, and leaving the impression that this is what Christianity is about.

Unless the congregation is being confronted, is being informed by the truth of God's Word, it will leave as empty and confused as when it came in, no matter how good it may feel about itself. Unless the congregation is learning to think God's thoughts after him in *this* world, one that is highly modernized and postmodern in its ethos, it will not be able to function with a Christian worldview. Parishioners will not be able to engage their world in a way that is both pertinent and faithful on Monday morning. Nor will they be able to think of their own lives adequately because, after all, they are still living in this world and not yet in heaven.

This, of course, assumes that this world is not friendly to Christian faith. But that is not what many of these very sensitive preachers are now assuming. They see no danger anywhere. They do not preach as if this world were perilous to Christian faith because they do not think it is. They preach, if that is still the right word to use, as if we had no enemies. The truth is that we do have enemies, and we do need to be able to recognize them.

It takes work for any preacher to toil effectively on both ends of this trajectory. What does this Word mean in this world? That is the preacher's question. Or, at least, it ought to be.

Why, we might ask, are so few working on both ends of the sermonic trajectory? The answers are, I believe, astonishingly simple. Those who have walked away from conscientiously biblical sermons have done so because they really do not believe that these sermons can actually "connect" with their postmodern hearers, that they will be understood, that they will do any good.

That being the case, a strange bond begins to bind the preacher and at least the more casual in the audience together. The preacher thinks biblical truth simply will not be able to resolve any real need in people's lives. About this the people agree. This is not what they have come to hear. They have come for encouragement and inspiration, to be uplifted, to be given some help for their psychological tensions, for all the bafflements of life, or simply to be amused. Preach a biblical sermon and they want to walk out.

But what about preachers who are anchored in the biblical truth and want to preach it? Why can't they anchor it in the world as we know it? Certainly, they believe that this Word, more than anything else, is what will nourish the soul. So, they set about their exegesis. But, given all the pressures of pastoral life, they must get their work done quickly. Mercifully, there are the commentaries!

The other end of their sermon's trajectory, though, is another matter. How does the preacher learn about the world people inhabit? Where does one find help in thinking about life in a modernized society, such as those in the West with their deepening postmodern ethos?

How does one come to understand how the biblical truth in a passage will intersect with the inner lives of those living in a modernized world? Rooting biblical truth in this context takes work, work that most pastors are apparently willing to skip. Or maybe have no time to do. They therefore preach the text and leave the application to God.

Are we surprised, then, that the evangelical church in the West is stumbling, that its biblical ignorance is growing and its worldliness is increasing? If the truth of Scripture is not being preached, biblical illiteracy is the outcome. If the truth of Scripture is not being applied in ways pertinent in the culture, then Christians are liable to inhabit two worlds, the world of Sunday morning and the world of the rest of the week. Of what use is it for a preacher to be relevant to the culture but irrelevant to the Scripture? If we have to choose, the church benefits far more from hearing a sermon that is relevant to Scripture, even if it lacks serious, insightful application, than from hearing one that has no serious biblical engagement.

Best of all is to hear sermons that arise from a biblical text and then bring that truth into the center of life as we know it today. Unless this happens, we are only feeding into the scourge of the modern church in which Christianity lives on in our private lives but disappears from our lives in public, in the workplace.

Preaching lives between two worlds, the world of God's truth and the world we inhabit in our minds and daily life. If preaching does not bridge these two worlds effectively, the church inevitably stumbles. Where preaching negotiates these worlds, there one is likely to find spiritual authenticity.

Sacraments

The second "mark" of the true church is that the sacraments are rightly administered. The Reformers were particularly concerned with the Catholic view that saving grace was conveyed in and with the sacramental form. What was clearly at stake was how we are encountered by Christ, what is the nature of his grace, and how we receive it. There has always been some room for different understanding of these matters, both in baptism and in the Lord's Supper, but none for any view of the sacraments that nullifies the Christian gospel. What we need to think about, then, is how our understanding here separates churches that are true from those that are not.

However, it is also true that the intensity of this older discussion has died down. Most evangelicals are not even in dialogue with Catholics, let alone in contention with them. We therefore need to see what *principle* was at stake, and then how we might apply this principle to our own situation.

The principle at stake is that salvation is to be found in Christ *alone*, by grace *alone*, through faith *alone*. Indeed, whatever is added to the work of Christ actually takes away from it, as J. I. Packer has argued. To say that our justification is not complete until we have added our works — as Catholics said then and as the Protestant New Perspective says now — is also to say that Christ's work on the cross was incomplete, and remains so until we ourselves produce that completion. To say that Mary should be added to Christ as an intercessor with the Father is to say that Christ by himself is inadequate to do this work. Whatever we say needs to be added to Christ's work in fact detracts from it. Only when we see Christ doing for us what we cannot in any way do for ourselves are we able to see that all the glory belongs to God for this and none comes to us.

This was the broad principle being engaged across several fronts at the time of the Reformation. Among these were the Catholic sacraments.

The sacraments can never be a substitute for the biblical gospel. That is the point. They cannot become an alternative to the gospel — as they had in Catholicism and have in subsequent Anglo-Catholicism — as if there were a different way of receiving forgiveness from God than trusting in the saving work of Christ alone. The sacraments undoubtedly point to this. They symbolize it. But they do not offer any detour around the necessary exercise of saving faith in the work of Christ on the cross. No wonder understanding all of this in a biblical way, and not confusing it with an ecclesiastical notion of how we find God's saving grace through the sacraments, is a mark of the true church!

If the "apostles and prophets" are the church's foundation on which it is built, then Christ is the "cornerstone, in whom the whole structure, being joined together, grows into a holy temple in the Lord" (Eph. 2:20-21). In what sense is Christ the cornerstone? In what sense is he the means of connection between adjoining walls? Quite simply, it is because of him, because of his death, because of his dying in place of sinners, and because of their union with him through faith that there is a church. Without the incarnation of the Son of God, his taking of our flesh, his bringing to completion what had been begun in Adam, his substitutionary death and justifying work, his resurrection and ascension, there is no church.

There is no true church that does not preserve this gospel. The true church declares that God's holiness being what it is, and sin being what it is, the only possible mediator between God and sinners is the God-man, Jesus Christ. To his work we can add nothing, and from it nothing can be taken.

If it is Christ *alone,* it is also by grace *alone* because the only contribution we make to the efficacy of his saving death is the sin from which we need to be redeemed, as William Temple declared. No addition can be made to Christ's work without simultaneously proposing something derogatory to his accomplishment. After all, if his work lacked something that is secured from the sinner before it becomes efficacious, then in itself it was incomplete before that addition. Being incomplete, it was therefore imperfect.

The gospel announcement, then, is that Christ's work on our behalf was perfect and completed in space, time, and history. The gospel offer is the offer of forgiveness to those who will recognize their own sinfulness, repent of it, seek God's acceptance through Christ, and receive that acceptance through him.

Here is a spirituality that begins "above," not "below." It does not begin in our yearning for the Other, our sense of emptiness, our psychological dysfunction, our reaching out to God, our moral effort, or our attendance in a church. It begins "above," in the counsels of God in eternity, in his unmerited favor through which he reaches into sinful lives that reject him, works in those lives a willingness to hear his Word and to receive his truth and to embrace Christ, who is its central declaration.

If we really want to be biblical in a careful and precise way, we will not think so much of the decision we make for Christ as of the decision God made for us in Christ. And we will not think that Christ merely dies for us because, as Paul says, sometimes "for a good person one would dare even to die" (Rom. 5:7). Indeed, in acts of heroism during times of war this happens quite often. Christ's death, however, was not simply an act of selfless heroism. It was a substitutionary death. The New Testament language is clear and insistent, as we have seen. He not only died, but he died in our place, for our sins: he gave himself "for our sins" (Gal. 1:4; 1 Cor. 15:3), he "bore our sins" (1 Pet. 2:24), he was "delivered up for our trespasses" (Rom. 4:25), he "bore our sins in his body" (1 Pet. 2:24), he is the propitiation "for our sins" (1 John 2:2; 4:10), and we are now "justified by his blood" (Rom. 5:9).

This language makes sense only in a moral world, and makes no sense whatsoever in the kind of therapeutic world most postmoderns today inhabit. Theirs is a world that is acutely aware of internal wounds, human brokenness, broken relationships, a spoiled and disorderly environment, rotten human structures, dehumanizing bureaucracy, inane and corrupted government, all of which cause pain and provoke outrage. But it is not a world where we ever — not ever — find ourselves face-to-face with a God who is justly angry, who is affronted by our sin and whose moral presence looms in front of us as the most awesome and destructive thing we will ever encounter. That is the God who is gone, at least in our minds. The "god" who is there is caring, cheers us on from the sidelines, commiserates with us, and so desperately would like to help us out but, alas, life is just a bit too complex for him (or her, or it).

No, it is not just that our systems are all amiss, that life is twisted with bruised and painful relations, but in and with all of this we have also sinned against *God*. We have sinned in a way that is utterly unpardonable without Christ. Not only do we feel bad about ourselves, our life, our society, our environment, or our world. It is *we* whom we need to feel bad about, more bad than we have ever realized, and not because we have our unsolvable personal "issues." No. Our most fundamental "issue" is with God, who will not be diverted from expressing his moral judgment on what we have done unless we find in Christ the "Rock of Ages" who was cleft for us. We need to be able to hide in him.

At stake here are two things. First, it is the *character* of the gospel that we have to preserve. This is important because it reveals the character of *God*. It is in the gospel, not first and foremost in the sacraments, that we see his mercy and justice. It is in the gospel that we see his holiness and grace. We see his holiness calling for his own death in the person of Christ, and we see his grace bearing that death in himself and thus paying our debt. And Christ did so, not because he deserved that death, or because we had any claim upon him, but because that is what God's kind of love does.

What is at stake, second, is the nature of spirituality. In protecting the character of the gospel in what we teach, preach, and believe, we also protect the true nature of spirituality. Spirituality that is authentic is not spirituality that is self-generated but what is supernaturally wrought. It is not what we find in ourselves but what we have in God the Father, Son, and Holy Spirit. Without the real gospel there is no justification before God and no regeneration in ourselves. Without regeneration there is no new life, no appetite for God, no capacity to live before him as those who know him. To know him through Christ, and to live before him with moral authenticity, is what true spirituality is all about.

If we mute the biblical gospel by our misunderstanding, or by our practice in the church, we destroy the possibility of spiritual authenticity in the church. In theory, most evangelicals assent to all of this. In practice, many evangelicals — especially those of a marketing and emergent kind — are walking away from the hard edges of these truths in an effort to make the gospel easy to swallow, quick to sell, and generationally appealing. They are very well aware of a deep cultural hunger for spirituality in the West, and they are trolling in these waters. The problem, however, is that this spirituality is highly privatized, highly individualistic, self-centered, and hostile to doctrine because it is always hostile to Christian truth. Evangelicals gain nothing by merely attracting to their churches postmoderns who are yearning for what is spiritual if, in catering to this, the gospel is diluted, made easy, and the edges get rounded off. The degree to which evangelicals are doing this is the degree to which they are invalidating themselves and prostituting the church.

Discipline

The third sign of the church's authenticity is its practice of discipline. This may seem odd to us today, and certainly in our postmodern moment it is often most offensive. Are not lifestyle decisions private, and who is to say that one person's choice is acceptable and another's is not? What business is it of any church to intrude into such matters? Besides, how effective can discipline be if the person being disciplined can simply go down the road and find a new church? Is it not also the case that, sinners being sinners, church discipline can give legalists and the hard-hearted who are handing out the discipline scope for their misshapen passions? All of which raises anew the question why the Reformers would have seen this as a mark of authenticity.

The fact is, though, that discipline is enjoined on all churches who wish to think of themselves as being in the New Testament mold. The seriously unrepentant are to be shunned (Matt. 18:15-19), the creators of dissension are to be avoided (Rom. 16:17; Titus 3:10), the immoral "removed" or excommunicated (1 Cor. 5:1-5, 11) and the idle admonished (1 Thess. 5:14). The church is to be cleansed of false teachers (1 Cor. 5:6-7; Rev. 2:2), and those who persist in sin are to be rebuked (1 Tim. 5:20; cf. Titus 1:13). Clearly, there is a wide range of possible circumstances in which we can put the name of Christ and the reputation of the church at risk. That being so, there is no one form of discipline. Discipline includes private rebukes, teaching for the purpose of correction, and what we might now think of as excommunication.

It would be foolish to suppose that the purpose of these disciplinary measures is to purge from the life of the local church all that makes it less than a "pure" church. The truth is, as long as there are sinners in the church, it will never be pure. It will never be pure this side of heaven. And, further, it is the Holy Spirit's work, applying the saving death of Christ, that actually brings about purity in thought, word, and deed. We can but exhort one another to this end.

However, when we are joined to Christ by faith, we are no longer our own. We now bear the name of Christ. It is his name that is besmirched by our actions. The principal purpose of discipline is to restore the name of Christ among his people and in the world. But there is more to it than this.

Why do some in the church wander from the core doctrines of the Bible and have to be rebuked? Why do some carry on sexual affairs as if this were a purely private matter and irrelevant to their Christian lives? Why is it that some pastors yearn for preeminence (cf. 3 John 9-10), demand attention, are authoritarian, build careers and empires, or are moneygrubbing? Why are some church members so disagreeable that they are the source of constant grief and divisions?

The simple answer to all these questions is that the holiness of God is not a pressing concern. It does not have the power to wrench around the disposition of people. It is not a present reality. At most it is a doctrinal point to be agreed to, but it is not a searing reality that enters our hearts like a sword. That is why we have no compunction about engaging in sexual immorality, self-serving and obnoxious behavior, or embracing beliefs that are unorthodox, biblically speaking. It is as if, in our minds, God is off in a distant realm, utterly pure though he might be, and we are in our own realm, living our lives as we want, giving expression to some of our dark impulses whenever the urge creeps up on us. And why not? God is there and we are here. That, no doubt, was the psychology present in Ananias and Sapphira when they engaged in their deception, and that was the reason for their rather drastic discipline (Acts 5:1-11).

In our modernized societies in the West, we are faced with an epidemic of lying, theft, abuse, rape, and other predatory behavior, but we are far more likely to blame it on bad self-image than on bad character. Even in the church, the story is not much different. We have seized upon the language of our therapeutic culture and insist that our preachers toe this line and speak to us in this language. What is often missed, however, is that this language comes out of a psychological world, not the moral world, and the chief consequence of this is that responsibility has vanished. We do not accept responsibility because we have no sense at all that we stand in the presence of a God of blazing, majestic purity. And when we lose this sense of the moral "over-againstness" of God, this opposition of what is Good to what is not, we lose all moral urgency. Indeed, we lose our gospel and the whole point of Christian faith.

This has become an especially pressing concern for the church today. What we see on all sides is the constant preoccupation with psychological wholeness as a substitute for biblical holiness. This inevitably changes the way we think about God. The God of the outside, who stands over against us in his holiness, loses his point for our lives. We find ourselves yearning for comfort, therapeutic comfort, and at the same time the self-discipline and sacrifice of a faith grounded in God's holiness have become distasteful to us. As this God, the God of the Bible, becomes remote to us, worship begins to lose its awe, his Word loses its power to compel us, obedience loses its attraction, and the church loses its moral authority. That is our situation today, and that is why discipline is so important in the life of the church.

The Old Testament frequently speaks about knowing God (e.g., Hos. 2:20; 4:1; 5:4; 6:6; Isa. 1:3). Plainly, much more than simply knowing about him is in view. This knowledge has consequences because God's is an intrusive moral presence. Those who know God will walk before him humbly (Mic. 6:8), not carelessly or with indifference, because they have come to learn that they can stand before him only because of his grace. They will be morally careful and reverent as a result. They will be in awe of him, living in "the fear of the LORD" (Ps. 111:10; Prov. 1:7; Job 28:28). Why is this? It is because of God's exclusive demand upon their loyalty and attention. He brooks no rivals. He allows no alternatives. This was a sore lesson that the Old Testament people had to learn over and over again. More than that, God's exclusive demand is what is to be reflected in everything we are and do. That was the basis of the Ten Commandments (Exod. 20:2-3), and it is the summons to be heard in the church today: "As he who called you is holy, you also be holy in all your conduct" (1 Pet. 1:15).

Holiness is not a matter of people simply cleaning up their lives on the outside, becoming civil as a matter of politeness only, or going along with biblical teaching because others are doing so. This is not biblical holiness. This is, at best, social niceness.

Biblical holiness begins with the Holy. But the Holy, by its very nature, can be approached only when we come as sinners. He is never accessible to us as consumers. We come in sackcloth and ashes, not as buyers. Indeed, we cannot approach the Holy at all on our own terms. We must see that the Holy has first approached us in Christ and, through him, reconciled us to himself. The revelation of the Holy would be unbearable were we to see it in any other way than from within Christ. In Christ, what we are seeing is God's holiness in its action on our sin. Without Christ we would have to bear that judgment in ourselves. What we see instead is holiness coming down in grace and, in Christ, going forth against our sin in triumph.

Holiness is therefore so much more than just a moral code or a set of rules. It is all about what is right because it is all about what God is in his utterly pure being. It is his being in its burning purity that drives us in the pursuit of what is right. And he has disclosed to us in Scripture, in a multitude of ways, what is true and right.

Without the holiness of God, sin has no meaning and grace has no point. God's holiness gives to the one its definition and to the other its greatness. Without the holiness of God, sin is merely human failure, but not failure before *God*. It is failure without the standard by which we know it to have failed. It is failure without guilt, failure without retribution, failure without any serious moral meaning.

Without the holiness of God, grace is no longer grace because it does not arise from the dark clouds of his judgment that covered the cross. Without God's holiness, grace would be nothing more than sentimental benevolence. It is this holiness that shows the graciousness of grace, its character as unmerited, because it also shows us the offensiveness of sin.

Without the holiness of God, faith is but a confidence in good fortune, optimism about our prospects, hope in some future happiness. It is not what takes hold of the one in whom God has wrought his propitiation. It is not that trusting in the utter reliability of the good character of God that makes his promises "Yes and Amen" in Christ.

Sin, grace, and faith are emptied of their meaning when they are separated from the holiness of God. "Love," as P. T. Forsyth wrote in *The Cruciality of the Cross*, "is but its outgoing; sin is but its defiance; grace is but its action on sin; the Cross is but its victory; faith is but its worship." That is really what this third mark of the church is all about. It is about the people of God showing the same kind of moral seriousness that is in plain sight on the cross. It is about the need to reflect that seriousness in the midst of all of life's conflicts and temptations. There is no one who is perfect. Nevertheless, despite the tentacles of sin that remain and reach into the soul, in the church we should see enough of Christ's conquest over sin that grievous violations of expected belief and conduct that flow from this redemption need to be addressed. The purpose of this is that the name of Christ and the reputation of the church are protected.

Into the Depths

These three marks of the true church, the signs of its authenticity, seek to verify whether the truth God has given the church is being preached, the gospel is being proclaimed, and the moral character and reputation of the church are being protected. However, each of these comes back to God. The test is whether the truth being preached is God's, the gospel being proclaimed is God's, and the holiness being sought is God's. An authentic church is one that is God-centered in its thought and God-honoring in its proclamation and life. It can be authentic only when it honors, reflects, and proclaims who God is and what he has done in Christ. These marks of an authentic church are asking deep but unavoidable questions. Are we preoccupied with God as he has revealed himself to us, with Christ as he has been given to us, and with ourselves, not simply as psychological selves, but as God's people in this world? These tests, in fact, take us to the very depths of who God is and test the church at the deepest level of its being.

Who Builds the Church?

Suppose we were to discover that the evangelical church in America today was not passing these very basic tests of authenticity with flying colors. What would we do? Think afresh about worship? Revise the Sunday school curriculum (if it still exists and if there is such a thing as a curriculum)? Ask if there are new, more innovative ways in which the church can rethink and rearrange itself?

The most important things we learn about the church when we come before God in this way are that the church is his, as we have seen, and that he is the one who builds it. Indeed, we have this in Jesus' own words. It was on the "rock" of Peter's confession that Christ said, "I will build my church, and the gates of hell shall not prevail against it" (Matt. 16:18). The New Testament uses many metaphors to speak of this process, but those of building and growing are frequent. And the key point is that this is *God's* work. The church needs to be led, taught, pastored, and organized, but it is God alone who builds and nourishes it.

This is Paul's main point in 1 Corinthians 3:1-15. What is the church and how does it get built? What is ministry in the church and how are we supposed to do it? These questions are obviously connected. What we think the church is will explain how we think it will grow. How we think the church grows, explains what ministry is. Paul had been driven to raise these questions because many people in Corinth were going about their life in the church in the wrong way. They were not spiritual in their understanding and behavior. Paul could not address them as "spiritual" (3:1) because they were seeing the church simply from within their own fallen perspective. They had to be spoken to as the children that they were (3:1).

Is not the evangelical church in the same boat today? That this is a moment of great weakness seems to be commonly agreed. What the remedy is has become a matter of debate. The parallels between our situation and the one in Corinth, however, are really quite striking. Would we not do well to ask, then, what they had not understood?

Paul's perspective on this matter is summed up in a few pointed words. How should we think of ourselves? The answer is as "*God's* fellow workers" (3:9; in Paul's Greek, the word "God" is placed first for emphasis). How should we think of the church? It is "*God's* field" and "*God's* building" (3:9). And why should we think of it as God's field and building? Because the church is his creation and only he can grow it. He gives it its qualitative growth inwardly, in terms of character and obedience, and its quantitative growth outwardly in terms of numerical expansion. We see this second truth at work in the early days of the church's life when we read that "*the Lord* added to their number day by day those who were being saved" (Acts 2:47, italics mine). All of this being true, it is *the Lord* who "assigns" the work in the church (1 Cor. 3:5), Paul says, to bring about its growth, nurturing, and training. The church's goals and functions, therefore, are *given* to it. They come, not from business manuals, not from cultural norms, and not from marketing savvy, but from what the Lord has told us in the Scriptures. It is in the light of these truths that we will be judged (1 Cor. 3:8). And this leads Paul to the heart of the matter. We sow and water, but it is *God* who gives the growth (3:6-7).

This last statement rests upon three New Testament doctrines. Each one is under siege in the church today, and each one needs to be preserved if we are to see again the full expression of God's excellency in the life of the church. And this is the key to the restoration of its full health.

GOD IS SOVEREIGN

First, when Paul says it is *God* who grows the church, he clearly is assuming that God is sovereign. God rules over all of life, bringing about his providential will, from the mighty events like the falling of empires to the most insignificant, like the falling of the sparrow. This means that within this world, kingdoms and cultures rise and fall according to his sovereign will. Paul says he has even established the nations' boundaries (Acts 17:26). Nothing, therefore, is more absurd than the panic that now grips the evangelical church. It is terrorized by the specter of postmodernity. Reading today's "how-to" literature, one has to draw the conclusion that the church's days are numbered unless we rush in to prop it up with our own know-how. God, you see, has more on his hands than he can possibly handle. Unless the church capitulates and kisses its (post)modern enemies, it is done for!

The desperate measures being proposed for these desperate times are often little more than a case of weak knees and unbelief. We believe altogether too little in God's sovereign control, otherwise we would not be in full retreat before the pressures and demands of the (post)modern world. We look like the soldiers of some sorry nation that are very brave when they are safe in their protected barracks but, at the first sight of the enemy, lay down their arms and run.

The truth is that there is nothing in our postmodern world that is a serious threat, or an insurmountable obstacle, to the will of God. This is true of his saving will as well. He is as sovereign in the way he begets faith today as he is over the sparrow that flies or falls. He will grow the church. Today, we no longer seem to believe this, and want to aid his cause by our weak and foolish capitulations.

WE ARE CAPTIVE

Second, this belief rests upon a conviction about human inability. This is why it is only *God* who can grow the church. The point is that only God can impart new, supernatural life. We can pray for people, seek God's blessing for the church, preach, counsel, and witness, but God alone gives the growth.

If it were only a matter of changing people's attitudes, we could grow the church. We could use marketing techniques, the best advertising, and we could bring in motivational speakers. We could grow the church as a successful corporation is grown.

The problem, though, is the problem we are up against. It is so much deeper than anything that might hinder a corporation from becoming successful. The problem is aptly summed up in some lines from Charles Wesley's great hymn. "Long my imprisoned spirit lay," he wrote, "fast bound in sin / and nature's night." That is the problem. It is the problem of innate hostility to the truth of God to which we are willing captives. We are driven by an unwillingness to yield to Christ's claims upon us. What is the solution? "Thine eye," Wesley wrote poetically, "diffused a quick'ning ray; / I woke — The dungeon flamed with light! My chains fell off, / my heart was free, I rose, went forth, and followed thee." He was speaking about the deep-seated inability of all people to know God, to honor him, or to obey him in and of themselves. This is an inability that marketing technique, psychological motivation, and generational pandering cannot touch. It is immune to all techniques of persuasion. It is only overcome supernaturally. Only *God* can grow the church. He does so first through regeneration and then by sanctification.

MEANS OF GROWTH

Third, this understanding about how the church grows must be linked to the means God has ordained for its growth. Paul says he planted the seed and Apollos watered. What was planted? What was the water?

What was planted was surely the truth God has given us in the Scriptures. How shall we call upon God and believe upon him, Paul asks elsewhere, unless we have a preached Word through which to respond (Rom. 10:14)? It is, James tells us, "of his own will [that] he brought us forth." But what means does God use? He brings us forth "by the word of truth" (James 1:18). How did the Thessalonians turn from their idols and believe on Christ? They "received the word" (1 Thess. 1:6) that had been preached in the full power of the Holy Spirit. That is the seed. The watering is the work of encouraging belief in the teaching of that Word, fostering obedience, and encouraging a life of God-centeredness to which that Word points.

Let God Be God over the Church

These three doctrines underlie Paul's simple affirmation that it is *God* who grows the church. What is interesting is that few in the evangelical world would actually contest this. The point of confusion comes in how this happens. What is the relation between the preaching of biblical truth and the church's growth? Between different kinds of worship and growth? Between music and growth? What must we do and what will God do? And under what circumstances will he do it?

The answer is found in a place hidden to human view. It is private. It is the place within our souls where our most personal thinking, wanting, yearning, and hoping originate. It is where all our ambitions, plans, and goals come together. So, what drives us? What do we really want? Do we really understand what it means to humble ourselves before God and forsake the self-sufficiency that is so natural and seems so sensible?

The outward appearance, as we all know, is one thing. We all know how to conform our speech and behavior to what is expected of us, don't we? We do so in pious ways, too.

The inward reality, though, may be something different. The curtain is pulled across the windows of our souls so that outsiders cannot look in. Before God, however, there is no hiding place. Before him we are what we are. It is in this inner sanctum that we determine whether we are going to build the church ourselves, or whether we are going to do much of it with a little help along the way, or whether we know, in a way that touches all our thought, every ambition for ourselves, every fiber of our being, that all we can do is plant and water, that it is God alone who can grow the church.

Letting God be God over his church, seeing him as its center and glory, its source and its life, is a truly liberating experience. It liberates us from thinking that we have to do, in ourselves, what we are entirely incapable of doing. That is, growing the church. We cannot do the work that only God can do. We can work in the church, preach and teach, spread the gospel, encourage and urge each other on, but we cannot impart new life. Nor can we ever sanctify the church. Indeed, we cannot even feed the church. It is God who supplies the food; we are simply called upon to serve it (1 Cor. 3:5). This, however, is precisely why Paul says, a little later, that "we do not lose heart" (2 Cor. 4:1, 16) but are "confident" (3:4; cf. 5:6).

While all of this is conventional enough, it is not common enough in evangelical churches. Lip service is paid to these ideas, but when we get really serious about "doing church" we turn to what we know best. We turn to structures and programs, appearances and management, advertising and marketing. Our preoccupation is with what we *do* and therefore with what we *control*. This is what animates the conversation among evangelical leaders, what fills the pages of magazines like *Leadership,* and what attracts pastors to the really big, important conferences. This is what they are willing to pay serious money to hear.

Alas! It is missing the point, if I may say so. What is of primary interest in a technological world is technique, for that, after all, is how we manage everything else. In the kingdom of God things are different. It is not that we do not do things, but that our doing is rooted in our being. Who we *are* is more fundamental than what we *do*. Character is more basic than action. Being mastered by God is infinitely more important than having the know-how to manage the church.

Letting God be God over the church means that he becomes foundational to its being, thinking, and doing. In a highly pragmatic culture, such as we have in America, doing cuts itself off from thinking. The only thinking that gets done, at least with respect to the church, is about the how-to questions. The kind of critical thinking, the serious evaluation that should go along with all of this, is impatiently brushed aside as irrelevant. If something works, if it is successful, that means that what was done has validated itself. What more needs to be thought about it?

I believe that today there is a deep yearning for churches in which

God is God. Those are the churches that most easily become the communities we have all lost, where relations are developed, even in this fallen world, in the sight of God. They are where people strive to be truthful in those relations, which really is the key to integrity, and integrity ties together our public and private lives. Churches, in fact, need to be communities that love the truth God has revealed and, in so doing, become serious and joyous about the God of that truth and intent upon serving him in his world. The church is not a business, not an experiment, not a product to be sold. It is an outpost of the kingdom, a sign of things to come in Christ's sovereign rule, which is now hidden but will be made open and public. Then all the world will bow before him in recognition of who he is.

And this, I dare say, is the only answer we have for the church's existence and service. It is the anticipation of that great day. It is pointing beyond itself to that great day. It lives in this world, but it lives because it has seen the glory of the coming of the Lord. This is the knowledge that changes everything. Business savvy, organizational wizardry, cultural relevance are simply no substitute for this. Unless the Lord rebuilds the evangelical church today, as we humble ourselves before him and hear afresh his Word, it will not be rebuilt.

Index

Aquinas, Thomas, 203
Aristotle, 144
Arminianism, 129
Augustine, 20, 203, 218

Bandy, Thomas G., 87
Barna, George, 9, 12, 13, 42, 43, 46, 47, 90, 131, 132, 166, 172, 173, 180, 182, 216, 229
Barth, Karl, 190
Beckett, Samuel, 110
Bell, Rob, 86, 87
Bellah, Robert, 70
Benedict XVI, 32
Berger, Peter, 68, 142
Bible. *See* Word of God
Bloom, Harold, 184
Britain, 17, 18, 34, 68, 149, 157, 179
Brunner, Emil, 68
Buddhism, 68, 95
Bunyan, John, 183

Calvin, John, 20, 177
Capps, Donald, 112
Carnegie, Dale, 149
Chalke, Steve, 129
Chesterton, G. K., 71
Christ, xiii, 8, 42, 45, 46, 49, 52, 56, 57, 62,

76, 80, 82, 88, 91, 117, 126, 128, 131, 133, 145, 167, 173, 174, 175, 188, 198, 200, 201, 202, 203, 213, 214, 216, 218, 222, 223, 224, 233, 234, 238, 240, 242, 249; ascension of, 192, 204-7; death of, 5, 7, 116, 123, 125, 129, 130, 177, 182, 190, 197, 198, 199-202, 207, 210, 219, 221, 234, 235, 236, 237; divinity of, 193-94; incarnation of, 50, 82, 83, 123, 193-94, 195, 197, 235; preexistence of, 196, 205; resurrection of, 177, 190, 199, 207, 235; virgin birth of, 86
Christian Century, 6
Christianity Today, 6, 8, 18, 19, 92
Church, xiii, 1, 3, 4, 7, 10, 11, 12, 13, 14, 15, 17, 18, 25, 26, 27, 28, 29, 30, 31, 34, 36, 37, 39, 41, 43, 44, 46, 49, 50, 53, 54, 55, 56, 57, 59, 60, 75, 84, 85, 86, 87, 88, 91, 92, 98, 102, 116, 126, 129, 130, 131, 133, 137, 150, 164, 170, 177, 178, 179, 180, 181, 182, 189, 194, 202, 204, 209, 214-16, 218-48
Churchill, Winston, xiii
Clinton, William Jefferson, 161
Coleman, Lyman, 137
Consumerism, 13-15, 25, 28, 29, 30, 31, 34, 35, 36, 38, 50, 51, 52, 53, 54, 57, 70, 111,

113, 123, 133, 151, 169, 182, 188, 189, 213, 222, 227

Cranach, Lucas, 202

Culture, 1, 2, 3, 4, 7, 8, 11, 12, 14, 15, 17, 20, 23, 31, 37, 43, 44, 48, 49, 53, 56, 60, 61, 67, 90, 92, 93, 98, 101, 105, 109, 110, 111, 117, 118, 122, 132, 135, 136, 138, 142, 146, 150, 154, 172, 176, 182, 183, 212, 216, 217, 223, 225, 227, 233, 249

Cushman, Philip, 112

Darwin, Charles, 105, 154

Delbanco, Andrew, 106

Doctrine, 2, 3, 4, 5, 6, 8, 10, 12, 17, 26, 39, 42, 43, 46, 47, 53, 54, 55, 56, 57, 84, 86, 87, 184, 189, 227, 228-29, 237, 239

Donnelly, William, 109

Drucker, Peter, 35

Eastern Orthodoxy, 17

Easum, William M., 87

Edwards, Jonathan, 20

Emergents, 4, 7, 12, 15-18, 20, 39, 41, 76, 78, 79, 86, 92, 98, 142, 178, 189, 210, 227, 237

Enlightenment, 1, 20, 32, 49, 61, 62, 68, 86, 105, 107, 108, 118, 157, 185, 203

Eschatology, 192-98, 202, 203-4, 205, 207, 220, 221

Europe, 2, 4, 5, 18, 32, 48, 49, 110, 157

Evangelicalism, 1, 2, 3, 4, 6, 7, 8, 9, 10, 11, 13, 14, 15, 16, 17, 18, 19, 21, 23, 24, 25, 26, 29, 36, 40, 42-43, 44, 46, 47, 48, 49, 51, 52, 54, 57, 62, 76, 84, 86, 91, 92, 122, 129, 131, 137, 138, 142, 157, 161, 165, 167, 169, 170, 178, 180, 181, 189, 210, 211, 212, 213, 214, 217, 218, 219, 226, 227, 229, 230, 233, 234, 237, 242

Evil, 100-102, 106, 124, 127, 130, 131, 133, 191, 192, 202, 204, 205-6, 206, 247, 249

Existentialism, 110, 154, 158

Faith, 21, 33, 44, 45, 51, 52, 84, 123, 130, 138, 169, 198, 205, 213, 217, 218, 234

Faludi, Susan, 140

Finke, Roger, 55

Forsyth, P. T., 130

Fromm, Erich, 165

Fundamentalism, 5, 18

Gallup, George, 42

Gergen, Kenneth, 135, 160

Globalization, 32, 33, 93, 176

Gnosticism, 184, 185, 228

God, xiii, 6, 7, 11, 18, 21, 30, 37, 45, 46, 47, 48, 49, 52, 53, 56, 60, 61, 98, 101, 102, 104, 106, 108, 109, 112, 116, 117, 118, 119, 121, 122, 124, 125, 131, 138, 144, 145, 148, 163, 165, 167, 175, 176, 178, 179, 180, 181, 182, 185, 186, 189, 190, 191, 192, 194, 195, 196, 203, 204, 205, 206, 207, 217, 220, 221, 222, 223, 225, 230, 231, 235, 243, 244, 245, 246, 247; goodness of, 115, 122, 144; holiness of, 99, 117, 125-26, 127, 128, 129, 130, 132, 133, 144, 173, 174, 192, 199-202, 216, 223, 224, 236, 237, 239, 240, 242, 249; image of, 108, 137, 153-55, 167; immanence of, 120, 123-24, 128, 133, 183; judgment of, 35, 45, 69, 71, 73, 74, 75, 77, 80, 82, 83, 84, 85, 86, 95, 125, 130, 168, 192, 209, 218, 236; love of, 99, 117, 129, 130, 199-202, 209, 224, 237; providence of, 100, 105, 106, 107, 121, 122, 205-6; transcendence of, 119, 120, 126, 128, 132, 133, 178, 183, 205; trinity, 99, 117

Gospel, 2, 13, 28, 51, 52, 57, 76, 89, 91, 92, 116, 123, 129, 137, 169, 200, 202, 212, 213, 214, 219, 220, 222, 229, 234, 235, 236, 237

Grace, 21, 42, 82, 117, 130, 143, 167, 174, 175, 177, 179, 192, 198, 201, 204, 207, 221, 225, 233, 234, 237, 240

Graham, Billy, 5, 18

Guinness, Os, 4

Henry, Carl, 5, 18

Index

Hinduism, 68, 69, 215
Hoefner, Herbert, 215
Holy Spirit, 53, 74, 76, 81, 85, 87, 123, 195, 205, 225, 226, 228, 237, 238, 246
Humanism, 49, 68
Hunter, James, 137
Hybels, Bill, 13, 27

Individualism, 11, 17, 39, 47, 61, 68, 69, 70, 106, 123, 136, 157, 158, 159, 166, 172, 183, 187, 237
Islam, 32, 33, 68, 72, 157

Justification, 53, 198-202, 219, 221, 234

Kant, Immanuel, 61
Katz, Stephen, 78
King, Martin Luther, 127
Kingdom of God, 196-97
Koran, 60
Kundera, Milan, 115

Langman, Lauren, 112
Lasch, Christopher, 112, 152
Las Vegas, 14, 24
Leadership, 92, 247
Lewis, C. S., 45
Liberal Protestantism, 2, 5, 6, 9, 15, 17, 19, 20, 26, 52, 95, 136-37, 142, 144, 230
Lindbeck, George, 17
Lloyd-Jones, Martyn, 5, 18
Luther, Martin, 20, 144, 177, 192, 198, 200, 202, 218, 219, 220, 226, 230

Madonna, 151
Mann, Alan, 129
Marketers, 5, 7, 9, 10, 11, 12, 13-15, 16, 18, 23, 25-30, 31, 34, 35, 36, 37, 38, 39, 40, 43, 44, 45, 46, 47, 48, 49, 50, 51, 52, 53, 54, 55, 57, 60, 92, 98, 111, 131, 132, 150, 182, 211, 213, 214, 216, 221, 227, 237
Marshall, I. Howard, 85, 87
Marx, Karl, 59, 157, 158

Maslow, Abraham, 138, 165
May, Rollo, 165
McLaren, Brian, 86, 87
Menninger, Karl, 163
Modernists, 20
Modernity, 16, 61, 157, 167, 184, 194, 202
Modernization, 3, 5, 20, 31, 34, 41, 52, 61, 63-67, 71, 86, 94, 99, 105, 108, 113, 114, 118, 119, 120, 122, 123, 141, 142, 157, 160, 184, 185, 186, 211, 217, 231, 232, 233, 239
Moral norms, 46, 60, 61, 62, 74, 93, 100, 102, 104, 106, 107, 109, 111, 112, 117, 119, 122, 127-28, 133, 137, 143-46, 148, 151, 154, 155, 158, 159, 162-63, 164, 165, 166, 170, 171-72, 174, 177, 179, 185, 191, 201, 213, 227, 236, 239
Moulton, John Fletcher, 170
Muhammad, 32
Myers, David, 67

National Association of Evangelicals, 6
National Council of Churches, 6, 26
Natural revelation, 190
Neoevangelicalism, 5
New Age, 95, 182, 183, 184
New Perspective, 234
Niebuhr, Reinhold, 63, 67

Ockenga, Harold, 5, 18

Packer, J. I., 5, 18, 234
Paganism, 45, 76, 121, 122, 132, 169, 176-78, 182, 188, 191
Pantheism, 121
Pearcey, Nancy, 40
Pelagianism, 57, 167
Plantinga, Cornelius, 103, 104
Pollack, William, 139
Postconservative, 16
Postfoundational, 16
Postliberals, 16-17
Postmodern, 1, 16, 17, 21, 36, 38, 41, 42, 49, 57, 59, 61, 62, 65, 69, 71, 72, 73, 74, 75, 77,

78, 79, 81, 87, 88, 92, 94, 97, 98, 100, 101, 102, 104, 107, 109, 112, 114, 115, 116, 117, 120, 122, 123, 124, 127, 129, 142, 155, 166, 167, 178, 179, 180, 184, 193, 197, 202, 217, 227, 230, 231, 232, 236, 237, 238, 244

Preaching, 26, 27, 29, 30, 37, 46, 55, 56, 82, 85, 89, 130, 137, 150, 181, 196, 204, 207, 214, 215, 216, 225, 229-33, 242, 246

Pride, 103, 104, 167-68

Protestantism, 1, 14, 19, 21, 27, 93, 95, 137, 143, 157, 174, 189, 209, 210, 218, 229

Putnam, Robert, 31

Rainer, Thom, 54, 55

Rationalism, 49, 62, 86, 107, 157, 186

Redemption, 45, 53, 56, 76, 80, 197, 221, 231, 235

Reformation, 6, 10, 20, 21, 143, 178, 203, 219, 225, 226, 233, 234

Reformed Protestantism, 16, 218

Relativism, 70, 73, 75, 93, 111, 114, 123, 124, 193

Religion, 27, 53, 60, 68, 71, 93, 118, 132, 136, 157, 165, 177, 179, 180, 181, 182, 183, 186, 187, 215

Rogers, Carl, 138, 165

Roman Catholicism, 9, 17, 19, 38, 52, 144, 157, 184, 189, 219, 226, 233, 234

Roszak, Theodore, 66

Russell, Bertrand, 207

Sacraments, 12, 215, 219, 220, 225, 236-37

Satel, Sally, 138

Schaeffer, Francis, 5, 18

Schorr, Daniel, 150

Scotus, Duns, 203

Scripture. See Word of God

Secularism, 18, 68, 71, 95, 101, 118, 157, 164, 186-87

Seeker-sensitive, 28, 40, 41, 45, 55, 56, 57, 131, 150, 178, 189, 210, 213, 216

Self, 11, 62, 63, 69, 103, 111, 112, 113, 115, 116, 123, 124, 137, 142, 147, 149, 158, 166, 169,

180, 183, 185, 207; autonomous self, 61, 87, 103, 104, 107, 109, 117, 120, 143, 168; self-abasement, 170; self-absorption, 90, 161; self-action, 138; self-actualization, 138; self-centeredness, 161, 237; self-commitment, 89; self-construction, 181; self-control, 151; self-deception, 140; self-desire, 109; self-directing, 153; self-discipline, 170, 171, 240; self-effacing, 194; self-esteem, 138, 139, 141, 156, 160, 169; self-expression, 151, 156, 202; self-focus, 11, 137; self-fulfillment, 138, 151, 166, 169, 170; self-generated, 237; self-giving, 194; self-gratification, 151; self-healing, 155, 164; self-help, 182, 195; self-image, 239; self-indulgence, 137, 132, 152; self-interest, 158, 159; self-mastery, 103; self movement, 62, 67, 103, 141, 142, 165, 166, 167, 168, 169, 170, 173, 174, 217; self-oriented, 181; self-pitying, 161; self-promoting, 163; self-realization, 148, 220; self-restraint, 170; self-righteousness, 104; self-sacrifice, 6, 148, 170, 194; self-satisfaction, 166; self-serving, 239; self-sufficiency, 177, 246; self-talk, 137, 138, 165, 178; self-violation, 159

Shakespeare, William, 85

Sin, 30, 45, 52, 57, 99, 101, 102-4, 126, 128-29, 130, 144, 163, 164, 166, 167, 168, 169, 174, 175, 176, 177, 179, 184, 189, 190, 191, 197, 198-202, 205, 206, 209, 221, 235, 237, 238, 245

Solzhenitsyn, Aleksander, 159

Sommers, Christina Hoff, 138

Spears, Britney, 151

Spirituality, 23, 43, 52, 53, 54, 56, 60, 68-69, 77, 88, 122, 123, 131, 132, 165, 166, 168, 169, 175, 176, 177, 179, 180, 182, 183, 184, 185, 186-92, 195, 196, 207, 237, 243

Stark, Rodney, 55

Stott, John, 5, 18, 228

Susman, Warren, 147
Sykes, Charles, 159

Temple, William, 235
Theology, 16, 40, 45, 48, 51, 105, 143, 193
Tocqueville, Alexis de, 211
Tolkien, J. R., 103
Trends, 3, 13, 90, 174
Truth, xiii, 1, 7, 8, 9, 12, 14, 17, 18, 21, 26, 45, 47, 49, 51-52, 53, 55, 56, 59-60, 70, 71, 76, 80-85, 88, 89, 90, 92, 93, 94, 95, 100, 102, 110, 111, 117, 120, 130, 131, 173, 174, 178, 179, 183, 203, 207, 224, 225, 227, 228, 229, 231, 233, 235, 237, 242, 245

Wal-Mart, 35-36
Warren, Rick, 13, 24
Weaver, Richard, 97
Wesley, Charles, 245
Western world, 3, 31, 32, 47, 48, 50, 65, 69, 71, 72, 73, 76, 88, 90, 93, 94, 98, 105, 108, 112, 113, 116, 118, 119, 123, 132, 143, 146, 153, 156, 157, 158, 164, 170, 175, 176, 179, 184, 210, 212, 223, 225, 226, 230, 232, 233, 237
Willow Creek Community Church, 13, 15, 16, 52
Wittgenstein, Ludwig, 78-79
Word of God, 3, 4, 5, 6, 7, 8, 9, 11, 12, 16, 20, 21, 27, 33, 39, 40, 42, 45, 47, 60, 72, 74, 75, 77, 78, 80, 81, 83, 84, 85, 86, 87, 88, 89, 90, 93, 98, 99, 100, 109, 117, 120, 124, 126, 127, 130, 131, 132, 167, 168, 173, 178, 179, 182, 183, 191, 192, 193, 195, 210, 211, 218, 223, 225, 226-30, 231, 232, 235, 240, 243, 246, 249
Worldview, 45, 46, 47, 54, 93, 95, 109, 110, 121, 136, 137, 167, 184, 220, 231
Wright, N. T., 85, 87

Yankelovich, Daniel, 135, 143